VIRGINIA WOOLF
THE PROFESSIO

This book explores Virginia Woolf's engagement with the professions in her life and writing. Woolf underscored the significance of the professions to society, such as the opportunity they provided for a decent income and the usefulness of professional accreditation. However, she also resisted their hierarchical structures and their role in creating an overspecialised and fragmented modernity, which prevented its members from leading whole, fulfilling lives. This book shows how Woolf's writing reshaped the professions so they could better serve the individual and society, and argues that her search for alternatives to existing professional structures deeply influenced her literary methods and experimentation.

EVELYN TSZ YAN CHAN is currently Assistant Professor of English at the Chinese University of Hong Kong. She completed her PhD on Virginia Woolf at the University of Cambridge in 2010.

VIRGINIA WOOLF AND THE PROFESSIONS

EVELYN TSZ YAN CHAN

The Chinese University of Hong Kong

CAMBRIDGE
UNIVERSITY PRESS

CAMBRIDGE
UNIVERSITY PRESS

32 Avenue of the Americas, New York NY 10013-2473, USA

Cambridge University Press is part of the University of Cambridge.

It furthers the University's mission by disseminating knowledge in the pursuit of education, learning and research at the highest international levels of excellence.

www.cambridge.org
Information on this title: www.cambridge.org/9781107657229

First published 2014
First paperback edition 2015

A catalogue record for this publication is available from the British Library

Library of Congress Cataloguing in Publication data
Chan, Evelyn, 1982– author.
Virginia Woolf and the Professions / Evelyn Chan.
pages   cm
Includes bibliographical references and index.
ISBN 978-1-107-07024-0 (hardback)
1. Woolf, Virginia, 1882–1941–Criticism and interpretation.   2. Literature and society–England–History–20th century.   3. Professions in literature.   I. Title.
PR6045.072Z574   2014
823'.912–dc23   2014002052

ISBN 978-1-107-07024-0 Hardback
ISBN 978-1-107-65722-9 Paperback

Contents

Acknowledgements

This book derives from the work I did for my PhD. I would like to express my deep gratitude to Trudi Tate, my PhD supervisor. I have benefited greatly from her generous help and guidance, and her continuing support and advice after my graduation. My secondary PhD advisor Alison Hennegan read through numerous early drafts and gave invaluable suggestions which helped to direct the work. Laura Marcus and Alex Houen read and commented on the PhD thesis as my examiners. Many of their recommendations have been taken up, and have improved this work substantially.

I also especially wish to thank two teachers to whom I owe a lifelong debt of gratitude. David Parker, to whom I dedicate this book, enthusiastically encouraged me to publish it. He has never ceased to be a source of immense support, always generously sharing his time and knowledge. Mimi Ching introduced me to Virginia Woolf in my undergraduate days, and has since then been unfailingly available for advice and guidance. They have both been the best mentors anyone could wish for.

My personal thanks go to four people. O. B. has always readily shared her time and wisdom with me and many others, and has been a teacher in life in an unofficial capacity. May has been a steadfast source of help and encouragement for as long as I can remember. Without her room in Oxford, my research into Woolf's holographs of *The Years* would not have been possible. Both she and Georg helped me to access necessary material while I was not in the United Kingdom. Arjan's abiding support and wisdom have sustained me while I worked on this book, and beyond.

The three anonymous readers for Cambridge University Press who read this book in its manuscript stages gave many invaluable suggestions that I gratefully adopted. I would also like to thank the copy editor, Alissa McGowan, and Ray Ryan, Caitlin Gallagher and Elizabeth Shand at Cambridge University Press for steering the book efficiently through the publication process.

Parts of this book have previously been published in journals. I would like to take this opportunity to thank the anonymous readers at these journals, and Mark Hussey at *Woolf Studies Annual*, for their helpful critiques of earlier versions of some of the material. Sections of the book, but mainly Chapter 4, first appeared in "Professions, Freedom and Form: Reassessing Woolf's *The Years* and *Three Guineas*," *Review of English Studies* 61.251 (2010): 591–613. The work is reused in this book by permission of Oxford University Press. Chapter 5 first appeared in an earlier form in "A Balancing Act: Specialization in *Between the Acts*," *Woolf Studies Annual* 18 (2012): 29–52. The work is reused by permission of Pace University Press. The contents of Chapter 1 have appeared in an adapted form in "The Ethics and Aesthetics of Healing: Woolf, Medicine, and Professionalization," *Women's Studies: An Interdisciplinary Journal* 43.1 (2014): 25–51. They are reused here with the permission of Taylor and Francis.

Extracts from Woolf's unpublished holograph drafts are quoted with the kind permission of The Society of Authors as the Literary Representative of the Estate of Virginia Woolf; and of The Henry W. and Albert A. Berg Collection of English and American Literature, The New York Public Library, Astor, Lenox and Tilden Foundations.

The work on this book was made possible by the Sir Edward Youde Memorial Fellowship for Overseas Studies, which funded my PhD studies at the University of Cambridge. A Direct Grant (project code 2010362) from the Research Committee at the Chinese University of Hong Kong enabled part of the research for this book.

Abbreviations and Symbols

Works by Virginia Woolf:

"AN"	"Anon" and "The Reader": Virginia Woolf's Last Essays
AROO	*A Room of One's Own/Three Guineas* (1929/1938)
BA	*Between the Acts* (1940)
CE	*Collected Essays*, 4 vols. (1966–67)
CSF	*The Complete Shorter Fiction of Virginia Woolf* (1985)
D	*The Diary of Virginia Woolf*, 5 vols. (1977–84)
E	*The Essays of Virginia Woolf*, 5 vols. (1986–2009)
H	*Virginia Woolf "The Hours": The British Museum Manuscript of Mrs Dalloway* (1996)
"HTG"	Holograph fragments of *Three Guineas*
"HY"	Holograph of *The Years*
"IL"	"Introductory Letter to Margaret Llewelyn Davies"
L	*The Letters of Virginia Woolf*, 6 vols. (1975–80)
MD	*Mrs Dalloway* (1925)
ND	*Night and Day* (1919)
O	*Orlando* (1928)
OBI	*On Being Ill* (1930)
P	*The Pargiters: The Novel-Essay Portion of* The Years (1978)
PH	*Pointz Hall: The Earlier and Later Typescripts of* Between the Acts (1983)
RF	*Roger Fry: A Biography* (1940)
TG	*A Room of One's Own/Three Guineas* (1929/1938)
TTL	*To the Lighthouse* (1927)
VO	*The Voyage Out* (1915)
Y	*The Years* (1937)

Symbols for holographs and typescripts:

\<text>	Insertion made by Virginia Woolf
~~text~~	Text cancelled by Virginia Woolf

The holograph of *The Years* contains many ellipses of its own. To avoid confusion, omission of text in these quotations is indicated with ellipses inside square brackets ([…]).

Introduction

When your secretary asked me to speak to you on Professions, she condemned me to several weeks of ... \<acute discomfort\>, ~~which I can~~ as you will understand when I tell you that ~~in my own~~ I have two proposals to put before you: the first is that all professional [*sic*] are to be avoided; & the second that several new professions must \<at once\> be invented.[1]

The chance is there before you, to be as unlike the professional man as possible.[2]

– Virginia Woolf, holograph notes

The two quotations with which this book begins – taken from three pages of holograph notes which Virginia Woolf wrote for her talk for the London/National Society for Women's Service on 21 January 1931 – provide a good snapshot of the underlying tension in Woolf's engagement with the issue of the professions. They simultaneously express her dissatisfaction with their present state – especially as they had become hegemonic, masculine institutions of economic and political interest and power – and her reluctance to disengage her argument for a new social order completely from professional organisation, so that any innovation is still imagined in the form of "new professions,"[3] and so that people who are as "unlike the professional man as possible"[4] are still professionals. As this book demonstrates, Woolf's life and work were deeply informed by such thoughts on and observations of the professions and their values, and these can be traced not just in the content of both her political and creative writing, but also in their form and aesthetics. Her search for alternatives to what she conceived of as professional methods and structures influenced and became part of her literary methods and experimentation. Her writing, in turn, tried to depict, vex and shape the professions so they could better serve the individual and society.

The purpose of this introduction – instead of repeating the evidence to follow in subsequent chapters which shows how Woolf engaged with the professions – is to trace and historicise her relevant thoughts and views on which the chapters will build. This is especially important for elucidating what the concept of "profession" meant for Woolf. She used the word differently in different contexts, accepting its existing meanings yet also resisting and destabilising them through her writing, in order to explore how professionals could engage ethically with the wider public, how the professions could be participated in to lead to meaningful lives, and how one's professional identity could be a vital part of oneself yet not compromise one's integrity as a person.

The Professions, the Public and the Private, and Women

A profession is an unstable combination of the private and the public, the personal and the social, the disinterested and the financial. The religious roots of the word "profession" suggest an activity which, besides fulfilling the public purposes of declaration, promise and avowal, is also personally meaningful and fulfilling.[5] Often used before the nineteenth century to refer to the three ancient professions of medicine, law and religion, the expansion of industrial society led to the translation of the term into the wider socioeconomic realm, so that one of the defining characteristics of "professional" work was its result in financial rewards.[6] As Samuel Taylor Coleridge writes in 1832, a significant change in the social structure in Britain occurred when the professions separated from the church.[7] With the church no longer possessing a monopoly over knowledge and learning, the gradual disassociation between religion and the professions led to a more heterogeneous, diverse society.[8] To enter a profession became less associated with answering a spiritual calling than with qualifications and certifications which would ensure – in a competitive commercial environment which was the legacy of nineteenth-century laissez-fairism – a decent and stable remuneration for services rendered.

The tension between private and public in the word shows itself in the thin line between the sincere enactment of professional ideals and their strategic espousal for the purpose of material rewards. Such a clash is present in the very etymology of the word "profession." The word derives from *profess-*, the past participle stem of the Latin word *profiteri*,[9] which refers to the acts of public statement, declaration and avowal.[10] The word's references to activities in the public eye or domain explain why the word "profess" itself can imply insincerity,[11] with professionals publicly avowing service ideals which they may not privately believe in. Yet owing to its public dimension, the word "professional" also entails the guarantee of objective standards and a certain level of competence, due to formal procedures of accreditation or qualification. Because of these special skills that professionals are seen to have, they often enjoy a matching social status and income.

For the professional women in Woolf's audience – for whom the speech from which the two opening quotations originate was drafted – the professions were an important way to enter and participate in the public sphere which they had historically been denied access to. The issues arising from this navigation for women with similar socioeconomic backgrounds to Woolf who wished to earn money doing brainwork had always preoccupied her in various ways. In her first two novels, *The Voyage Out* (1915) and *Night and Day* (1919), the two female protagonists, both young women, have had no formal education,[12] yet show potential in specialised areas. In the sense that they could be making their living on work which is also personally meaningful to them, Rachel Vinrace could be a professional pianist and Katharine Hilberry a professional mathematician, but they are not. There is a latent rift already present in their characterisation between the notion of an individual and literal "profession" of oneself to a fulfilling activity in which lies one's interest and talent, and a socioeconomic conception of profession which is located more firmly in the public sphere. *The Voyage Out* describes a conversation between Rachel and Terence Hewet, revolving around the politics of the professions and their genderedness:

> "There's no doubt it helps to make up for the drudgery of a profession if a man's taken very, very seriously by every one – if he gets appointments, and has offices and a title, and lots of letters after his name, and bits of ribbon and degrees.... What a miracle the masculine conception of life is – judges, civil servants, army, navy, Houses of Parliament, lord mayors – what a world we've made of it! Look at Hirst now.... [N]ot a day's passed since we came here without a discussion as to whether he's to stay on at Cambridge or to go to the Bar.... And if I've heard it twenty times, I'm sure his mother and sister have heard it five hundred times. Can't you imagine the family conclaves, and the sister told to run out and feed the rabbits because St. John must have the school-room to himself.... But St. John's sister –" Hewet puffed in silence. "No one takes her seriously, poor dear. She feeds the rabbits."
>
> "Yes," said Rachel. "I've fed rabbits for twenty-four years; it seems odd now." (197)

Rachel's so-called rabbit-feeding has taken the place of formal education. She possesses little basic knowledge such as "[t]he shape of the earth, the history of the world, how trains worked, or money was invested, what laws were in force, which people wanted what, and why they wanted it, the most elementary idea of a system in modern life" (26). Yet Woolf writes, no doubt from personal experience:

> [T]his system of education had one great advantage. It did not teach anything, but it put no obstacle in the way of any real talent that the pupil might chance to have. Rachel, being musical, was allowed to learn nothing but music; she became a fanatic about music.... At the age of twenty-four she ... could play as well as nature intended her to, which, as became daily more obvious, was a really generous allowance. (26)

Rachel's unconventional education has not prepared her for a public profession, but has allowed her to exercise her intrinsic talent to the full. Her death cuts any future possibilities short, but even before she dies, the novel hints at the difficulties she would have faced in pursuing her talent as a public profession. She is engaged to be married to Terence, whose demands are already intruding on her practice of music:

> "No, Terence, it's no good; here am I, the best musician in South America, not to speak of Europe and Asia, and I can't play a note because of you in the room interrupting me every other second."
>
> "You don't seem to realise that that's what I've been aiming at for the last half hour," he remarked. "I've no objection to nice, simple tunes – indeed, I find them very helpful to literary composition, but that kind of thing is merely like an unfortunate old dog going round on its hind legs in the rain."[13] (276)

Terence trivialises her ability as a hobby, and in so doing encloses it within the preserves of the private sphere. Although Rachel dies before the conflict comes to a head, in *Night and Day*, Katharine consciously wishes to break free from the constraints of her sheltered upbringing:

> "I suppose you're one of the people who think we should all have professions," she said, rather distantly, as if feeling her way among the phantoms of an unknown world.
>
> "Oh dear no," said Mary at once.
>
> "Well, I think I do," Katharine continued, with half a sigh. "You will always be able to say that you've done something, whereas, in a crowd like this, I feel rather melancholy." (45)

However, Katharine is unable to connect her talent in mathematics to her desire to have a public profession and be productive in this sense. In a subsequent short story, "A Woman's College from Outside" (1920), Woolf imagines women receiving formal university education at Newnham College at the University of Cambridge, "for the purpose of earning [their] living[s]" (*CSF* 146). Like in the two novels just mentioned, Woolf has yet to engage fully with materialist specificities. As Patrick McGee has pointed out, Woolf, looking at the college "from Outside," creates primarily a "dream of a feminine universe."[14]

Katharine's longing is echoed by Elizabeth in *Mrs Dalloway* (1925), who comes from a similar socioeconomic background and likewise yearns for a future of professional productivity. She thinks:

> And every profession is open to the women of your generation, said Miss Kilman. So she might be a doctor. She might be a farmer. Animals are often ill. She might own a thousand acres and have people under her.... And she liked the feeling of people working.... In short, she would like to have a profession. She would become a doctor, a farmer, possibly go into Parliament, if she found it necessary, all because of the Strand." (149)

The city's bustling activity entices Elizabeth with a sense of professional purpose. Yet her highly romanticised notion of the professions is problematic: Any profession, it seems, is a possible avenue for the assertion of individuality. Elizabeth's view is less of an insistence on professing herself to one particular line of work for which she possesses special aptitude, and more one of seeing the professions in general as a way to escape the historical restrictions of the private sphere for women. But what Elizabeth here ignores are the practical considerations of how to successfully bridge the public and the private, to negotiate between social ideas of productivity and personal interest, which are crucial to a fruitful relationship between oneself and one's profession.

All three young women in Woolf's novels share a troubled relationship with the professions, and reflect facets of Woolf's own ambivalent relationship with them that were to be engaged with even more fully in her writing from the late 1920s onwards. Such early representations of the question of how – and significantly of whether – to transfer one's personal "profession" to the socioeconomic sphere, to subject one's talent to its scrutiny and evaluation, foreshadow the full-blown professional anxieties experienced by the later Lily Briscoe in *To the Lighthouse* (1927) and Miss La Trobe in *Between the Acts* (1941), both of whom will be discussed in Chapter 3. The "professional" activities of these two characters maintain, with difficulty and at some sacrifice, a precarious autonomy from financial concerns.

Woolf thought carefully about how women should participate in the elaborate systems of financial and social recognition of the professions. She wrote about the topic right before and when it first became a legal right for women to earn money in the professions on the same basis as men, with the passing of the Sex Disqualification Removal Act in 1919. After the passage of the act, the continuing issue of women's income seemed a sequel to what Leonard Woolf described as "the great dilemma of the nineteenth century," that is, "the question whether the establishment of political equality would not inevitably lead to a demand for economic equality."[15] Many of the questions Woolf had when she was thinking about the professions revolved around this fundamental issue of money.[16] Material reality dictated that it was necessary to perform socially product-ive work, and the professions were the most suitable type of such work for people of her background; yet she was keenly aware of the limitations of the professions, and harboured a desire to escape the restrictions and hypocrisies of such bureaucratic systems, to realise what she would call in *The Years* (1937) "a world in which people were whole, in which people were free" (285). In her notes in 1933 entitled "Draft of Professions," for instance, she asks: "What is the need of employment? To escape from the house. To have money, to enjoy life. But how can we enjoy it without some money? But how much?"[17]

In the 1920s and 1930s, her works increasingly address the potential disadvantages of women's entry into the professions. The mission of the London/National Society for Women's Service, Woolf's speech for which was referenced at the beginning of this introduction, was to "obtain economic equality for women by propaganda and non-party political work," and to distribute "information for women's education, economic oppor-tunities, and 'freedom for women in pursuit of their work.'"[18] Its focus on economic opportunities for women in the public sphere was reflected by the audience for the speech: "some hundreds of younger professional and business women,"[19] whom Woolf would later in her diary describe as "well dressed, keen, & often beautiful" (*D* 4: 7).[20] Although the exact version of the speech is lost, the holograph on which it was based foreshadows what she was to discuss at length later:

> And you are bound to find when you come to practise your innumerable professions that your difference of outlook is bringing you to loggerheads with some respected ... <chiefs> of your profession. But one of your most amusing and exciting experiences will be precisely on this account – ~~when you~~ <that you will have to> make your profession adapt itself to your needs, your sense of values, your common sense, your moral sense your sense of what is due to humanity and reason. ~~I have no right to speak; but~~ as a mem-ber of the general public, who sometimes has to employ lawyers, then archi-tects, then builders, then doctors, stock brokers and so on – I can assure you that I think it is high time ~~you got to work upon these professions and brought them rather more into line with common sense.~~ <that these ancient and privileged professions came more in touch with human needs.> (*P* xv)

Lois Cucullu has argued that in this speech, Woolf's "peroration is simple and direct: social reproduction now rests with the expert class; either join it or become its object."[21] But this ignores Woolf's criticism of this expert class, and her emphasis that women had to make it "adapt itself to [their] needs." Professions, which were established to address "human needs" and render their services accordingly, had in Woolf's eyes become so "privileged" that they had paradoxically become detached from those needs. Departed from "moral sense," "humanity and reason," the professions needed an overhaul from the outside. The professional women whom Woolf was addressing were given the task of using their female "difference of outlook" to transform the professions to be "more in touch with human needs" for the benefit of themselves as well as the "general public." To Woolf, the importance of the difference of the woman – whose "experience is not the same" and whose "traditions are different" (*P* xii) and in whom she saw the power to change society – meant that she thought it imperative that this difference was valued and preserved. But this gave rise to contradictory impulses in Woolf – on the one hand she supported such societies as the National Society for Women's Service, who made it their objective to help women enter the professions, and on the other she feared that the difference of the woman would be effaced by this new environment, that women would be locked in the same system as men. Therefore, in *A Room of One's Own* (1929), the narrator writes: "I thought how unpleasant it is to be locked out; and I thought how it is worse perhaps to be locked in" (21). And in *Three Guineas* (1938), a work which she called "my book on professions" in its conception stage (*D* 4: 102), she describes professionals as imprisoned in a dance "round and round the mulberry tree, the sacred tree, of property" (199). When she depicts the only female doctor in her fiction, Peggy Pargiter in *The Years*, Woolf does not represent her as receiving the fulfilment from her work that decades of feminist campaigning had fought for. Instead, as we will see in Chapter 1, being a doctor has made Peggy bitter, twisted and trapped (*Y* 257–58).

Although the focal point of investigation in this book is not the relationship between the public and the private, nor is the aim of the book to subsume every aspect of Woolf's engagement with the professions under this larger rubric, it is part of the pattern which emerges from her response to the professions, and which enables us to connect the discussion on Woolf and the professions to existing debates on Woolf and the public/ private. As critics such as Anna Snaith and Melba Cuddy-Keane have persuasively demonstrated, Woolf was seeking the right balance between these two realms, constantly traversing the boundaries between them.[22]

This book, with some continuity, shows how she attempted to shape the professions so that they could become individually and personally, not just materially and socially, more rewarding pursuits. Her hope for them was, to use a phrase she applied to literature, one of "perfect integrity" (*CE* 2: 145), of wholeness and meaningful unity, so that their practitioners could lead through them full lives without the need to preclude essential facets of their being. As she writes in *The Years*, "[t]he soul – the whole being.... It wishes to expand; to adventure; to form – new combinations," not to live "screwed up into one hard little, tight little – knot," "[e]ach in his own little cubicle" (216). But Woolf was also aware that this ideal was difficult, if not impossible, to realise in the actual world. Her writing became the site where she could both critique the existing professions and imagine alternatives to them.

In the preceding discussion, the issue of the professions has been looked at as a feminist one. But although Woolf's concern with the professions may have begun as a feminist issue, it was a much larger topic for her, as I have started to suggest. Her portrayal of male professionals in her work, for instance, testifies to a wider concern about the professions as both social institutions and personal vocations. In *Mrs Dalloway*, Sir William Bradshaw, a Harley Street psychiatrist, is perhaps as much imprisoned within the "social system" (*D* 2: 248) as Septimus is, trapped in his own unyielding "sense of proportion" (109) and understanding little else beyond this limited and meagre view of life. In *The Years*, North, on his return to England after farming in Africa, is asked by everyone about his plans, and his sister Peggy predicts that he will go down the conventional path for someone of his background: "You'll marry. You'll have children. What'll you do then? Make money. Write little books to make money" (286). Yet what North really wants is not to be restricted by the conventional way of living for someone of his class, but "[t]o live differently ... differently" (309). In *Between the Acts* (1941), Giles, a stockbroker, is trapped within his "job in the city": "Given his choice, he would have chosen to farm. But he was not given his choice. So one thing led to another; and the conglomeration of things pressed you flat; held you fast, like a fish in water" (30–31). That the professions were satisfactory personally, and not just economically, was essential to all members of society, male or female.

The Professions: A Historical Overview

The historical relevance of Woolf's concern with the professions is not limited to the prelude to and aftermath of the Sex Disqualification Removal

Act. Woolf's portrayal was situated in what Louis Menand and Lawrence Rainey call "the new consumerist and professionalist society" of the time.[23] It was marked by a proliferation of writing which first attempted to theorise the professions, as people were starting to think more widely about their roles, and as they were becoming a more general concern in discussions on the well-being of society as a whole. The earliest book-length studies on the professions appeared in Britain at the very end of the nineteenth and the beginning of the twentieth century. *Unwritten Laws and Ideals* (1899) is a compilation of essays, edited by E. H. Pitcairn, on a number of professions by experts in their own fields who outline their history. The book sets out to describe "the Unwritten Laws" that professions operate by, and the "Ideals" these embody.[24] It includes chapters not only on the three ancient professions of medicine, law and the religious order, but also on, for example, vice-chancellors, schoolmasters, "boys at public schools," banking, music and art.[25] *Professionalism and Originality* (1917) by F. H. Hayward is a systematic, chapter-by-chapter critique of the professions. Hayward equates professionalism with ordinariness and mediocrity,[26] yet at the same time asserts that professionalism is necessary to modern society for several reasons: as "an important link with the past," because it is "one of the chief agents by which social heredity is handed down"; as a form of "specialization," because "all affairs of life demand, at some point or other, specialist training"; and because it allows the satisfaction and pride of being skilled in one area, and performing work in it with merit.[27] His argument in the book is that "[t]hough Professionalism exists for the purpose of achieving certain desirable ends (Health, Justice, Education, etc.), it is frequently an enemy to the realization of those ends – It loses contact with the facts of Life and the needs of Society" (9). This echoes Woolf's own view in the holograph version of her 1931 speech. The most comprehensive book on the subject is perhaps *The Professions* (1933) by A. M. Carr-Saunders (with whom Woolf was acquainted)[28] and P. A. Wilson, which considers the general characteristics of the professions, treating a range of occupations beyond "certain vocations of ancient lineage which by common consent are called professions, law and medicine among the foremost," because "[t]here are many other vocations which, though more recently and therefore less firmly established, are nevertheless usually granted professional rank."[29] The justification for the book is that in the past few years "the interest of the public in professionalism has become more direct and immediate, because numerous practical problems relating to the organisation of the professions and to the availability of professional services have had to be faced."[30] These included the expansion and state organisation of medical service, the regulation of professional education, and the establishment of state registers for new professions. But beyond such practical concerns, professionalism, the authors point out, has also become "one of the themes most debated by political theorists," as "there are few associations more important or powerful than those formed by professional men."[31] They locate "a new wave of professional association" at the beginning of the nineteenth century, and criticism of the "exclusiveness, selfishness, and slothfulness of their fossilized corporations" as accompanying this rise. They state that "[o]pinion was then, and long remained, hostile to professional association as it was then understood."[32] Included in the book as examples of professions which had established elaborate administrative structures are law, architecture, engineering, medicine and stock-broking, the same ones that Woolf named in her speech as her own examples of "ancient and privileged professions" (*P* xv). The book explains at length their professionalising process: Although all had existed in some form or other in previous centuries, many had not organised themselves into the massive administrative bodies that attracted Woolf's criticism until the nineteenth century and beyond, and changes in their organisation were still ongoing in her time.[33] Despite their own specificities, all the professions that Woolf named shared similar characteristics of professionalism: a historical tradition of the practice, intricate levels of organisation, and often concerns with social status and prestige.

The lucidity in the analyses of the professions provided by Woolf's contemporaries is in contrast to the difficulties late eighteenth- and nineteenth-century social commentators faced in theorising the professions, when they were still an emerging social category. In the late eighteenth century, Adam Smith labelled professionals as part of the "unproductive labourers," whose services may be important in the functioning of society, but whose labour did not add value to a material object which lasted beyond the duration of service-provision.[34] Claiming that only productive labour "replenishes circulating capital and so contributes directly to the wealth of nations,"[35] Smith effaced the emergent professional class in his very effort at describing them. In the nineteenth century, Karl Marx highlighted above all the hierarchical relationship between the capitalist bourgeoisie and the manual labourer, the latter adding value to material which is appropriated by the former.[36] This model was at the expense of a more accurate description of the middle class at the time, which Matthew Arnold more perceptively describes as "cut in two in a way unexampled anywhere else," consisting "of a professional class brought up on the first plane, with fine and governing qualities, but disinclined to rely on reason and science," and of an "immense business class," "brought up on a second plane, cut off from the aristocracy and the professions, and without governing qualities."[37] In the mid-nineteenth century, the word "professionalism" emerged in the English language, coming into existence as the need arose to conceptualise common qualities which the expanding category of professions were thought to share. The earliest example which the *Oxford English Dictionary* (*OED*) gives of its first meaning as professional quality, conduct, system or method is in 1856. The earliest example of its second meaning, as the work or status of a professional as opposed to that of an amateur,[38] occurs in 1884. Towards the end of the nineteenth century, negative evaluations of the word start to appear in the list of sources for the word given by the *OED*. In 1895, for instance, *The Educational Review*, warning against overspecialisation, recommends that the "student should not lose sight of general cultivation and fall into stark professionalism."[39]

We can observe shifts in the definition of what constituted a profession by looking at changes in the categories used by the national censuses in Britain in the nineteenth century. As W. J. Reader notes, in the national census in 1841, only certain people working in the clergy, law and medicine were designated as professionals.[40] Under the clerical profession were only two subcategories: "Clergyman," and "Minister and Clergyman." Under the medical profession were seven, of which the last two were "Corn-cutter (Chiropodist)" and "Midwife." In contrast, in the census in 1851, under the heading "Persons in the Learned Professions (with their immediate Subordinates)," each of the three previous main categories was further divided into two. The medical profession, for instance, now consisted of the categories of "Physicians and Surgeons" and "Chemists and Surgical Instrument Makers." The occupation of "Midwife" was no longer to be found under either of these two. In addition, "Persons engaged in Literature, the Fine Arts, and the Sciences," under which are "Authors," "Artists," "Scientific Persons," and "Teachers," comprised a separate class, excluded from the heading of "Learned Professions."[41] In 1861, for the first time, census authorities broadened their definition of the professions. "Persons engaged in the Learned Professions or engaged in Literature, Art, and Science (with their immediate Subordinates)" were grouped together, and this category, together with "Persons engaged in the General or Local Government of the Country," and "Persons engaged in the Defence of the Country," were now the three orders under the main heading "Professional Class."[42] The concept of the professional class was thus being expanded to accommodate an increasing number of occupations which involved brainwork, but the classification of occupations as professions beyond the religious order, law and medicine was uncertain and subject to continuous change, and even certain subcategories under the three ancient professions could be variously included and excluded, as in the case of midwifery.

The distinction lies in the prestige value of the word "profession," which the word "occupation" lacks. A profession is an elaborate artificial social construct, which operates by creating and manipulating ideologies of the scarcity value of specialised intellectual labour or brainwork. Although a wider sense of the word "profession" is any occupation by which someone makes a regular living, the *OED* writes under this definition that the 1908 version of the dictionary notes that the word is "[n]ow usually applied to an occupation considered to be socially superior to a trade or handicraft."[43] An early example of this distinction comes from F. D. Maurice's *Lectures on the Education of the Middle Classes* (1839), in which he states that a "[p]rofession in our country ... is expressly that kind of business which deals primarily with men as men, and is thus distinguished from a Trade, which provides for the external wants or occasions of men."[44]

If nineteenth-century political writing still struggled with theorising the emergent figure of the professional,[45] this problem was increasingly recognised and addressed in the twentieth. The inadequacies of Marx's description of social strata, though still highly influential, had become too noticeable to ignore. William MacDonald, in *The Intellectual Worker and His Work* (1923), states that "[t]he classical theory of economic organization, rigorously and elaborately developed in industrial England," which "conceived of society as divided for economic purposes into two great classes, capitalists and labourers," ignored the prominence and prevalence of intellectual work.[46] MacDonald defines intellectuals as "persons who are not capitalists or employers, or whose support is not derived from invested funds or the earnings of others; all whose work is not primarily manual, clerical, or routine; and all whose intellectual effort, whether narrow or extended, is not spent in the regular production of a material product."[47] The "learned professions," which he sees as a distinct subcategory of intellectual work, are treated in a chapter of their own. These are the three ancient professions of medicine, law and religion, and the newer profession of engineering, which he includes because of the rigorous and extended study requirements in special schools which this work is now predicated on.[48] The professions are distinct in that their practitioners both enjoy legal rights not available to outsiders and must abide by legal obligations which, if not fulfilled, may result in punishment.[49] Medicine and law, for example, have strict entry requirements set down by the state, which forbids their practice by people who do not fulfil them.[50] These two professions "have long since developed a strong professional solidarity, and professional codes of ethics bind the members of those professions to the observance of certain standards of conduct and provide penalties for unprofessional acts."[51]

In the early twentieth century, both established and aspiring professions claimed the pursuit of higher ideals, and attempted to project an image of social and intellectual superiority to set themselves apart from mere trade. Carr-Saunders and Wilson identify "the raising of status" as almost always one of the "declared objects" of newly formed societies aspiring towards professional standing. This is because "[t]he members of the first formed of these societies were very conscious that they had no social prestige and that their occupations were not 'fit for gentlemen.'"[52] (302). At the same time, as we have seen, this also had the opposite effect of attracting criticism of such ideal-espousal as hypocrisy. Harold Perkin, in *The Rise of Professional Society* (1989), which gives a historical overview and analysis of the professionalisation of British society, describes the attributes of professional ideology: the concepts of "human capital," "highly skilled and differentiated labour," and "selection by merit defined as trained and certified expertise."[53] To translate these into an assured income, the professions need to have created and ensured a market for their services by, for example, turning their services into a scarcity by restricting access to training, making entry into a profession difficult, and by the establishment of qualifying associations which control the terms on which services are provided.[54] A profession is thus a closed organisation, limiting the free availability of both service and training. In order to protect the status and rewards of their work, professionals had to affirm and defend the quality and scarcity of their service, potentially leading to "individual arrogance, collective condescension towards the laity, and mutual disdain between the different professions."[55] The rhetoric of "persuasion and propaganda" which professions use to raise their status means that their members, instead of having their services evaluated in the free market, can provide their services in a protected environment and set the conditions and the rates of remuneration themselves.[56] This enables them to earn more money and have more security than if professional organisation had not been successful. In this processes, money, status and power are interchangeable: They represent what Perkin theorises as the sides of a three-sided pyramid of equal worth, so that more of one thing can translate into more of another.[57]

Although this analysis of the professions comes from a book published in the 1980s, the dynamics of professional ideology was already well-known in Woolf's time, and, as this book shows, can be observed in Woolf's own work. In 1917, Hayward writes in a chapter on "The Self-Concern of Professionalism" that "[p]rofessionalism seeks to acquire power, privileges, or emoluments for itself"[58]; and in another chapter on "The Cultivation of Complexity" that "[p]rofessions strenuously support complicated laborious methods if these bring profit or influence," and "show a tendency to create work of a doubtful, useless, or mischievous kind, or to prevent its abolition, in order to justify their existence as professions."[59] Although the emphasis of the professions on intellectual work and their self-proclaimed distance from the immediacies of commercialism made the professions attractive prospects for people from educated backgrounds, Woolf could not help but view them suspiciously, describing them towards the end of the 1930s as "the public world, the professional system, with its possessiveness, its jealousy, its pugnacity, its greed" (*TG* 199). Her works show her to be aware of the ideology on which the professions operated, and which writers such as Hayward addressed: They claimed removal from blatant commercialism and the corrupting marketplace, but were in more indirect ways highly implicated in the financial interests which they attempted to disavow. Thus professional anti-commercialism is also rooted in commercialism, its real purpose to protect professionals' financial interest.

Woolf's early political engagement with the professions can be traced to her involvement with the Fabians from the 1910s onwards, for whose social vision the professions were essential. This possibly contributed to her own political views on the professions, which would problematise those of the Fabians. Woolf was familiar with Fabian politics through her association with Sidney and Beatrice Webb, two prominent members of the Fabian Society, and her husband's work for the *New Statesman*, the periodical which the Webbs founded in 1913.[60] On 22 January 1915, Woolf attended a meeting of the Fabian Society on the topic of "The Conditions of Peace," which discussed amongst other things the "[m]ain causes of war: the fact that the separate nations are the supreme social groups, mutual fears of national safety, the natural pugnacious instinct of men."[61] The relationship between "supreme social groups" and "the natural pugnacious instinct of men" was to form the basic premise of her own treaty on the conditions of peace in the prelude to the Second World War two decades later, in the form of *Three Guineas*. The meeting struck such a chord in Woolf that she wrote afterwards in her diary that "I have now declared myself a Fabian" (*D* 1: 26). This was not a small statement from Woolf, who was usually reluctant to be categorised into any group, although she did not maintain this position in later decades.

The Fabian vision to create a collective society without class distinctions based on the historical determinants of land and capital and without gender inequality appealed to Woolf's sense of democracy. But theirs was also a vision of society led by an elite force of intellectuals and professionals in which social ills would be solved by professional and bureaucratic means.[62] The Fabians' views on the necessity of expertise in the organisation of society can, for example, be observed in their opinion on the concept of cooperation, which was Leonard Woolf's focus in his book *Co-operation and the Future of Industry* (1918). Woolf's contact with this topic can be traced back to the first Fabian conference she attended in July 1913 on "the Control of Industry," including issues such as "Co-operation and the 'Self-Governing Workshop'; Profit Sharing and Industrial Co-partnership; the present organisation of Trade Unionism in Great Britain, Germany and Belgium."[63] Woolf's notes on the conference reflect the Fabian preoccupation with the power relations between wage-earners and consumers at the time: "Nothing ignoble in being a consumer ... Man wage-earner can make his power felt, woman consumer very little power. Wage earner's view predominates."[64] In subsequent written reports on the same topic which were published in the *New Statesman*, the Webbs criticised both the organisation of industry by the association of producers and by that of consumers. Cooperative associations of producers, also termed self-governing workshops, in which producers both owned the equipment for production and operated it to make products which they shared among themselves, had mostly failed because the producers lacked knowledge of consumer markets. In addition, there was little workshop discipline: Since the workers were also the owners of the plant, the manager of the workshop was hired by these workers to supervise and advise them while they were in fact also his employers.[65] Cooperative associations of consumers, in which groups of consumers supplied themselves with the products they needed, had been more successful, but had failed to extend their influence beyond certain types of products and the working class, and had neglected workers' interests.[66] What was needed was a centralised system of organising these two groups with such disparate interests and such specific shortcomings. The solution, the Webbs argued, lay in "vocational organization for both producers and consumers," a step towards which had already been taken in the formation of trade unions, but which were only the "crude beginning of a far higher and more complex system" – such as the associations found in the professions of medicine and law. In this, producers, "with all the power behind them of a completely organized industry," would negotiate with consumers, who would "settle which commodity or service he will command at the price that these conditions make necessary."[67] In effect, what the Fabians were proposing was their own version of the professionalisation of the entire industry.

The fourth written report on the same topic of "the Control of Industry" as the conference that Woolf had attended in 1913 appeared in the *New Statesman* in two parts on 21 and 28 April 1917, and was on the issue of "Professional Association." Here, the Webbs argue for what they call the most important function of professional associations: to combat the "immunity from expert criticism" of "all enterprise on a large scale, and therefore especially in Government and in Consumers' Co-operative Societies," by allowing the professions to use their specialised knowledge to offer advice and criticism.[68] Even though drawbacks to professional organisation are identified, such as their exclusiveness, which has among other things led to the "long fight made by one profession after another to exclude women," and possessiveness, which causes them to "attempt to exact from the community a higher remuneration or easier conditions of employment," the Webbs point out that "[w]ithout some protective development there is always a danger of any group being so crushed down as to be incapable of rendering its full service to the community."[69] To mitigate the impulses for self-protection from the opposing camps of service providers and users, the Webbs argue for a "composite authority" of representatives from the professions, from service users, and from the state, in which the interests of all parties can be represented and negotiated. Even within a profession there should be "'stratified Democracy,' in which the affairs of each grade or special section are dealt with separately by that grade or section" to ensure that the voices of expert specialists within each profession are not drowned out "in the undistinguished mass of the rank and file pursuing the old routine."[70] The society that the Webbs describe is informed by professional expertise in all areas.

This book aims to show how Woolf participated in this and other contemporary critical theorising of the professions and their ideology in British society. She was influenced by this context of debates to formulate her own political and aesthetic responses to the professions in her writing – ones which, as we will see, disagreed with those of the Fabians, for all her early enthusiasm for their ideas. But Woolf's awareness of the problems and potential disingenuousness of professional ideology did not mean she could dismiss them outright: By the twentieth century, the professions and their ideology had proliferated to the extent where their influence was felt across all strata of society. Occupations which were previously considered just those were now jostling for a share in this power by claiming professional status themselves. The brainwork of the professions may be worthwhile intellectually, but the process of institutionalisation which many professions had to undergo, and their implication in financial interest despite their public claims to the contrary, also meant that they could be dehumanising, with competition for an excessive amount of social and financial reward obscuring any benefits from intellectual rewards and a balanced, well-deserved income. Woolf engaged with these issues via the criticisms she voiced in such essays as *A Room* and, even more ardently, *Three Guineas*. Even in these essays, however, her attempts to disparage and escape the professions were tempered by a sense of inextricability: The professions were too important – especially for women who had been denied access to the public sphere in previous centuries – to dismiss entirely. What we find in them are rhetorical strategies to balance criticism of the professional system with a reacquisition and renewal of it, moulding it into an improved, more democratic, and more accessible version. What we find in some of her novels in the 1920s and 1930s are similar attempts, channelled at times through the aesthetics of the writing, to rescue the concept of "profession" from itself by a greater emphasis on its more personal and original attributes. These included those of economic disinterestedness and the idea of a whole-hearted pursuit of a worthwhile vocation, which Woolf was only too aware the public version of the professions did not always live up to.

The Professions in Literary Modernism: Existing Debates

One of Woolf's goals was therefore to destabilise the notion of a "profession," taking certain values for further use and attempting to minimise or discard other characteristics. In that her appropriation of certain aspects of existing professional ideology was not mainly to make favourable claims for her own work, she defies the model of literary modernism which critics have convincingly applied to some male writers, who shared a desire for exclusivity in the field, and who arguably saw formal innovation as a way to gain professional status. Such scholarship builds on the description of the complex relationship between art and money in the early twentieth century, such as that provided by Peter Keating in *The Haunted Study* (1989), to look at how authors used professional ideology to position themselves more favourably in the literary marketplace. It posits modernist innovations as attempts to professionalise the literary vocation at a time when professionalisation was a major force in British society. Since professional organisation protected against direct competition in the market, and the professions claimed to provide services not for the sake of money, but for higher service ideals, their values could be used to counter commercialism. David Trotter has argued that the obsession with professional status of some male modernists, such as Ford Madox Ford, D. H. Lawrence and Wyndham Lewis, led to the experimental urge that forms their modernism.[71] Louis Menand has shown that the pursuit and elevation of objective form by T. S. Eliot became part of the movement to imbue literature with the professional values of objectivity, tradition and esotericism, as the field of literary studies became institutionalised as a university subject.[72] As Eliot declared, "Surely professionalism in art is hard work on style with singleness of purpose."[73] Yet, as we have seen, and as both Trotter and Menand have pointed out, the professions, in their own way, also try to maximise private profits: Their social negotiation processes establish artificial control over the market, and increase income. Menand therefore argues that "the modern artist belongs to the moment when capitalism, entering its corporate phase, provided its professional class with a set of values that present themselves as preindustrial in origin."[74] He points out that writers and academics who espoused such values ignored the fact that professionalism could be seen not just as a reaction against capitalism, but ironically also as a perpetuation of capitalist values, in what he calls the "double motive" of professionalism.[75]

Thomas Strychacz has similarly argued, in the context of American modernism, that there was both a mismatch and an affinity between writers and professional expertise: although writers had to sell their work "as commodities on the market" and could not strictly speaking be seen as experts in a field of specialized knowledge, modernist writers seemed, in their demarcation of "a space that exists culturally, economically, and linguistically apart from mass culture and the imperatives of the mass market," to reap some of the knowledge-based social rewards that were similar to those awarded to professionals.[76] Joyce Piell Wexler, in her discussion on D. H. Lawrence, Joseph Conrad and James Joyce, sums up the issue by saying that "[m]odernists ... found that art and popularity were antithetical claims. Only after failing to attract as wide an audience as they felt they deserved did modernists make their texts difficult."[77]

Competition, self-interest and money: these are not on closer inspection any more distant from professionalism than other social ideologies. Woolf, however, unlike some of her contemporaries such as Eliot, did not keep silent about its potential for disingenuousness. This becomes especially obvious in *Three Guineas*. In its draft, she writes that "if people are highly successful in their professions they are failures as human beings" ("HTG" 60). In the published version, such blunt remarks are replaced by more polished, but no less damning, attacks on the professional system.

She points out the close link between claims to social superiority in the professions, whether "by dressing differently, or by adding titles before, or letters after their names," and their "advertisement function": They serve, she states, "the same function as the tickets in a grocer's shop" (*TG* 137–38). Woolf therefore differed from some of her male contemporaries: As a woman writer, her attitude towards the professions was perhaps developed via a different perspective, and her political tendencies diverged from some of theirs.[78] Some critics have already written about this discrepancy, and a few comparisons between Eliot's version of "professional" modernism and Woolf's version already exist.[79] This book addresses the need for a more extended and in-depth focus on Woolf's engagement with professional values, looking at her as a writer in her own right and on her own terms.

Despite the existence of the short studies which argue for important differences between her views on professionalism and those of her male contemporaries, Woolf has recently become more directly implicated in the same arguments. In *Expert Modernists, Matricide, and Modern Culture: Woolf, Forster, Joyce* (2004), Cucullu posits a Woolf whose modernist aesthetics were really attempts to exploit the ideology of expert culture in professional society.[80] One of the results of my study is to problematise such attempts to situate Woolf as another modernist writer who manipulated the marketplace for her own gain, who pretended to divest herself from the marketplace in creating a modernist practice and aesthetics but actually used this feigned disavowal for her own advantage, to gain cultural and economic capital. In other words, this would be a Woolf who went with the times, appropriating professional ideology and reaping its material and status rewards. Such a view would be based on what Jennifer Ruth calls "the hermeneutics of suspicion" in her critique of scholarship on the relationship between nineteenth-century fiction and professionalism which reads into authors' and characters' claims of professional merit the specious attempt to divest themselves from the marketplace.[81]

This book does not rest on the assumption that such a hermeneutics of suspicion is always unjustified, but rather that it becomes problematic for reading Woolf. She was obviously not unaware of professional ideology and the potential for hypocritical disavowal from material concerns: One of the goals of this book is to show this. Nor was she uncompromised in duplicitous claims of anti-commercialism, as will become clear in Chapter 2. But what this book also reveals is that she was too aware of professional ideology, and too consciously and vocally critical of it, to use it unscrupulously. When reading Woolf's works and life closely, the claim that she deliberately and consistently utilised and manipulated the selfsame ideology she so passionately deplored in her writing – and tried to deplore in her life, earnestly although not always successfully – to gain more of the very same material rewards she condemned, is not convincing. Care must be taken to avoid overapplication of the hermeneutics of suspicion. Is it, for instance, possible that Woolf publicly disavowed money concerns because she really was afraid of the corrupting power of money, and not because she actually wanted more of it? This book shows that Woolf's criticism of the professions was on the whole not a device to gain more status or money, but comprised a sincere attempt to build a better society, a "new world" in which "we will be free" (*Y* 217).

Professionalism and Woolf's Early Short Stories

Some of Woolf's earlier short stories demonstrate how she imagined possibilities beyond received notions of professionalism, and this section briefly discusses these by way of introduction into subsequent literary analysis. "The Journal of Mistress Joan Martyn" (1906) and "A Dialogue upon Mount Pentelicus" (1906) engage with the tension between individuality and imagination on the one hand, and professional academic discourse on the other. In the first story, the narrator, Rosamond Merridew, a documentary historian, advocates the importance of "certain digressions" in the historian's academic discourse. These depict scenes from historical subjects' lives and are products of her imagination rather than based on hard-and-dry facts. "It is well known," she says, "that the period I have chosen is more bare than any other of private records; unless you choose to draw all your inspiration from the *Paston Letters* you must be content to imagine merely, like any other story teller" (*CSF* 35). As a private narrative, the sixteenth-century journal by Joan Martyn challenges the reader to go beyond factual historical dissection and discourse, and engage with her personally and imaginatively. Leena Kore Schröder has argued that Merridew was modelled on F. W. Maitland, Professor of the Laws of England at the University of Cambridge, whom Leslie Stephen asked to write his biography (published in 1906).[82] Maitland's methodology, Schröder points out, put great emphasis on sources of subjects' personal experiences, so that the lives he wrote portrayed three-dimensional human beings, showing their public as well as their private sides.[83] In other words, Maitland was able to create a distinct academic discourse which, while still professional in the sense that it was ensconced within the academy, moved away from an emphasis on fact as "truth" and on "the sterner art of the Historian" as necessarily distinct from the art of imagination (*CSF* 35). His work exemplifies the possibility to incorporate both the public and the private into the professional, to allow a personal, sympathetic engagement with subjects as human beings alongside a more objective, factual narrative, by which the word "professional" does not need to be defined.

In "A Dialogue," two men in a group of Englishmen on a trip in Greece argue about how to view the country, the people and its civilisation. The first thinks the epitome of beauty achieved by the ancient Greeks is never to be surpassed; the second that such views do not see Greece, but merely take it as a text to be inscribed with whatever the scholar exalts: "Indeed there is no reason why you should read their writings, for have you not written them?" (*CSF* 66). The debate is interrupted by the unexpected arrival of a Greek monk, whose immediate presence confounds all attempts at fixation, "[s]uch was the force of the eye that fixed them" in return (67). Flesh-and-blood human beings resist the discourse in "which etymologists define," and "which archaeologists can dispute" (66), which attempts to inscribe and dissect academically but fails to engage with people as people. Instead, they and their lives, if to be analysed by these disciplines, should be captured by methodological shifts in professional discourse such as those effected by Maitland.

"The Mark on the Wall" (1917) continues this questioning of the limits of social conceptions of valid, professional knowledge, and to counter types of epistemological prioritising which threaten to confound and invalidate a freely roaming imaginative mind.[84] "The Mark" is, like Woolf's essay "Modern Fiction" (1919), famous for expressing her modernist questioning of narrative structure and reality. Woolf's quest in the story for a style that explores the (un)knowability of the other would eventually lead to her experimental breakthrough in *Jacob's Room* (1922), in which the narrative claims to depict Jacob's life, yet simultaneously undercuts its own ability to represent and understand him. The narrator in "The Mark" deliberately forestalls discovering what the mark on the wall really is by remaining resolutely at a distance from it while allowing her mind to speculate freely. This imaginative space leads her to reflect on the nature of knowledge itself. "[L]earned men," she thinks, are no more than "the descendants of witches and hermits who crouched in caves and in woods brewing herbs, interrogating shrew-mice and writing down the language of the stars." The accepted factual and objective knowledge they create are mere "superstitions." Therefore, "[a] world without professors or specialists" would be "a very pleasant world." Erupting freely into imaginative metaphor, she imagines this to be "[a] quiet spacious world, with the flowers so red and blue in the open fields," in "which one could slice with ones thought as a fish slices the water with his fin, grazing the stems of the water-lilies, hanging suspended over nests of white sea eggs ..." (87). If only, she laments, "it were not for Whitaker's Almanack [and] the Table of Precedency!" (88). There are multiple accounts of truths that require individual exploration beyond the boundaries set by "professors or specialists" (87) which are too rigid and allow for too little imaginative, sympathetic engagement with others and the world.

The story has recently been read as an example of Woolf drawing on naturalist approaches to resist patriarchal ways of ordering,[85] and to counter rigid forms of classification and taxonomy prominent in the Victorian life sciences.[86] Such new insights into Woolf's methodology and perspective have their bearing on her attitude towards professionalism as well. Woolf's use of natural imagery here is one early example of the ways in which she explored the mind's flight from standardised professional methodology that sought to define a set version of reality and truth.

One last example of Woolf's preoccupation with potential conflicts between one's personal interests and socially recognised professions prior to the works from the 1920s and 1930s is the story "Solid Objects" (1918). John, an aspiring politician, takes his fascination with collecting extraordinary objects such as stones and glass to such an extreme that he ruins his professional career. Collecting objects for their own sake for no other reason than a search for beauty in them is, after all, not a social profession. "Pretty stones," his friend Charles tells him as he leaves at the end of the story, trivialising John's activities, which by contrast John takes to be more important than anything else. John fails to balance or reconcile his private and public worlds, with a passionate interest in the former which is an ill fit with his formal profession in the latter. Such socially untranslatable private interests are often called "amateur" interests. But although the word "amateur" is derived from the Latin verb *amare*, to love, in its modern use it barely captures John's obsession with his objects, and is easily obscured in the shadow cast by the much more imposing word "profession." In these examples drawn from Woolf's earlier short stories, then, we can already observe Woolf attempting to conceive of alternatives to customary ways of participating in the professions.

Methodology and Structure

This study focuses on how Woolf engaged critically with the social, political and economic phenomenon of the professions at the beginning of the twentieth century, with implications for how she thought about the dilemmas modern individuals faced in being integral selves, in trying to live whole, fulfilling lives. The methodological basis on which this study builds its arguments comprises a firm placing of Woolf in her historical context, rather than a fixed theoretical framework. The study is informed by later sociological theories of the professions and the patterns of professionalisation, such as those provided by Magali Sarfatti Larson, Harold Perkin, Keith M. Macdonald, Ann Witz and others.[87] However, these are not used either to underpin or to encase it. Instead, this book is driven by Woolf's own views and those circulating in her context, which would have been readily available to her. It shows how Woolf tapped into related debates, and contributed to them by questioning the professions and their ideologies; and how she acceded to their value to society – such as the opportunity they provided of a decent income and the usefulness of procedures of professional accreditation – but simultaneously resisted them. Although later social theories, such as those by Perkin, will occasionally be used as critical material, the focus is on elucidating Woolf's thinking – and the results of that thinking in her work – using the social background of her own times, and on representing the issue of professionalism as she encountered it. At times, because women's issues were so important to the question of the professions for Woolf, the study may seem to take on a feminist perspective. However, this is not so much part of a preconceived systematic approach as it is the result of following the process of Woolf's own thematic choices in her writing and thinking.

The chapters will draw on a variety of works by Woolf. The objective is not to be exhaustive or strictly chronological throughout, but rather to explore in depth works and themes which are particularly relevant to professional issues, and allow these, rather than chronology, to guide the study. The book will focus on several major novels: *Mrs Dalloway* for its depiction of doctors and the professional medical system; *To the Lighthouse* and *Between the Acts* for their two women of vocation; *The Years* for its latent concerns with the professions for building a better society, as observed from its holograph; and *Between the Acts* again for the larger issue of the force of specialisation at the heart of professionalisation. But all chapters will make some use of Woolf's essay *Three Guineas*, the only book which she made clear was devoted to the professions as the core theme, and which is, in effect, the linchpin of this study.

The aim of this study, as should now be obvious, is not to fit Woolf into existing theories and models of literary modernisms, or to provide a paradigm of literary professionalism in early twentieth-century Britain.

What it sets out to do instead is to provide new ways of looking at Woolf and her work by exploring how she interacted with the issue of the professions. Representations of professional characters exist in literature from various periods, and many, if not most writers at the beginning of the twentieth century wrote about them. But Woolf does not seem to be just another author whose works merely included professional characters. She actively engaged with the problems posed by the professions and their values, in her thinking, life and work, aesthetically, philosophically and politically, which makes the topic of the professions a rich area of investigation for her.

The book is structured around two parts. Part I focuses on two specific professions which played a major role in Woolf's life: the medical profession and what she called the "profession of literature" (*TG* 188), and three women artists: Woolf herself, Lily Briscoe in *To the Lighthouse* and Miss La Trobe in *Between the Acts*. Chapter 1 explains how Woolf's political and aesthetic engagement with medicine (one of the most powerful professions in the early twentieth century) and with the doctor figure is closely related to wider debates in society on medical professionalism. In so doing, it reassesses the view that Woolf was, in the face of the medical profession, merely a victim, and argues for a more politically empowered view of Woolf – one which shows she actively sought to improve medicine, using her aesthetics in her novel *Mrs Dalloway* and the woman figure in her essay *Three Guineas* to counter the dehumanising tendencies in its professionalising processes.

Chapter 2 investigates Woolf's views on the relationship between literature and professionalism. For literature, professionalisation was a difficult and to a certain extent incongruous process. Writing can be seen as professional work because it is brainwork; but because it is based on such indefinite qualities as creativity and imagination, it is not a field which can be easily standardised, one of the main procedures for professionalisation. The chapter historicises and problematises the terms "amateurism" and "professionalism" for literature, showing how Woolf both applied and subverted them, constantly using them as reference points to circle the dilemma of what the profession of literature should entail – how it could both be driven by one's personal vision and be taken seriously by others, be done out of love and allow a living to be made, be private and public.

Chapter 3 continues from the relationship between art and professionalism by looking at Woolf's two fictional women of vocation, Lily Briscoe and Miss La Trobe. It argues for ways in which we can consider them as "professional" while they are removed from material concerns and formal institutions. Through this, it demonstrates how Woolf reconfigures the idea of professional work in art so as to realise in her fiction some of the claims of sincere devotion to work made by professional ideology (such as economic disinterestedness) and discard some of its deleterious characteristics (such as the very implication in the economic interest it feigns removal from).

Part II focuses on the interactions between literary aesthetics and political and economic context in Woolf's last two novels, which respond more generally to the effects of professionalisation and specialisation on life in human society. Chapter 4 makes use of holograph versions of *The Years* to show that Woolf's ambivalent feelings towards women's entry into the professions not only informed her political views in *Three Guineas*, but also shaped her aesthetic decisions during the extensive rewriting process of *The Years*. Through this, it reconsiders Woolf's use of such devices as ellipses, truncations and omissions in the novel. It argues that the vision underlying the novel is possibly even more sweeping and radical than the solutions proposed in *Three Guineas*, and that Woolf's views of the professional system became the basis for her vision of freedom in a new type of society. Chapter 5 focuses on the larger force of specialisation which underlies the professionalising process, and proposes Woolf's concern with how to reach the right amount of specialisation as a new way to explain and reconcile the seemingly contradictory aesthetic forces of fragmentation and unity in *Between the Acts*.

PART I

Two Professions and Three Women of Vocation

CHAPTER I

The Ethics and Aesthetics of Medicine

I want to criticise the social system, and to show it at work, at its most intense.

– D 2: 248

Professionalism tends to be unchivalrous, tyrannical, or cruel towards the weak committed to its care.[1]

During his consultation with the Harley Street nerve specialist Sir William Bradshaw in *Mrs Dalloway*, Septimus compares both Bradshaw and Dr Holmes, who was previously consulted for his mental symptoms, to "human nature": "Once you fall, Septimus repeated to himself, human nature is on you. Holmes and Bradshaw are on you. They scour the desert. . . . The rack and the thumbscrew are applied. Human nature is remorseless" (107). The image of "human nature" as "the repulsive brute, with the blood-red nostrils" conveys the horror of the force of tyrannical power which represses social deviations into conformity, and which authority figures such as Holmes and Bradshaw represent. Septimus calls only the two doctors "human nature." Although the metaphor suggests that all humans are capable of the cruelties the doctors inflict, they are singled out as agents of the cruelties of the "social system" (D 2: 248).

This view is historically significant. By the twentieth century, the medical profession had become established as one of the most powerful professional institutions of all time, and had come to be regarded as a principally representative example of the kind of social order that professional systems created.[2] This had come about not least importantly because of the legislation of medical practice in the nineteenth century, which organised it into one single profession. The two most important parliamentary acts in this regard were the Apothecaries Act of 1815 and the Medical Act of 1858. The Apothecaries Act was the first of its kind, arising out of the desire by apothecaries, or general practitioners, for a formal controlling body that would protect their interests in the face of competition from druggists and "improper persons."[3] The act required licensing by examination of a large number of medical men. Since the training of such medical men was now standardised, regulated and certified by the Society of Apothecaries, the act increased their public standing and power,[4] although this did little to mitigate intra-professional competition between general practitioners, surgeons and physicians, which would continue well after the act.[5]

The Medical Act of 1858, also in part a response to competition from perceived outsiders, led to the founding of the General Medical Council (GMC) as the overseeing authority of all existing licensing medical bodies.[6] It established a national register for legally recognised medical practitioners, which helped define the legal boundaries of the medical profession. Although the unqualified were not banned outright from practice, which was a disappointment to the qualified, they were henceforth forbidden from posing as medical practitioners.[7] The act was the first step towards the national regulation of medicine as one single profession and the establishment of a monopoly of doctors' services. Although the tripartite structure of medicine remained, doctors saw themselves increasingly as members of a common profession with common interests, whose authority was backed by such huge national organisations as the GMC and the British Medical Association (BMA), the professional association for doctors.

By the early twentieth century, by setting medicine apart from mere commercial trade and positing the pursuit of higher ideals such as public service as the goal, the attempts at professionalising medicine were largely complete. Restricting access to training had turned medical services into a scarcity, entry into the profession was more difficult, and organisations such as the GMC and the BMA controlled the terms of services. This successful organisation of medicine into a national profession also meant that it was, and saw itself as, a sociopolitical body whose task it was to serve the greater good of society. The scientific positivism on which medical science was based was now mapped onto a sociopolitical positivism of a national medical profession, dictating that it should be equally logical, rational and objective, and lead to normative laws and standards.

This chapter, moving away from biography and psychiatry,[8] and from Woolf's role as a "female victim of male medicine,"[9] aims to explore Woolf's engagement with medicine as such a professional and professionalised practice. It argues for the importance of the contextualisation of Woolf's literary critique of doctors within wider debates in British society on the medical profession. This alternative focus will allow us to see that Woolf and her writing responded actively to the problem of medical professionalism by advocating a more humanistic medicine, with the incorporation of ethical values such as sympathy and trust, and with doctors who could go beyond their customary methods of empirical analysis and thinking. This new emphasis can also attune us to an even wider range of possibilities for reading the novel, for instance as a key text in the field of the medical humanities. Marcia Day Childress, for instance, has described her use of *Mrs Dalloway* to explore issues of medical ethics, pointing out that it can stimulate doctors' examination "into the ethical challenges, responsibilities, and rewards of professional life," and heighten their awareness of "varieties of voice and experience encountered in practice."[10] This is a role which Woolf herself had already hinted at in the novel. In one of the few direct glimpses into Bradshaw's candid thoughts in the novel, he thinks of Septimus:

> The fellow made a distasteful impression. For there was in Sir William, whose father had been a tradesman, a natural respect for breeding and clothing, which shabbiness nettled; again, more profoundly, there was in Sir William, who had never had time for reading, a grudge, deeply buried, against cultivated people who came into his room and intimated that doctors, whose profession is a constant strain upon all the highest faculties, are not educated men. (106–07)

Here Woolf suggests there are other dimensions to the education and cultivation of human beings that are not sufficiently addressed in medical training and thinking, which may account in part for Bradshaw's uncannily mechanistic thinking. In focusing excessively on a normative view of his patients' conditions, Bradshaw neglects moral and creative aspects of human experience and existence, to the detriment of both himself and his patients, and in ethical if not professionally procedural violation of the Hippocratic oath – to do no harm.

Woolf's censure, however, was not a categorical dismissal of the medical profession or its practitioners, and the two doctors in *Mrs Dalloway* should not be construed to represent the entire profession, for all the sweeping remarks Woolf could make in her diaries and letters, in her anger and frustration, about doctors as a group. In fact, doctors themselves disagreed at times, as Carr-Saunders and Wilson point out, with the perceived "self-regarding motives" of their own professional organisation, the BMA. The authors write that "[n]ot a few medical men in each generation have been uneasy about the policy of the Association. There is and there has long been an undercurrent of opinion that its forceful, unsleeping, and ubiquitous activities are undignified."[11] And they too could be aware and openly critical of the potential for hypocrisy in their own profession.

In 1934, for instance, the speaker, Lord Macmillan, says at a lecture on "The Professional Mind" to the Medico-Psychological Association: "There was more lip service nowadays to lofty social motives, but the pursuit of selfish aims under the guise of public good was not an unknown phenomenon."[12] Woolf's satire of doctors in the novel aimed to bring this "undercurrent" to the surface, to improve medical practice for both practitioners and patients.

The first part of this chapter relates Woolf's portrayal of the ideal-espousing meretriciousness of the doctors in *Mrs Dalloway* to the professionalisation of medicine. It argues that Woolf's criticism focuses on the dehumanising effects of medical professional ideology, and that she sought to shift the emphasis on the public in the medical profession back to the individual, its macroscopic view of society back to a personal consideration of the human patient. She chose to respond to this only on her own terms, most notably in *Mrs Dalloway*, "On Being Ill" and *Three Guineas*, as opposed to other political avenues familiar to her through her correspondences with Margaret Llewelyn Davies, described in the second part of this chapter. The final two parts explore Woolf's aesthetic interventions in *Mrs Dalloway*, and her rhetorical strategies in *Three Guineas*.

"A Whited Sepulchre": Sir William Bradshaw and the Discourse of Medical Professionalism

One famously acerbic passage on Bradshaw in the novel highlights the sinister pursuit of power beneath the veneer of superficially admirable and respectable ideals:

> Worshipping proportion, Sir William not only prospered himself but made England prosper, secluded her lunatics, forbade childbirth, penalised despair, made it impossible for the unfit to propagate their views until they, too, shared his sense of proportion ... ; Sir William with his thirty years' experience of these kinds of cases, and his infallible instinct, this is madness, this sense; in fact, his sense of proportion.
>
> But Proportion has a sister, less smiling, more formidable.... Conversion is her name and she feasts on the wills of the weakly, loving to impress, to impose, adoring her own features stamped on the face of the populace. At Hyde Park Corner on a tub she stands preaching; shrouds herself in white and walks penitentially disguised as brotherly love through factories and parliaments; offers help, but desires power.... This lady too ... had her dwelling in Sir William's heart, though concealed, as she mostly is, under some plausible disguise; some venerable name; love, duty, self sacrifice.

How he would work – how toil to raise funds, propagate reforms, initiate institutions! But conversion, fastidious Goddess, loves blood better than brick, and feasts most subtly on the human will. (109–10)

Woolf highlights the deceptive performativity of Bradshaw's role as a famous nerve expert, depicting his unique expertise and experience, on which he has built his charismatic reputation, as a glossy cover for his hidden and true motive of conversion – to propagate fixed ways of thinking and acting on the populace.[13] Bradshaw's professional image (as having "thirty years' experience" and an "infallible instinct" in the diagnosis of "madness") contradicts his own description of his field as "this exacting science which has to do with what, after all, we know nothing about – the nervous system, the human brain" (108).[14] Woolf shared some of the scepticism expressed in this passage with others in her time. In 1917, Hayward, in his book *Professions and Originality*, argues:

In the case of the medical profession,

(1) Knowledge,
(2) Money,
(3) Medical prestige,

may each be regarded as more important than the claims of kindness or humanity.[15]

Two decades later, an article in the *New Statesman and Nation* remarks on "the unwillingness of the public to accord to the medical profession the place the profession thinks it ought to have. It is all a part of the impatience with closed professions and mysteries."[16]

The language Woolf draws on to deride Bradshaw's self-aggrandising rhetoric is closely related to the language employed by the profession itself at the time. The words Bradshaw uses, such as "Proportion" (112), and "love, duty, self-sacrifice" (110), which serve as the advertising slogans for his cause of conversion, were part of the vocabulary of a self-promoting medical profession which sought to expand its influence through presenting its sociopolitical influence as necessary, beneficial and altruistic. As the first example of many to follow in this chapter, an address by Sir Bertrand Dawson on "The Future of the Medical Profession" in 1918 to the West London Medico-Chirurgical Society draws on such notions to justify an expansion of the clout of the profession: "With so much of the flower of our manhood sacrificed for the great cause, the rearing of a healthy race has become a supreme necessity."[17] He argues for the need to found a "Ministry of Health" to serve as the "brain" of the "body politic" of the profession, which will lead to greater national well-being and prosperity.[18] The novel similarly links Bradshaw's work and esteem as a specialist to England's economic growth and power, with the two in a symbiotic relationship together.

The trope of the medical profession as a massive engine of progress which emerges from Bradshaw's portrait can also be found in much of the discourse used by the BMA at the time. The organisation frequently described the role of medicine in all-encompassing terms, viewing the population as a homogeneous group rather than as discrete individuals, and health as a universal concept with common criteria. In an address in 1921, the president of the BMA cites from *A New Chapter in the Science of Government* (1919), which states that because "the whole hygiene of the folk requires its [the medical profession's] utmost and careful consideration in all its aspects, it is determined to be adequately represented in the government of the country." He proclaims that the profession is a "power that is essential to the well-being of the people, to be encouraged and fostered as one of our great national assets."[19] "[T]he whole medical profession of the country," he says, "is now in process of organizing itself into a vast unified guild of a medico-political kind, which later will embrace the entire world."[20] This is being achieved through "our ever-growing efficiency," which is "a gain all along the line; an advance that is quite as marked in the socio-politico-medical world as it is in the strictly scientific, and all purely professional and aiming at improvement of the health and welfare of the people with proficiency as our goal, ever mindful that the standard of our efficiency is the measure of the value of our services to the State."[21] Medicine will not just heal the patient; it will heal the whole nation, and perhaps even the world. What is remarkable in this address are the compound words ("medico-political" and "socio-politico-medical") which attempt to link medicine with other areas, reflecting the ambitions of the profession for the expansion of its sphere of influence, an ambition which is very similar to Bradshaw's.

Such continued professionalisation would of course ensure not just national welfare, but also professional welfare. In the same lecture on "The Future of the Medical Profession," Sir Bertrand argues for the necessity of "secur[ing] [for the profession] that proper influence in public affairs which, to the detriment of the state, is now so sadly lacking." Whereas "[i]n the United States the medical profession occupies a leading position in the life and counsels of the American nation," in England, he laments, "although doctors in their individual capacity enjoy the confidence and even the affection of their *patients*, yet as a profession their influence is small and their advice regarded as of small account." This, he says, "must change, and let us see to it that we come into our kingdom."[22] This last metaphor, used to assert doctors' rightful position in Sir Bertrand's mind, brings to mind the very similar desire to conquer and convert that Woolf identifies in Bradshaw. In 1923, an article on the profession in the *British Medical Journal* (*BMJ*) asserts that "[t]he record of ninety years' work shows that professional organization, directed with wisdom and imagination, can successfully combine service for its members with service for the public."[23] The question that the passage in *Mrs Dalloway* raises is if this combination could really be achieved so straightforwardly, or if it requires deeper introspection than such facile claims allow.

In the novel, Woolf similarly words Bradshaw's idealism in explicitly sociopolitical rather than medical or occupational terms. Bradshaw's planned confinement of Septimus into a home is "a question of law" (106).[24] Bradshaw's consulting room is no longer private, and legal and social conventions must dictate its workings. Conversely, Bradshaw's verdicts do not just exert power in his consulting room, but also in the public arena. He preoccupies himself with the establishment of public laws: at the party towards the end of the novel, Bradshaw and Richard Dalloway discuss "that Bill, which they wanted to get through the Commons." There was "[s]ome case, Sir William was mentioning, lowering his voice. It had its bearing upon what he was saying about the deferred effects of shell shock. There must be some provision in the Bill" (200–01). His public work overshadows his work with individual patients. When his overworked state is described, it is not because he is devoting too much individual time to his patients, to each of whom he metes out "three-quarters of an hour,"[25] but because he works on large-scale public projects: "How he would work – how toil to raise funds, propagate reforms, initiate institutions!"[26] But this macroscopic and public view of healing, indicating a mass and impersonal approach to medicine, could come at the expense of the individual patient like Septimus. If the ideals of the medical profession had by now expanded into other areas of society, reality sometimes remained mired in inequality, manipulation and extortion. *Mrs Dalloway* describes how power is abused by these new authority figures to "feast[] on the wills of the weakly," and to decide that "this is madness, this sense; in fact his sense of proportion" (109). The metaphor of a feast is telling: doctors do not simply destroy "the wills of the weakly," but, as with food, assimilate these "wills" into the system to empower and substantiate. This feasting created an endless cycle of demand and power consolidation, which is perhaps one of the main reasons why both Holmes and Bradshaw refuse to release Septimus from their care, even when neither Septimus nor Rezia want it.

Sue Thomas has connected the conversation between Bradshaw and Richard Dalloway to the *Report of the War Office Committee* presented to Parliament in August 1922, which described shell-shock symptoms and recommended treatment methods such as "deliberate insistence on the illegitimacy of nerves as a symptom of illness," and "the minimization of sympathy for the patient."[27] Alex Zwerdling has pointed out that this document does not show much consideration for such patients, making no distinction between shell shock and cowardice or disobedience.[28] Despite the proclaimed authority of medicine as a science to be widely applied to heal both humans and society, and the certitude of diagnosis displayed by such physicians specialising in mental health as Bradshaw, the *Report* shows that consensus on diagnosis and treatment had yet to be reached on shell shock. Woolf expresses such uncertainty in the novel. Claiming to represent the "truth" (*H* 147) of science and norms, doctors instead "differed in their verdicts" (*MD* 162). Although "Holmes said one thing, Bradshaw another," "judges they were; who mixed the vision and the sideboard; saw nothing clear, yet ruled, yet inflicted" (*MD* 162). We can therefore understand Woolf's choice of shell shock as a socially relevant and timely example to use to detract from particular types of self-professed medical authority.

Apart from the view by medical doctors specialising in mental illness, however, there was an alternative understanding of the mind emerging at the periphery of the medical profession in Britain: the field of psychoanalysis. David Eder, one of the founders of the London Psychoanalytic Society in 1913 (which later became the British Psycho-Analytic Society in 1919), authored *War-Shock: The Psycho-Neuroses in War Psychology and Treatment* (1919), a notably more sympathetic account of soldiers who suffered from what he preferred to call war shock rather than shell shock, because he saw soldiers' mental problems as deriving from their psychological response to the horrors of their context.[29] The book recorded his experiences as an army doctor in the First World War, and his accounts were based on his belief in the need for

> a close personal relationship with the patients, allowing them to talk at their ease, asking few questions, but gathering their life-history, earlier characteristics, their dreams past and present, the details of their symptoms, and their mental and physical condition, both at the time when the disease occurred and subsequently.[30]

This is a wholly different approach from that by Bradshaw in the novel. As Michael Whitworth has pointed out, Bradshaw, in contrast to psycho-analysts, often refers to Septimus as a "case," showing that he is unlikely to treat and listen to his patient as a fellow human being.[31] Being one of the first doctors to apply Sigmund Freud's ideas to shell shock, Eder saw it as "a variety of hysteria," and advocated psychotherapy (in the form of hypnosis, suggestion and persuasion) as treatment.[32] He specifically sounded a note of caution about the Weir Mitchell cure with which Woolf was famously treated, the "rest cure" which consisted of a regime of enforced rest and (over)feeding,[33] thinking it "the very reverse of rational treatment."[34] The regimen, he writes, "is most unsuitable for cases of war-shock among soldiers – it prolongs their illness and may sow the seeds of a more permanent psycho-neurosis."[35]

As Nicole Ward Jouve has pointed out, although Woolf had family and friends who ascribed to psychoanalysis and even practised it, she herself was often distant, even hostile, to the emerging psychoanalytic profession.[36] We may expect the cool response from the medical profession to psychoanalytic approaches – which handled mental illness so differently from prevailing medical methods in focusing on a personal and searching analysis and examination of each patient's life – to make Woolf inclined to a more favourable treatment of psychoanalysis. This would seem particularly the case when we consider her hostility towards the entrenchment of such harmful and ineffective standard methods as the Weir Mitchell treatment. Jouve offers a sound explanation for Woolf's attitude, suggesting that Woolf did not just resent "the fictions of psychoanalysis," but also disapproved of and felt threatened by how Freud proclaimed his theories as science, in doing so aligning himself, in her mind, to some of her incompetent and abusive doctors.[37] Despite the central concept of the unconscious, psychoanalysis was to be described in scientific language and terminology, and to use the same processes of strict empirical validation as medical science.[38] Its efforts to institutionalise itself as a legitimate branch of medical science meant that it was one of many forms of brainwork aiming for professional status in this period – something which Sarah Winter, applying the sociological theories of Magali Sarfatti Larson on the professions, has called "Freud's professionalizing strategies."[39] Like other branches of medicine, psychoanalysis attempted to establish its own legitimacy, and imposed fixed readings of the human psyche in professional/scientific language and terminology.

Woolf's response to psychoanalysis in the 1920s is notable for its deflation and ridicule specifically of the scientific basis of psychoanalysis, and we can read this as part of her reaction against the same in the medical establishment. Writing about James Strachey's plans to conduct psychoanalysis for a living in 1918, she says: "Poor James Strachey was soft as moss, lethargic as an earthworm. James, billed at the 17 Club to lecture on 'Onanism,' proposes to earn his living as an exponent of Freud in Harley Street. For one thing, you can dispense with a degree" (*D* 1: 221). Woolf's comment is double-barrelled: Psychoanalysis, which one can become an expert in without a degree, can hardly be called a science; but since a medical degree does not guarantee real knowledge and expertise either, one may as well do without. With the Hogarth Press about to publish Freud's *Collected Papers*, she dismisses the psychoanalytic readings of patients as fictions posing as science: "We could all go on like that for hours; and yet these Germans think it proves something – besides their own gull-like imbecility" (*L* 3: 135).[40] And in a review of J. D. Beresford's *An Imperfect Mother* entitled "Freudian Fiction" (1920), Woolf writes, perhaps no less satirically than in her portrayal of Bradshaw, that

> A patient who has never heard a canary sing without falling down in a fit can now walk through an avenue of cages without a twinge of emotion since he has faced the fact that his mother kissed him in his cradle. The triumphs of science are beautifully positive.... [B]efore the end of the book the medical man is left in possession of the field; all the characters have become cases; and our diagnosis is now so assured that a boy of six has scarcely opened his lips before we detect in him unmistakable symptoms of the prevailing disease. (*E* 3: 196–97)

At this point, Woolf conflates "the medical man" and the psychoanalyst. The similarities of psychoanalysis as an aspiring branch of the medical profession may account for why it could not be a viable alternative to psychiatry to Woolf. But this did not prevent Woolf from using Freudian ideas such as "infantile fixation," "Oedipus complex" and "castration complex" (254–55) in *Three Guineas* – for both their novelty in her own novel argument (that patriarchy and war were linked, and that the same aggressive impulses underpinned the professions), and for their claim to scientific authority in an essay which, as Zwerdling has written, deliberately takes on an "elaborate scholarly apparatus."[41]

The bigger issue of contention to Woolf, however, would remain with the mainstream medical profession rather than the newly established psychoanalytic branch. Directing our discussion back to the former, we have seen that its espousal of professional ideals, and its establishment of qualifying certification and associations to ensure not only standards of service, but also power and monopoly, follow the pattern of professionalisation

as described by Perkin. There is one important aspect remaining to be
discussed that is often the focus of sociologists of the professions, and
of Woolf: that of money, or more specifically of how much should be
enough for remuneration of medical services. As I have pointed out, professionalisation derives from the desire not just for power, but also for
financial independence and gain, which can itself be better consolidated
by anti-commercial rhetoric. An article in the *BMJ* in 1922 entitled "The
Profession of Medicine" describes it as "a calling which the general public
and public authorities have come to look on as partly a form of philanthropic service," which the writer says is a "compliment" that "would be
more welcome if it were less a cloak of meanness." Judgments on money
matters in medicine must be made by people within the profession itself,
because "the aims and requirements of modern medicine are still imper-
fectly understood by many lay persons," and "the financial interests of the
profession and the objects and methods of medical science are in constant
risk of attack from one quarter or another."[42] The writer therefore argues
for greater financial and professional autonomy from the state, even as
medicine had been cooperating with the state in its establishment of professional monopoly. Another article with the same title in *The Times* in
1921 warns that "[a]lready the public has begun to lower its opinion and
to speak of this great profession in terms of commerce." "Professions," the
writer says, "are not called into being: they develop out of noble minds,
and derive their sustenance from the general recognition of this nobil-
ity." Where before, "love and honour" were "always willingly accorded"
by merit of doctors' professional identity alone, now the "position in our
national life" which the medical profession occupied has been brought
down. This, the writer argues, "[n]othing but a return to ideals can
stay," which derive from doctors' sense of "vocation"[43] and "professional
spirit."[44]

The decorousness of such arguments and statements belie anxieties
about the loss of professional authority and financial control, and were in
part responses to accusations that medical appeals to professional values
were really for financial interests. The BMA was often accused "of seeking to further interests of the profession at the expense of the public."[45]
The *BMJ*, for example, reports that in a meeting of the Fabian Society
in 1927, W. A. Robson argued that any public policy by the BMA only
shows interest in "the private pockets of the doctors," and never in
"public welfare." This, he added, "showed what would come of giving the
professional men a free hand so long as their professional organization
was untouched."[46] In a point that I will return to when discussing Woolf's

stream-of-consciousness technique in the novel, although Woolf might have agreed with Robson's views, her psychological method – unlike the weight Robson places on "public benefit" – prioritises private, personal and individual well-being, on which she bases all propositions for public benefit.

Woolf's criticism in *Mrs Dalloway* of Bradshaw's excessive wealth, which symbolises as well as contributes to the social status he enjoys, addresses this context. Bradshaw's hunger for power, status and money does not end with the attainment of "enough to live upon" (*TG* 218), even though he is a top-earning physician. His "motor car," for example, is "low, powerful, grey with plain initials interlocked on the panel" (*MD* 103); as Septimus comments, "[t]he upkeep of that motor car alone must cost him quite a lot" (108). The room in which Bradshaw receives his patients has "valuable furniture"; "his income was quite twelve thousand a year"; and "Lady Bradshaw in ostrich feathers hung over the mantelpiece" (111). All of these represent as well as reinforce the validity of his "sense of proportion" (109). But in a passage which describes Lady Bradshaw waiting in the motorcar outside while Bradshaw is paying medical visits to the rich in the country, Woolf depicts the emptiness and restrictiveness of the excessive money he makes:

> Her ladyship waited with the rugs about her knees an hour or more, leaning back, thinking sometimes of the patient, sometimes, excusably, of the wall of gold, mounting minute by minute while she waited; … respected, admired, envied, with scarcely anything left to wish for … ; too little time, alas, with her husband, whose work grew and grew; … while she waited. (103–04)

Lady Bradshaw is waiting both for and on her husband. The "wall of gold" has grown too tall; it imprisons her, blocking her from seeing that the linear growth of the wall results in no horizontal movement, no actual displacement. The lengthy sentence begins as it ends, with Lady Bradshaw waiting. The stagnant lady in the stagnant car feigns advancement where there is none, as Bradshaw feigns healing even when there is only subjugation.

Such earlier attempts to "criticise the social system" *D* 2: 248 in the novel would later find full expression in *Three Guineas*.[47] In this essay, she quotes from the biography of William Broadbent, a prominent physician, to stress the importance of not making an excessive income:

> Take the doctor's profession next. "I have taken a good deal over £13,000 during the year, but this cannot possibly be maintained, and while it lasts it is slavery. What I feel most is being away from Eliza and the children so

frequently on Sundays, and again at Christmas." That is the complaint of a great doctor; and his patient might well echo it, for what Harley Street specialist has time to understand the body, let alone the mind or both in combination, when he is a slave to thirteen thousand a year? (195–96)

Woolf sees such an income not as a well-deserved reward for the provision of services, but as so extreme that it obliterates the doctor's private life and impedes his most basic duties. One of the main purposes of professionalisation, namely the protection of the income of service providers, seems to have become warped beyond its well-intended origins: immediate money-making in the medical profession is now a disease in itself, conquering doctors' entire lives and thwarting genuine improvement in medical science.

If we return to the 1910s as part of the context of such issues, we can see how Woolf responded to the social debate on political reforms to mitigate the commercial side of medicine in the form of the National Insurance Acts. The next section demonstrates Woolf's carefully peripheral participation with the issue in her writing. Unlike activists such as Margaret Llewelyn Davies, Woolf did not seek to remedy problems within the medical profession by formulating responses to specific political issues. Although both Woolf and Davies tried to shape the medical profession into one which was less competitive and money- and status-driven, their approaches were very different. This characterises Woolf's engagement with the professions in general: Although perhaps no less political, her response was often more broadly conceptual.

Medicine and Money: Comparing Woolf with Margaret Llewelyn Davies

The conflict in medicine between money and service standards had been an especially contentious issue during the previous centuries, as medicine was being organised into a protected, unified but also stratified profession. John Pickstone describes how, in the eighteenth century, medicine was informally structured, its services and products seen as market commodities which advertised in mass newspapers.[48] Gradually, however, medical practitioners wished to elevate the status of their work above mere trade.[49] At the beginning of the nineteenth century, it seemed to some doctors necessary self-protection: medical professionalisation was a desperate attempt to improve practitioners' livelihood, with some doctors bidding for Poor Law vacancies, and others subjected to aggressive bargaining strategies by Friendly Societies.[50]

The possibility of easing the incompatibility between money and service in the form of creating a national system of salaried doctors working for the state was widely considered in the first decades of the twentieth century.[51] In 1905, the BMA had initially proposed – in response to the excessive competition in the profession and the low rates of remuneration to doctors provided by local societies – a "Public Medical Service, to be organized by the profession itself." But the plans for National Insurance halted this idea of self-organisation, and the BMA instead set out to try to change the provisions under the scheme so that the profession would retain better control.[52]

A few years after the implementation of the National Insurance Act (1911), which introduced a mandatory contribution system for workers who earned less than £160 a year towards medical care,[53] the possibility of implementing a full state medical service was being heatedly debated. The main advantage cited was that it would "set the practitioner free from the competitive struggle."[54] A leading article on the medical profession in the *BMJ* in 1923 comments retrospectively on the series of acts: "If the freedom of family practice has been restricted by the Insurance Acts and Regulations, they have probably rendered it easier for a doctor to make an assured income out of attendance on working-class patients."[55] Such an "assured income" meant that doctors who attended poor patients were less tempted to make decisions in favour of their own material interests. The acts were a step towards recuperating what F. Lawson Dodd in 1927 described as "a declining popular faith in regular medical practice," brought about by "the acquisitive commercial system based upon intense individualism and competitiveness, which had invaded medical practice."[56] But the fundamental conflict between materialism and idealism in the medical profession remained. In 1935, a letter to the *BMJ* entitled "State-Organized Medicine: A Point of View" says:

> [T]he whole principle of medical service wherein a doctor is paid when a patient is ill and receives nothing when he is well is wrongly conceived. It is putting too much responsibility upon the shoulders of a practitioner to expect him to choose equitably between two lines of treatment when the bread-and-butter of his family depend upon his choice.... [U]ntil human nature is changed, or until the doctor is paid a salary for performing his proper function – that of maintaining his patients in health – such abuses, which threaten to discredit the profession in the eyes of the laity, will continue.[57]

Woolf was certainly aware of the debates, which, although with helping the working classes in mind, attempted to address issues similar to ones she herself was concerned about. In *The Voyage Out*, when Evelyn

Murgatroyd names "the Insurance Bill" as one of the "[q]uestions that really matter to people's lives" (235), she is referring to what became the Insurance Act in 1911.

Associations such as the Women's Co-operative Guild (WCG) were actively involved in shaping the medical part of the insurance scheme. The WCG lobbied for including dependants – namely wives who were not in paid employment and their children – under its provisions. The basis of this proposition was that, as Davies put it, "the woman contributes equally with the man to the upkeep of the home and the family income in reality is as much hers as the man's."[58] Some of their suggestions were subsequently incorporated into the final 1911 act, which included "a voluntary health scheme for non-wage earning women" and maternity benefits.[59]

Virginia Woolf's involvement with the WCG was initiated through Leonard Woolf, whose interest in the cooperative movement brought him into contact with Davies, the secretary of the WCG from 1889 to 1921.[60] Together with Leonard, Woolf attended its Annual Congress in Newcastle in June 1913, an event which was later recorded in her introduction to *Life as We Have Known It* (1931). After the act, the WCG continued to fight for better maternity and infant health care, and part of their campaign was the publication of a collection of letters from working women on their experience of childbirth and motherhood, which Woolf read in December 1914 and advised Davies to publish (*L* 2: 54). They appeared in September 1915 in the book *Maternity: Letters from Working Women*. The book was reviewed favourably by *The Times Literary Supplement*,[61] and the very same day that this review appeared, Woolf wrote to Davies: "Did you see your very warm review in the Times? Your Guild I find quoted everywhere" (*L* 2: 65).

The letters in *Maternity* were real examples used to support the arguments in the introduction and the conclusion on how the existing medical system could be transformed to help the working-class woman and her children better. The goal of the reforms was the levelling of the amount and quality of health care provided to working-class and middle-class women.[62] The suggestions in the book often encouraged the professionalisation of women health service providers. For example, under the heading of "Women Health Officers," it states that "[t]he status of Health Visitors should be raised, their salaries being increased, and three qualifications being required – i.e. midwifery, sanitary, and nursing certificates." The services of midwifery and nursing "should be organised by the Public Health Authorities," and "[l]onger training for midwives should be required," so that "an adequate salary [can be] secured to them." This would be the "only way of securing skilled attention for women" and "at the same time securing adequate payment for midwives."[63] It also asks for the establishment of "Maternity & Infant Centres," to which it would be "[d]esirable to appoint women doctors as municipal officers," and suggests that "working women should be elected onto councils and serve on public health committees."[64] In the end, it stresses the necessity for "partnership between the women concerned, the medical profession, and the State" to ensure that "the best results of democratic government can be secured for the mothers and infants of the country."[65] However, the beneficiaries of such a sweeping vision would not just be "mothers and infants," but also their many female service providers – the demand for whom would increase, and whose working conditions would be improved and standardised. The qualifications of women who already worked in the medical profession – but who, due to a lack of a proper certification and training system, were not earning the respect which they deserved – needed to be formalised. Women doctors in maternity and infant care had a unique role to play, and should be allowed full opportunity to contribute. The working woman's voice needed to be included in all these matters. All these arguments suggest that the WCG's goals were more than just improved health care for working-class women and their children. They were also trying to further women's entry into the historically male domains of politics and the professions by consolidating the position of women already working peripherally in the medical profession, and increasing the importance of those women who were fully qualified doctors. To shape these areas to women service providers' and receivers' needs would allow them to gain a voice, and gradual empowerment.

Woolf would not likely have disagreed with such arguments, which resembled hers in some ways. But what is noteworthy, although not surprising, is her limited engagement with the topic in her writing, for all its importance at the time, and for all Woolf's interest in the medical profession itself. The only other time when the Insurance Acts are mentioned, apart from the instance already referred to in *The Voyage Out*, is in *Night and Day*, when Katharine Hilbery, the upper-middle-class heroine of the book, and Mary Datchet, an independently minded suffragist, have the following conversation after a lecture on the Elizabethan use of metaphor:

> "They're exactly like a flock of sheep, aren't they?" she [Mary] said, referring to the noise that rose from the scattered bodies beneath her.
> Katharine turned and smiled.

"I wonder what they're making such a noise about?" she said.

"The Elizabethans, I suppose."

"No, I don't think it's got anything to do with the Elizabethans. There! Didn't you hear them say, 'Insurance Bill'?"

"I wonder why men always talk about politics?" Mary speculated. "I suppose, if we had votes, we should too."

"I dare say we should. And you spend your life in getting us votes, don't you?"

"I do," said Mary, stoutly. "From ten to six every day I'm at it." (45)

It is not entirely clear which of the many Insurance Bills at the time Katharine is referring to, but it would likely be one of the amending bills to the 1911 National Insurance Act. The National Health Insurance Act of 1918, for instance, changed contribution and benefit arrangements for women. Under the 1911 Act, women who had been insured before marriage but who did not work afterwards could become voluntary contributors. The National Health Insurance Act of 1918 removed this option but allowed such women to continue to receive some sickness and maternity benefits up to two years after the date of marriage.[66] The activities of the WCG, seen in the context of the conversation between Katharine and Mary, were attempting to shape ongoing social legislation such as the "Insurance Bill" (*ND* 45) to include women's voices, even when women did not yet have the vote. Yet Woolf's treatment here is peripheral: Even the politically engaged Mary refrains from direct engagement, curiously satisfied with relegating it to the male sphere.

The importance of the work done by Davies and such societies as the WCG was of interest to Woolf, and for all her ambivalence towards the working classes (which I will return to at the end of Chapter 4), her response to reading the letters in *Maternity* was a sympathetic one. That such issues received only two sporadic references in her writing should be noted in a discussion which attempts a politicised reading of Woolf's engagement with the medical profession. The easiest explanation would be that Woolf's preoccupation with money, status and power was grounded in the middle-class perspective she took in both *Mrs Dalloway* and *Three Guineas*, that this marked the boundary of her engagement with the medical profession, and that she seemed interested to merely a limited extent in the affordability of medical services in her writing. The only reference to doubts about Septimus's ability to afford medical fees is when the narrative describes Holmes's reaction when it is clear that Septimus is not improving under his care: "And if they were rich people, said Dr. Holmes, looking ironically round the room, by all means let them go to Harley

Street; if they had no confidence in him, said Dr. Holmes, looking not quite so kind" (*MD* 103).

But besides seeing Woolf's minimal engagement as class restrictiveness on her part, it may also be due to her tendency to deal with the issue from a broader and less politically restrictive perspective. In other words, Woolf seemed more concerned with the possible overall results, relevant across all classes, of the processes of professionalisation to medicine – a highly standardised and potentially dehumanising approach to medical treatment, which not only fails to help Septimus, but causes his death. The next section elaborates on her vision for the medical profession, one arrived at through quite a different approach from that of women activists such as Davies.

Remedies

In *Three Guineas*, Woolf relates some of the characteristics of the medical profession described in the previous sections directly to war. The essay criticises "the public world, the professional system, with its possessiveness, its jealousy, its pugnacity, its greed" (199), and points out that the professions "make the people who practise them possessive, jealous of any infringement of their rights, and highly combative if anyone dares dispute them" (191). Woolf concludes from examples from biographies of various successful professional men that they "cause us to doubt and criticise and question the value of professional life – not its cash value; that is great; but its spiritual, its moral, its intellectual value. They make us of the opinion that if people are highly successful in their professions they lose their senses" (197).

At the same time, Woolf would have known that doing away with the professional system for medicine was not a viable option: Amateurs could not consistently be relied on to have achieved the level of competence – vital in the curing of illness – which professionalism guaranteed. But the situation was not entirely irremediable: Women, she writes, who had been historically deprived of the very things the doctors in *Mrs Dalloway* are hungry for, based on "a different sex, a different tradition, a different education, and the different values which result from those differences" (239), are "immune without any trouble on [their] part from the particular loyalties and fealties which ... endowments and privileges engender" (207). Their difference is now crucial to fostering the opposing values of "ridicule, censure and contempt," which are "so essential for sanity, and so invaluable in preventing the great modern sins of vanity, egotism, and megalomania"

(207), faults the doctors in *Mrs Dalloway* are guilty of. Thus Woolf imposes specific conditions for women who wished to enter these masculine institutions, writing that "[i]f you refuse to be separated from the four great teachers of the daughters of educated men – poverty, chastity, derision and freedom from unreal loyalties – but combine them with some wealth, some knowledge, and some service to real loyalties then you can enter the professions and escape the risks that make them undesirable" (204). That way, she tells women, "you can join the professions and yet remain uncontaminated by them," and even possibly reverse some of the development which has led to abuse: "you can rid them of their possessiveness, their jealousy, their pugnacity, their greed" (208). What was needed was a balance between these lessons taught by women's "unpaid-for education" and "unpaid-for professions" (203) in the past, and men's paid-for education and professions; between "common sense" (*P* xv) and professional privileges.

In the section in *Three Guineas* on the donation of the narrator's second guinea to a society which promotes the entry of women into the professions, Woolf uses the pronoun "you" to address these women directly. However, since, as she argues, "the enormous professional competence of the educated man has not brought about an altogether desirable state of things in the civilized world" (198), ultimately educated men must also change for fundamental improvement to take place. Woolf chooses not to impose the conditions on men directly, however, merely structurally incorporating this section into the narrator's overall response to the barrister – who is a representative of male professionals – and his request to help prevent war. Although they would not much deprive women of existing material benefits, they would take away many from men. This is also why the narrator can wield more power over the women: Their "poverty" means that the guinea she donates the women, although constant in money value, is in real value worth significantly more to them than it would be to male professionals, so that she is able to "exercise the right of potential givers to impose terms" (163). In contrast, the third guinea, to be given to the society against war which the barrister belongs to, is "a free gift, given freely, without any other conditions than you choose to impose upon yourself" (272). Men's historical advantage meant they would need to give up some of these privileges voluntarily.

Woolf's portrayal and critique of medicine in both *Mrs Dalloway* and *Three Guineas* can thus be read as a constructive subversion of certain traits in its professionalisation. Her depiction of the "social system" (*D* 2: 248) was not merely autobiographical, but arose out of a real desire for change, in the hope of providing an alternative to its "old worn ruts"

(*TG* 231). When in *Three Guineas* Woolf recounts how Sophia Jex-Blake and other female medical students were barred from entering the Royal College of Surgeons to take their exams (189–90), the implication is that an exclusion of women would not just be women's loss but also men's, who would be rejecting an alternative force which could help improve their profession, their lives, and "the civilized world" (198). Women, trained to be fully qualified doctors, could retain and disseminate their alternative viewpoint derived from historically cultivated values so that a better, more sympathetic medical system could result.

Nor did Woolf only consider the patient's point of view in such an improvement of medicine. Woolf's more sympathetic description in *Three Guineas* of the real-life Sir William Broadbent as "a slave to thirteen thousand a year" (196), having little time to spend with his wife and children, perhaps also throws a slightly more compassionate light on Bradshaw in *Mrs Dalloway*, the possibility for which we may easily overlook in the novels' direction of our sympathies towards Septimus. The drive for status, money and power has deadened Bradshaw's emotions. He is all appearance but little substance, and has trapped himself in his overbearing view of Proportion. Portrayed as misguidedly power-hungry, he is as much imprisoned within his own mindset as Septimus is imprisoned within the "social system" (*D* 2: 248) which has made doctors absolute "judges" (*MD* 168). Although Bradshaw revels in his power, Woolf also describes his work as "toil" (110), and "the responsibilities and privileges of his profession" as "onerous" (104). Woolf's depictions of both the fictional and the real doctors show that she could sympathise, to a certain extent, with practitioners who called their own work slavery. Since "the professions have a certain undeniable effect upon the professors" (*TG* 191), doctors themselves needed healing from the potentially debilitating effects of their own profession.

Yet Woolf had perhaps exaggerated when she wrote that women could resist the temptations of the professions "without any trouble" (*TG* 207). The danger was that women, with the passing of the Sex Disqualification Removal Act and their gradual entry into the professions, would be assimilated into these institutions and add to, instead of counter, these attributes. Woolf's most haunting depiction of the possible detrimental effects of the professional system on a woman is focused on Peggy in *The Years*. Peggy's profession as a doctor has swallowed her whole being, and she has lost the possibilities for additional roles, such as maternity, which womanhood can bring, so that she regrets that "[s]he would have no children" (290). Unlike Holmes and Bradshaw, whom Woolf represents as unaware of their own imprisonment within their limited ideas and values, Peggy is only too painfully self-conscious of the limitations of her scientific, empiricist thinking. The description of her thoughts at the family party towards the end of the novel is telling: "What is the tip for this particular situation? she asked herself, as if she were prescribing for a patient. Take notes, she added. Do them up in a bottle with a glossy green cover, she thought. Take notes and the pain goes. Take notes and the pain goes, she repeated to herself as she stood there alone" (257). She thinks that "I'm good … at fact-collecting. But what makes up a person – (she hollowed her hand), the circumference, – no, I'm not good at that" (257–58). Inept in areas outside medicine, all she can fall back on in this social setting are her powers of objective analysis, but these fail to offer the comfort she seeks: "Time was getting on. An hour is sixty minutes, she said to herself; two hours are one hundred and twenty minutes. How many have I still to stay here?" (281). Despite her best intentions, she finds she cannot get out of the "groove" of being "hard; cold," "merely a doctor" (259). Her case is a chilly reminder that women, if they wanted to become doctors, might have to "profess the same loyalties that professional men have professed for many centuries" (*TG* 195), at the risk of ending up like the real Broadbent, or even like the fictional Holmes and Bradshaw.

This section has described Woolf's advice on how to improve the professional system underpinning medicine, arguing that the conditions which Woolf set out for women in *Three Guineas* also applied to men, so that both professionals, whether male or female, and the general population, including patients such as Septimus, could benefit. The next and final part returns to *Mrs Dalloway*. It shows that the novel's descriptions of doctors' impersonal and apathetic approach to medical treatment suggest the need for more personal trust and sympathy,[67] concepts often gendered female by Woolf, in a profession which had been objectifying these qualities away. In view of the large-scale changes and progress that the medical profession sought, some would have considered this a regression; but Woolf was precisely seeking improvement via a return to basic values, so that "these ancient and privileged professions [would come] more in touch with human needs" (*P* xv).

Humanising Healing: Stream of Consciousness, Sympathy and Trust

In the long passage quoted earlier, Woolf's choice of representing Bradshaw's thinking – by translating Bradshaw's word "Proportion" into the narrator's word "Conversion," which serves "to override opposition,

to stamp indelibly in the sanctuaries of others the image of herself"
(*MD* 112) – indicates a deliberate break between the narrator's and the
character's point of view. This sets the representation of Bradshaw apart
from that of other characters in the rest of the novel, whose voices usually
blend almost seamlessly with the narrator's because of the ways in which
Woolf uses free indirect thought representation (FITR), which shapes the
novel's stream-of-consciousness narrative. With FITR, characters' thoughts
are still moderated and described by a third-person narrator (hence "indirect"), but many aspects of the character's direct thoughts, such as the
lexis or the tone the character uses, come freely through (hence "free").[68]
FITR in the novel achieves two purposes: psychological intimacy with the
characters, and the technical merging of narrator and character so that it
becomes difficult to distinguish between them. The result is that the novel's stream-of-consciousness technique applies both to specific characters'
individual streams of consciousness, and the larger stream of interlinked
consciousnesses created by the narrative, which fluidly connects the narrator with characters, and characters with each other. But when describing Bradshaw, a subtle change occurs: The narrator's voice dominates,
allowing us only limited access and disrupting the non-judgmental com-
mingling of narrator and character.[69] In a novel which otherwise provides
deep psychological insight into and indeed enables and enhances readers'
sympathy for characters because of its particular way of rendering consciousness, Holmes and Bradshaw, though essential to the development
of the novel, remain distant from the reader – their descriptions lacking
emotional depth, their relationship with their patients as impersonal as
our relationship with them. All we know of Bradshaw's thoughts are his
views on Proportion, which the narrator immediately criticises for being a
guise for his hunger for power (*MD* 108–09). The closest Woolf comes to
conveying a sympathetic emotional response in the doctors is an external
description of Holmes's reaction to Septimus's suicide as he bursts into his
flat: "Dr. Holmes came in – white as a sheet, shaking all over, with a glass
in his hand" (164). But even at this crucial moment, we are not given any
access to Holmes's internal thoughts.[70]

Woolf had, in fact, experimented with the representation of Bradshaw's
thoughts while writing the novel. In one of the drafts, Bradshaw tries to
resist feeling any sort of human emotion, positive or negative, towards
Septimus, thinking this "unprofessional": Bradshaw "felt . . . unprofession-
ally, some human rancour" (*H* 134). If the doctor "~~attempts to give more~~,"
"~~<loses his> sense of the normal~~," has "~~some ill-guided spasm of sympa-
thy~~," or "fails to maintain that poise of mind . . . which directs him, in

spite of his sympathy (for the doctor has ~~his~~ feelings like other men) …
no good would … result" and "he fails in his profession" (*H* 149). This rare
instance of self-awareness and candour from the draft is finally removed
from the published version to render Bradshaw even more loftily distant.
Most of the thoughts that readers have access to are impersonal and professional, with his deeper intention, that of "Conversion," judged by the
narrator. The method with which the doctors treat patients is mirrored by
how the novel treats the doctors.

Woolf's series of short stories related to *Mrs Dalloway*, which have
been compiled and edited by Stella McNichol into a volume entitled *Mrs
Dalloway's Party* (1973), are narrative experiments which explore the issue
central to the medical ethics formulated in the novel: the possibility for
interpersonal understanding, communication and sympathy with others. In these stories, Woolf's use of free indirect thought again results in
a blending between the narrator and characters, with the narrator's representation and penetration, and characters' private, minimally mediated
thoughts, rendering boundaries between individuals porous without anni-
hilating them. Characters become, as Nena Skrbic has written, at the same
time both "ordinary and exceptional," both "profoundly sympathetic and
deeply flawed."[71] Woolf conducts two exercises in sympathy with two male
professionals, both barristers, in two stories which follow each other in
her holograph book[72]: Prickett Ellis in "The Man Who Loved His Kind,"
and George Carslake in "A Simple Melody." Prickett histrionically asserts
his humbleness and self-sacrifice: Working pro bono for the common person, he sees himself as "a plain man, an ordinary human being, pitted
against the evil, the corruption, the heartlessness of society" (196), and "as
the wise and tolerant servant of humanity" (197). In the overdetermina-
tion of his altruism and his desperation for approval, he becomes arrogantly condescending towards others. Yet the narrative thwarts readers'
moves to look down on Prickett and divest themselves from him, preventing them from judging him from an external, superior position. Instead,
we are made sympathetically, even painfully, aware of Prickett's vulnerable
humanity because of the close representation of his thought. George provides a different contrast, harbouring dreams of a harmonious humanity
by imagining people walking together on a heath, forming "a beautiful
picture, a very beautiful picture" (207). Such walking would significantly
be done while "silent" (201), because whereas "[t]hese states of mind when
one is walking, in company, on a heath, produce a sense of similarity,"
"social converse, when everyone wants to shine, and to enforce his own
point of view, produces dissimilarity; and which is the more profound?"

(206). As Christine Reynier points out, George's vision of similarity and silence are extreme, completely "assimilating the other rather than accommodating him." But I would not go to the extent of saying that this means that Prickett represents "a typically non-ethical attitude."[73] Spoken discourse can be as tyrannical, oppressive and assimilating, as we observe in the conversations of diagnosis between Septimus and his doctors in *Mrs Dalloway*.[74] What is needed is a type of sympathy which balances between the private and the public, a balance which Woolf's use of free indirect discourse experiments with. George's mistake is that he thinks the impossible task of complete harmony desirable, whereas human sympathy is best predicated on a respect for idiosyncratic differences between individuals that cannot and should not be erased. To attain such sympathy is difficult. Miss Merewether, with whom he converses on "his small nephew at Wembley," only feels that George is "a dark horse, a queer fish. There was no saying what he was after. Had he any affections[?]" (207). Although her attempt at understanding him on a deeper level is not successful, the very attempt itself is significant, and one which Bradshaw, blinded by professional knowledge and procedure, omits when diagnosing and fixing Septimus confidently as soon as Septimus enters his office. Woolf's narrative methodology, both in these stories and in the novel, calls attention to sympathetic engagement between characters and between readers and characters, while nevertheless retaining a respect for individuality.

Although both Prickett and George are highly flawed, with vulnerabilities which lend them easily to negative judgment, Woolf's use of FITR suspends judgment, prioritising instead understanding of and sympathy with the characters in all their petty imperfections as fellow human beings. That Woolf deliberately minimised, and even withheld, the same level of thought representation when describing the doctors in *Mrs Dalloway* is an aesthetic withholding of sympathy, one which has political use. The narrative only expresses those thoughts by the doctors that are professionally applicable, which it renders in dispassionate professional discourse. If the doctors have more private thoughts, Woolf is not allowing their full expression. Woolf's representation mirrors the superficialities of the doctors' diagnostic conversations with their patients, which need to be supplemented by ethical sympathetic engagement.

Bradshaw's belief is that professional productivity and efficiency can only be achieved by the doctor's emotional dissociation from the human suffering he deals with on a daily basis. But the possibility is also, as Hayward writes, that such "'selfish indifference to human life' … may be apparently a matter of sheer carelessness or indifference, without any dominating motive of any kind."[75] Bradshaw's ability to detach himself emotionally might not be a measure of his professional competence, but of his inhumanity,[76] and it is this possibility that the form of Woolf's representation of his thinking encourages, making him one of the most horrifyingly mechanistic characters in her fiction. Hayward writes that "[i]t is the passionlessness of Professionalism that is the root of its inefficiency and treason."[77] *Mrs Dalloway* likewise shows, in its form as well as its content, that at times, in the impersonality of the doctor-patient relationship, the possibilities for healing are lost. If professionalism means for the doctor to suppress entirely, or not to have, human emotions, this is to the detriment of both doctor and patient.

For Woolf, there seemed to be two key ethical concepts which could help temper a dehumanising treatment of patients, and allow an emotional affinity in the doctor-patient relationship which some aspects of the professionalisation of medicine, such as its concerns for enlarging the power and influence of medicine through organisation and politicisation, threatened to remove: sympathy, as we have seen, but also trust. These are some of the conceptual correlatives to Woolf's stream-of-consciousness technique, which destabilise boundaries between the self and others without rendering the notion of individual identity meaningless. They are important when applied to the dynamics between the professional service provider and receiver, and especially between the doctor and the patient, whose relationship should be a careful balance between formality and intimacy, impersonality and closeness.

Trust is key in the relationship between professional service providers and receivers: Because professional expertise is beyond laypeople, they must believe that professionals are both knowledgeable and have their best interests at heart.[78] However, for Woolf, this needed to go beyond the type of automatic trust in the doctor figure within society, which she found problematic. In her advice to friends, she would reiterate that doctors should not be blindly trusted. In 1907, for instance, she warns her friend Violet Dickinson indiscriminately against them: "O melancholy creature why do you see specialists? I wish to god you wouldnt. What you want, probably, is air and food and good society. . . . [A]ll I can say is, why do you see doctors? They are a profoundly untrustworthy race; either they lie, or they mistake" (*L* 1: 306). Fifteen years later, she says the same to Lady Ottoline Morrell: "Still there is little trust to be put in doctors – as I think you know" (*L* 2: 526). Woolf seemed to believe that unthinking trust could put patients in a dangerously complacent situation, and that a different type of trust was needed, based on a more personal view and relationship.

Woolf's first novel contains an early example of her scepticism. In *The Voyage Out*, when Rachel is ill with fever towards the end of the novel, Terence suspends his judgment of Rodriguez's character because of his claims as a doctor: Because "Terence respected the medical profession from hearsay, [this] made him less critical than he would have been had he encountered the doctor in any other capacity" (315). In doing so, he makes the mistake of looking at Rodriguez only as a doctor, and not as a person. Significantly, it is a woman, Rachel's aunt Helen, who is able to see through Rodriguez's professional position and evaluate him more accurately, although in Terence's own biased view she had "taken an unreasonable prejudice against him" (315). When it is clear that Rachel is becoming worse, and Terence forces himself to confront Rodriguez, he is finally able to look past his own favourable prejudice of medical doctors, and it is as if he sees Rodriguez for the first time: "He was determined to see for himself what kind of man he was. His confidence in the man vanished as he looked at him and saw his insignificance, his dirty appearance, his shiftiness, and his unintelligent, hairy face. It was strange that he had never seen this before" (319). That it takes Terence a conscious effort to "see" Rodriguez properly suggests how powerfully entrenched the social identity of a doctor is. Not only, then, should doctors treat patients as individual human beings: patients and their friends and family should do the same with their doctors. Woolf is espousing a medical ethics of personal, one-to-one human interaction, one which may still need to draw on such social identities as doctor and patient, but does not do so exclusively.

In *Mrs Dalloway*, Rezia's emotional agony after visiting Bradshaw also arises out of the stark contrast between her initial automatic trust in Bradshaw and her subsequent sense of disillusionment and abandonment, leading to the breakdown in the relationship between Bradshaw and his two clients: "Never, never had Rezia felt such agony in her life! She had asked for help and been deserted! He had failed them!" (*MD* 108). It is a failure which is not just professional, but also ethical and personal: The language Rezia uses is that of a moral appeal from one person to another for aid, and of having this request fall on deaf ears. In these two instances in both novels, therefore, Woolf highlights the importance of looking beyond the subtle social forces which construct and consolidate common readings of the doctor as trustworthy by virtue of his professional identity alone. In the case of Bradshaw, there seems to be little trustworthy about him as a person underneath his surface identity as an esteemed doctor:

> [Sir William] made a fine figurehead at ceremonies and spoke well – all of
> which had by the time he was knighted given him a heavy look, a weary

look (the stream of patients being so incessant, the responsibilities and privileges of his profession so onerous), which weariness, together with his grey hairs, increased the extraordinary distinction of his presence and gave him the reputation (of the utmost importance in dealing with nerve cases) not merely of lightning skill, and almost infallible accuracy in diagnosis but of sympathy; tact; understanding of the human soul. (104)

Here, again, the narrator's ironic voice dominates, interrupting the flow of Bradshaw's thought and his own judgment of his work which is put in parentheses. Unlike in the passage on Bradshaw and Proportion quoted earlier, the narrator is able to convey a deep sense of distrust through these interruptions without using any overtly negative descriptors. It is Bradshaw's appearance at ceremonies, his weariness, his grey hairs and his knighthood which give people the impression of his phenomenal abilities. The use of the word "sympathy" here is also ironic: True sympathy would involve emotional affinity, through which there is a levelling of hierarchy. But Bradshaw's exercising of power only serves to make the doctor-patient hierarchy even more extreme. It is therefore crucial to see past these professional trappings, not so as to do away with professionalism, but rather to remove from it its "unreal loyalties," such as its "medals, honours, degrees" (*TG* 219) – superficialities which Woolf thinks do not reflect the real human being, and detract from rather than benefit real service. These are what Clarissa struggles to penetrate, in order to see Bradshaw as he really is. At the party in the evening, she thinks: "He looked what he was, a great doctor. A man absolutely at the head of his profession, very powerful, rather worn" (200). She is therefore puzzled by her instinctive aversion to him: "she did not know what it was about Sir William; what exactly she disliked" (201), "[y]et – what she felt was, one wouldn't like Sir William to see one unhappy. No; not that man" (200). Clarissa's perspicuity and intuition are able to sense the nature of the flesh-and-blood human being and the potential for brutality underneath Bradshaw's distinguished professional identity. Although Clarissa and Septimus never physically meet, this moment of intuition connects Clarissa's strand of the narrative with that of Septimus, who has experienced Bradshaw's cruelty firsthand.

Therefore, to prevent abuse of the automatic trust which the public often readily accords doctors, such trust should only serve as the starting point for gradually building up a beneficial doctor-patient relationship. One article in *The Lancet* in 1935 says: "In most trades and professions you have to establish your bona fides in some definite way," but "if you are a doctor in this country you have only to put up a brass plate on your gate with your name and degree on it, and people will accept you as a matter of course. They will believe your diagnosis, swallow your medicine, and take the items of your bill on trust."[79] Problems arise when some doctors misuse this trust to cover up limitations in their knowledge or their lack of sympathetic engagement with their patients. Instead of taking unfair advantage of this professional trust, perhaps doctors could make good use of it to build a better relationship with patients, one based on real trust and sympathy. The stream-of-consciousness technique in *Mrs Dalloway* – which enables sympathy between the narrator, characters and readers, so that a deeper human understanding, the type which would allow Bradshaw to treat his patients better, is forged – serves as an aesthetic model for this process. In her refusal to probe doctors' emotional depths, Woolf excludes the doctors from this process aesthetically, just as she excludes them from a deeper understanding of their patients in the novel. Automatic professional trust alone, on which the doctors in the novel wholly rely, fails to create meaningful and healing engagement between patient and doctor.

A more personal approach to healing was envisioned by Woolf not just in *Mrs Dalloway* and *Three Guineas*, but also in the essay "On Being Ill," written in November 1925 (*D* 3: 46), a few months after *Mrs Dalloway* was published. It describes the shift in interpersonal relationships induced by illness. Writing about sympathy for the ill, Woolf mockingly states that "sympathy we cannot have. Wisest Fate says no. If her children, weighted as they already are with sorrow, were to take on them that burden too, adding in imagination other pains to their own, buildings would cease to rise; roads would peter out into grassy tracks" (*OBI* 11). The only people who can afford to "dispense[]" sympathy are "the laggards and failures, women for the most part (in whom the obsolete exists so strangely side by side with anarchy and newness), who, having dropped out of the race, have time to spend upon fantastic and unprofitable excursions" (11). Woolf pits sympathy humorously against the "goal" which "civilisation points to" (11), in contrast to the first long passage quoted from *Mrs Dalloway*, in which national progress and prosperity is interdependent with Bradshaw's exercise of power. Women who embark on such "fantastic and unprofitable excursions" do not receive training or pay and have "dropped out of the race" (*OBI* 11): They do not have to earn their living or support their husbands. Woolf significantly associates sympathy with the type of woman who, because of her inferior social position, can paradoxically afford the luxury to feel it and act on it, just as illness means that one can be "irresponsible and disinterested and able, perhaps for the first time for years, to look round, to look up – to look, for example, at the sky," which would normally be "impossible" (*OBI* 12–13). Woolf is linking these women, whom she humorously calls "the laggards and failures," to the ill patient: Their marginalised social standing gives them the time and space for the unconventional, outside the boundaries set up by the need to work for money. What is lacking in the relationship between Septimus and his doctors is precisely such voluntary and gratuitous sympathy, as opposed to the standardised response which doctors are trained to give to specific symptoms.

The language Rezia uses to describe Bradshaw's abandonment ("She had asked for help and been deserted! He had failed them!" [108]), and Septimus's subsequent death, recalls Woolf's earlier short story "Sympathy" (1919). Here, a notice in the newspaper on the death of a friend's husband, Humphry Hammond, stops the narrator in her tracks. Although her sympathetic engagement is confounded by the difficulty of understanding and describing the other, and in the end even made slightly ridiculous by the discovery that it is the not the friend's husband who died, but his father who has the same name, the narrator's act of stopping and of reflection is described with the single noun which is the story's title, "Sympathy." Putting *Mrs Dalloway* alongside this story, Bradshaw's act of "desert[ion]" is an ethical "fail[ing]" that derives from his carrying on procedurally, without stopping to consider Septimus as an individual human being. To our knowledge, Septimus's death only derails him to the extent of making him arrive late at Clarissa's party. Although death is "a defiance" and "an attempt to communicate" (*MD* 202), it still seems unable to stir Bradshaw emotionally. In contrast, the news of this stranger's death stops Clarissa in her tracks in the midst of the busy work of a party hostess, as it stops the narrator in "Sympathy." Retreating to a private room to reflect on her personal response, Septimus's death propels her not only into some form of a sympathetic engagement with Septimus, but also into an epiphany of her own place in life.

Doctors' lack of sympathy came when the patient was at his or her most vulnerable, and was at times validated by the standardisation of medical treatment – not just, as we have seen, in terms of diagnosis, but also in terms of legal rules and requirements. When Bradshaw tells Rezia that Septimus will be taken to "a delightful home in the country where her husband would be perfectly looked after," Rezia protests that "her husband did not like doctors. He would refuse to go there." Bradshaw then explains that Septimus "had threatened to kill himself. There was no alternative. It was a question of law" (106). Roger Poole has connected this to Woolf's own experience of mental breakdown in 1913, noting that Leonard Woolf, in his autobiography *Beginning Again* (1964), writes:

> In those days, if anyone was in Virginia's mental state, dangerously suicidal, it was customary to certify them. The procedure took place before a magistrate who, on a doctor's certificate, made an order for the reception and detention of the person either in an asylum or a nursing home authorized to take certified patients. Doctors were naturally unwilling to take the risk of leaving a suicidal patient uncertified in a private house.[80]

The law, the Lunacy Act of 1890, which was in force until its repeal in 1959, is an example of the potential impersonality of the medical system. The act stipulated that "privately paying patients could not be admitted to psychiatric facilities without the order of a justice of the peace."[81] This order could be obtained by a petition made by the spouse or relative of an "alleged lunatic," accompanied by two medical certificates.[82] But the requirement for a petition by a relative could be circumvented by a statement of a reason why, so long as the petitioner had seen the subject within fourteen days.[83] Similar rules applied to urgency orders, but with this time span shortened to two days.[84] So although on the one hand, the law meant that doctors could no longer confine alleged "lunatics" without a formal procedure, on the other, the provisions were sufficiently flexible to allow for a petitioner who was not a family member or a relative to apply for the involuntary admission of a patient, as long as he or she had seen the patient either within two or fourteen days. This may be one explanation for Bradshaw's planned uninvited visit to Septimus, and for Septimus's determination to avoid him at all costs. The act therefore both provided protection against as well as legitimised and justified confinement through its procedural formalities. Standard procedures were to be followed in the case a patient had mental illness and threatened suicide, and these meant that the patient could be put in an institution even when his or her spouse disagreed. I am not arguing that there was no valid rationale behind such a system. But more sympathetic consideration of each patient as a separate human being, meriting individual advice and help, was also vital.

Doctors' professional distancing, done in the name of efficiency, order and procedural standards, did not necessarily mean that patients' private space was preserved and respected, but possibly the opposite. This was problematic because there was a private aspect about illness which doctors at times, because of their power and their lack of sympathy or real emotional response, seemed to violate. In "On Being Ill," Woolf writes that "[h]uman beings do not go hand in hand the whole stretch of the way. There is a virgin forest in each; a snowfield where even the print of birds' feet is unknown." In illness, "we go alone, and like it better so" (12). So when Bradshaw thinks that "[h]ealth we must have; and health is proportion" (108), this sweeping and generalising view of "health" makes it a concept that is too devoid of individuality and humanity, so that no private space remains. Septimus is exposed and judged according to Bradshaw's "Proportion," reached by social and medical convention and embodied by these representatives of "human nature" (107), so that he thinks of the doctors that "he was in their power! Holmes and Bradshaw were on him! The brute with the red nostrils was snuffing into every secret place! 'Must' it could say!" (161). Finding his private space violated and seeing no possibility to maintain it in a life lived in society, he opts for death by jumping out of the window, but not without reflecting that he does not want to jump at all, thinking that "[l]ife was good" and "[t]he sun hot" (164). Woolf represents this as a tragedy borne out of the ubiquity of the power of the medical profession, one which she suggests has reached beyond its proper bounds, right into the "secret place" which should be every individual's preserve. Applied in the right way, sympathy would be a humane response which engages, but does not impose or encroach upon patients' private space against their will.

The question then is how genuine sympathy can be a part of professional medical service. The medical profession widely regarded what Bradshaw in one of the drafts of the novel calls the "poise of mind," which a doctor uses to ignore his emotional response, as necessary for the doctor not to "fail[] in his profession" (*H* 149), crucial to its proper functioning. At the lecture on "The Professional Mind" in 1934 mentioned earlier in this chapter, the speaker says that "[t]he role which the doctor was required to play must react on his mental and moral make-up." The doctor's "constant contact with suffering" does not mean that he is "callous," and the "certain calmness" which he must have "in the presence of the emergencies and tragedies of life" should not "be mistaken for unconcern."[85] Such suppression of his "natural sympathies" is necessary for his effective work.[86] As "professionally oracular" figures,[87] doctors possessed knowledge beyond laypeople's understanding, and the advice they gave patients was wise yet necessarily beyond their comprehension. Patients must then assume that doctors are "calm," not "callous" or "unconcern[ed]."[88] In other words, they must trust that doctors cared, and sympathised with their plight. Woolf, however, seemed to believe that too few doctors genuinely did. But if they could, a healthier "poise" could possibly be attained, so that medical service could be both professional and personal. I have shown that the balance which Woolf's stream-of-consciousness technique strikes between characters as individuals and as interconnected, both with each other and with the narrator, is interrupted once Woolf describes the two doctors. The doctors seem too professional, too detached from their patients as suffering individuals, and their thinking too congruous with macroscopic medical discourse. This narrative break is then the aesthetic equivalent of the rift they will need to bridge to negotiate a mutually beneficial balance between professionalism and intimacy.

Later, in the politically explosive late 1930s, such earlier thoughts on the medical profession become the foundation for Woolf's thoughts on a professional ethics which should apply more generally. Her satire of medicine in *Mrs Dalloway*, then, and her advice in *Three Guineas*, sought to redress imbalances in the current medical system derived from decades of continuing professionalisation, without undoing some of its benefits, such as basic standards of service and a gradually widening access to medicine. She makes this clear in *Three Guineas*, where she recommends that the "outsiders" living by the conditions she imposes should still base their work on professional structures:

> The outsiders then would bind themselves not only to earn their own livings, but to earn them so expertly that their refusal to earn them would be a matter of concern to the work master. They would bind themselves to obtain full knowledge of professional practices, and to reveal any instance of tyranny or abuse in their professions. And they would bind themselves not to continue to make money in any profession, but to cease all competition and to practise their profession experimentally, in the interests of research and for love of the work itself, when they had earned enough to live upon. (*TG* 237–38)

Such people would in essence be both outsiders and insiders at the same time: they would be fully qualified professionals, but practise the professions differently from before. In this lay their power to change the professions, so that in medicine, for instance, patients such as Septimus would be treated more humanely. The advantages, and indeed the necessity, of entering the professions should therefore also come with moral, personal and social responsibilities: with intellectual rigor and integrity, intrinsic interest in the work, and as part of an individual and human way of living, where being a human being takes precedence over being a doctor. Such passages as the above attempt to rescue the concept of "profession" from its social manifestation and return to the essence of professional work as personally worthwhile pursuits, which Woolf, as we have seen in the case of medicine, was only too aware the public version of the professions did not always live up to.

Woolf's last doctor was Octavia Wilberforce, who, unlike Peggy, was content with being single and childless, and seemed to have reached a good balance between her profession and her individuality. Lilian Furst, for example, writes that Wilberforce "would seem to have accomplished what Woolf defined as the most difficult task facing the woman in a male-dominated profession: to establish herself without succumbing to the jealousy and rivalry Woolf believed endemic to the professions."[89] When Woolf first meets her, she is pleasantly surprised by her first impression: "in she came – a very fresh coloured healthy minded doctor, in black, with loops of silver chain, good teeth, & a candid kind smile which I liked" (*D* 5: 49). This is the beginning of both their real friendship and doctor-patient relationship, a combination notably absent in Woolf's associations with male doctors throughout her life. The visits they paid each other were both friendly gatherings and medical consultations, neither strictly professional nor merely personal. Wilberforce, concerned about Woolf's health, regularly brought over "great white bottles of milk & cream" "with her market womans basket" (*D* 5: 351). Wilberforce's personal history, which is introduced during their first meeting and which Woolf wanted to write a history on, could have been put alongside the biographical examples used in *Three Guineas* of women who fought patriarchy to enter the professions: "from that we slipped to education – she had none: to families – she had 9 in family; & they coerced her, though unwanted, through pressure of anti-quated family feeling & propriety, to stay at home. Only through a great struggle did she break off & become a doctor" (*D* 5: 49). After qualification, Heather Levy points out, Wilberforce's priority was not to make as much money as possible, but to use her expertise to serve patients. Instead of opening a more lucrative and prestigious private office in London, she set up a rest home in Backsettown for overworked women.[90] Wilberforce was therefore in many ways the antithesis to the fictional Bradshaw. This woman doctor and friend was not able, in the end, to prevent Woolf from taking her own life; but her powerful example was on Woolf's mind until almost the very end. In her very last diary entry, dated a few days before her suicide, Woolf writes: "Octavia's story. Could I englobe it somehow?" (*D* 5: 359). If Woolf had lived on, a new and different story about the medical profession may have emerged, and the second fictional woman doctor who would have been at the centre of this story may have been happier than Peggy.

Furst believes that Woolf thought the achievements of individual women "did not destroy or even fundamentally change the patriarchal system she attacked in *Three Guineas*," and that women doctors did not change Woolf's mind about a profession with which she had had so many marring early experiences.[91] Since women doctors such as Wilberforce were still a recent addition and a minority in a profession which had been developing for centuries, this was perhaps only to be expected. But their importance to Woolf's hopes for a better medical system should not be underestimated. Although Woolf only met her belatedly, Wilberforce seemed a living instance of the insider/outsider who could provide a type of medical service in which "professional" and "personal" were not necessarily antagonistic to each other. Such women could, if not immediately reverse the rut of the medical establishment, for now at least mark out and explore alternative paths which demonstrate "how we can enter the professions and yet remain civilized human beings" (TG 204), helping to realise a future in which "the professions ... will be practised so that they will lead to a different song and a different conclusion" (TG 181).

CHAPTER 2

Virginia Woolf, Amateurism and the Professionalisation of Literature

In 1931, Woolf reviewed a biography on Edmund Gosse which had appeared after his death in 1928. She writes:

> Even the most superficial student of letters must be aware that in the nineteenth century literature had become, for one reason or another, a profession rather than a vocation, a married woman rather than a lady of easy virtue. It had its organization, its functions, its emoluments, and a host of people, not primarily writers, were attached to its service. (*CE* 4: 84)

Woolf's differentiation between literature as a "profession" and as a "vocation" can be understood by looking at the historical development of the word "literature" itself. Samuel Johnson's dictionary in 1755 had described literature as "learning, skill in letters."[1] Gradually, in the late eighteenth and nineteenth century, it came to mean literature as an entire field and industry.[2] Barbara M. Benedict writes that this change represented "the evolution of the book trade from a relatively haphazard, loose-knit craft into a professional, profit-seeking industry" and "the transformation of writers from gentlemen dilettantes into professional authors."[3] It is important to note that while the development of literature into a commercial commodity was closely related to the professionalisation of literature, the two developments were not identical. Professionalisation may arise for financial reasons, but literature did not become professionalised merely because it became something produced for money. Here, with the word "vocation," Woolf seems to mean a more individual pursuit of literature, possibly for money but without the organisational structures she names in the next sentence; and with the word "profession," the institutionalisation, with its own distinct characteristics, of activities involved with writing, including those of material benefits.

The distinction which Woolf makes between the two words, and the way in which she syntactically parallels "vocation" with "a lady of easy virtue," seem odd, considering how closely related the two words are to each other. Like "profession," the word "vocation" has strong religious roots, referring to the station God calls upon one to fulfil. Like "profession," it was extrapolated to apply in a more general sense to one's occupation. Unlike it, however, the etymology of "vocation" comes from *vocare* in Latin, which means to call or summon.[4] In this sense it is synonymous with the word "calling," referring to God's summons to salvation or service.[5] The agent of *vocare* is external to the person practising the vocation, appealing to the person's intrinsic qualities which make him or her suitable for particular ways of service, whereas the agent of "profess" is the person practising the profession, whom Woolf, as we have seen, often thought of as acting out of self-interest, the true motivation behind his or her public espousal of ideals. The way she uses "profession" here, associating it with such institutional aspects as "organization," "functions" and "emoluments," is the main sense which this chapter will focus on; the next chapter will address the potential sense of "profession" in her work as what she refers to here as "vocation."

Census data seem to confirm that the change of the perceived status of authorship to that of a profession happened largely in the nineteenth century. In the 1841 census, authors – among such other occupations as artists and musicians – were categorised under "other educated persons," separate from working-class occupations although not yet securely belonging to the professional class;[6] a total of 167 people classified themselves as "Author."[7] In 1851, authors were still considered a separate class from professionals, listed under "Persons engaged in Literature, the Fine Arts, and the Sciences." But the category was further divided into the two major groups of "Author" (436 people) and "Editor, Writer" (1,302 people), perhaps accounting for the dramatic increase in the total number of people who saw themselves as belonging to either one of these categories.[8] In 1861, census authorities broadened their definition of the word "profession," and for the first time authors were accorded semi-professional status.[9] They were listed under "Persons engaged in the Learned Professions or engaged in Literature, Art, and Science (with their immediate Subordinates)," which was subsidiary to the main classification of "Professional Class."[10]

In the early twentieth century, professional values were becoming sufficiently prevalent in British society for the field of writing to be under mounting pressure to professionalise itself.[11] Despite this, and despite the trend observed in the census data above, the professional status of writing was, in Woolf's time, not without its ambiguities. The activity of writing was caught in the identity conflict of, on the one hand, largely being regarded as a profession, while on the other hand considered less of one than, for example, medicine and law. As Carr-Saunders and Wilson point out, this difficulty was because of its dependence on such characteristics as creativity and imagination, complicating the institutional establishment of training and qualifications.[12] This chapter explores how Woolf used the focal points of amateurism and professionalism to triangulate the desired position of writing, yet how at the same time these focal points undermined the possibility for any stationary theory of an ideal profession of literature. In applying the positions of amateurism and professionalism, I follow in the footsteps of an article by Patrick Collier entitled "Virginia Woolf in the Pay of Booksellers: Commerce, Privacy, Professionalism, *Orlando*," which cogently argues that Woolf moved along "the continuum between the extremes of artistic self-enclosure and commercialism, private and public writing, complete fidelity to one's idiosyncratic expression and complete sell-out to the market."[13] But instead of focusing on patronage and audience, this chapter further probes and vexes the two terms of amateurism and professionalism themselves, historicising their relationship and showing how Woolf destabilised them in her efforts to conceive of a better profession of literature. It argues for even further problematising of the view of the figure of the amateur as her ideal (albeit one which she was aware was almost impossible to realise), and that of the professional as her counter-ideal.

Unlike Woolf's negotiations with the medical profession, her shaping of the profession of literature is less able to be phrased in terms of an attempt to displace overly public concerns towards a greater consideration of the private individual. Rather, as will become clear, they defy the boundaries which sole considerations of the public and the private would impose. For instance, she celebrated the notion of literature as a personal pursuit, yet also worried about the potential freedom and absence of rigid standards in literary writing; and she valued the public recognition of one's writing, yet asserted the need to resist the influence of external public demands.

Institutional English

It is significant that Woolf's comment on the professionalisation of literature in the nineteenth century appeared in relation to Gosse. Of the "host of people" attached to literature, Woolf writes with sarcasm, Gosse was "one of the most eminent": "He welcomed strangers, addressed bodies, celebrated centenaries, presented prizes, and represented letters on all occasions and with the highest delight in the function" (*CE* 4: 84). In fact, Woolf had met Gosse on 27 October 1926, when she attended a lecture that Vita Sackville-West gave to the Royal Society of Literature. She writes scathingly of this event in her diary: "I never saw the whole hierarchy of lit. so plainly exposed. Gosse the ornament on the tea pot: beneath him file on file of old stout widows whose husbands had been professors, beetle specialists doubtless, meritorious dons." Gosse, "drawing round the lot of them thicker & thicker, the red plush curtains of respectability" (*D* 3: 115), was to Woolf the epitome of the professional man of letters, both earning his money from writing, and deriving from his professional identity the intellectual and cultural status which enabled him to move in high society and satisfy "his appetite for social life" (*CE* 4: 85).

In "The British 'Man of Letters' and the Rise of the Professional," Josephine M. Guy and Ian Small write that the pre-eminence of "the Victorian sage," or "the cultural critic or distinguished 'man of letters,'" did not derive from institutional modes of recognition, but from "the prestige of the individual," or from who he was, and that professionalisation in literary criticism began only in the late nineteenth century, as exclusive scholarly communities and formal standards for academic writing were formed, which became the new sources of authority – in this case professional authority.[14] We can compare this position to Woolf's representation of Nick Greene in *Orlando* (1928). The fifteenth-century Greene, who "was a very famous writer at that time" (*O* 59), depends on wealthy patrons such as Orlando to make a living. He has "a face seamed, puckered, and drawn together," and suffers, or purports to suffer, ill health, having had "the palsy, the gout, the ague, the dropsy, and the three sorts of fever in succession; added to which he had an enlarged heart, a great spleen, and a diseased liver" (60–61). The nineteenth-century Greene, however, "so neat, so portly, so prosperous, with a cane in his hand and a flower in his button-hole, with a pink, plump face, and combed white moustaches" has clearly "risen in the world": "he was a Knight; he was a Litt.D.; he was a Professor. He was the author of a score of volumes. He was, in short, the most influential critic of the Victorian Age" (192–93). Greene's formal titles and honours would be described later in *Three Guineas* as "the fruits of professional culture – such as directorships of art galleries and museums, professorships and lectureships and editorships" (*TG* 225). For Woolf, the eminent Victorian man of letters who was attached to academic institutions already embodied the beginnings of the professionalisation of literature in the nineteenth century. The original source of their authority may have been their individuality, but their derived formal titles and honours amplified it until it was perhaps impossible to see the effects of these sources of authority separately.

In Woolf's time, English as an academic subject was a relatively recent phenomenon. In 1848, A. J. Scott, professor of English at University College, was still lamenting the treatment of English literature as mere recreation.[15] The sense of literature as a leisurely pursuit is expressed by Terence in *The Voyage Out*, when he introduces himself to the others:

> "I was educated at Winchester and Cambridge, which I had to leave after a time. I have done a good many things since – "
>
> "Profession?"
>
> "None – at least – "
>
> "Tastes?"
>
> "Literary. I'm writing a novel." (131)

Terence's classification of novel-writing under "tastes" brings into play all its gentlemanly associations. Yet this view had been slowly changing. The efforts to found English schools at new and existing universities throughout the nineteenth century culminated in their establishment at the universities of Oxford and Cambridge at the beginning of the twentieth century, the two universities which had been the most resistant towards the institutionalisation of the subject.[16] English literature, as Woolf was aware, was being redefined into a specialised academic discipline.[17] It was becoming part of the "the public world, the professional system" (*TG* 199), with its institutions and its forms and ceremonies; yet at the same time it was becoming less public, less accessible to the public at large and to public debate.

On the surface, Woolf's aversion to such institutionalisation is undeniable. The essay "Why?"[18] shows how passionate her antipathy was to the institutionalisation of English, and the artificial hierarchy it created and reinforced. One question that arises in the essay is: "why learn English literature at universities when you can read it for yourselves in books?" Although the narrator claims that "it is foolish to ask a question that has already been answered – English literature is, I believe, already taught at the universities" (*CE* 2: 281–82), she chooses to address it regardless by describing how her friend, who is a publisher's reader, responds to the issue. This friend is incited to "a flood of lamentation and vituperation," which the narrator summarises: "All I could gather was that this lecturing about English literature – ... all this passing of examinations in English literature, which led to all this writing about English literature, was bound in the end to be the death and burial of English literature." The friend asks: "Is poetry better, is fiction better, is criticism better now that they have been taught how to read English literature?" In reply to her own question, "she read a passage from the manuscript on the floor. 'And each the spit and image of the other!' she groaned, lifting it wearily to its place with the manuscripts on the shelf." The imposition of teaching and standards gives rise to uniformity, of dubious value in literature and criticism. The issue is linked in the same essay to the broader concerns of building a freer society without the restrictions of academic specialism and hierarchy which the practice of university lecturing promotes:

> [W]hy continue an obsolete custom which ... incites the most debased of human passions – vanity, ostentation, self-assertion, and the desire to convert? Why encourage your elders to turn themselves into prigs and prophets, when they are ordinary men and women? Why force them to stand on a platform for forty minutes while you reflect upon the colour of their hair ... ? Why not let them talk to you and listen to you, naturally and happily, on the floor? Why not create a new form of society founded on poverty and equality? Why not bring together people of all ages and both sexes and all shades of fame and obscurity so that they can talk, without mounting platforms or reading papers or wearing expensive clothes or eating expensive food? (*CE* 2: 281–83)

Thus what Woolf seemed persistently against was the type of university education that claimed authoritative monopoly on how to read and write. Related to the academisation of literature was the establishment of separate formal training requirements for journalistic writing, the other facet of Woolf's writing career. In *The Years*, Sara, who is Elvira in the holograph of the novel, seems to decide against taking on the job at the newspaper office of her own accord. But the holograph shows her dismissed from the office of "the bothered editor of a great newspaper" ("HY" 7: 3) at least in part because of her lack of formal education. The editor asks her for her qualifications in writing, and she is forced to answer that she has "no training, no education, not a letter to my name." She is then immediately sent to a "Mrs Potts" in "another department," "where they deal with those stains in tablecloth; how to fry fish in batter; & – she took the newspaper cutting – Lady Cynthia had chosen a huge hat to wear with her wide skirt of green" ("HY" 7: 3). The implication is that writing about the domains of housekeeping, fashion and gossip does not require any higher education or training, whereas more serious journalism does. The semi-formal educational and professional qualifications which Elvira/Sara does not have were becoming more widely requested and accepted as proof of a writer's professional competence.[19] Elvira/Sara's refusal to "[j]oin the patriarchy, sell my soul" ("HY" 6: 120) by writing solely for money is also a refusal to participate in the qualification process which the gradual institutionalisation of English was setting up.

But Woolf's position is also more nuanced than would appear from essays such as "Why?." What she was averse to was the hierarchical arrangement of university education in English – whether in the spatial arrangement of the lecture room, or the academic honours bestowed upon lecturers. However, Woolf herself had in fact taught classes on literature and composition at Morley College, a school for working adults, for three years, from 1905 to 1907. These had been very different from lectures at large universities. Her audience of working-class women meant that she had to create a teaching approach suited to them.[20] In her English history classes, for example, she recounts "talk[ing] from notes, with as little actual reading as possible," showing pictures, and lending books to students, with the goal not "to make them know anything accurately," but "to prepare the soil for future sowers." Although the report she wrote of her teaching shows her exasperation with the goals of the college, which according to her "prefer[red] the safeness of mediocrity to the possible dangers of a high ideal," and wanted her to switch to more instrumental subjects like English composition,[21] it shows, as Cuddy-Keane has pointed out, how Woolf desired an alternative way of teaching that would be dialogic instead of monologic, without necessarily being less intellectual.[22] "[D]ifficult ideas," she writes in "Why?," should be "read, thought over, discussed" "by the fire in winter, or under an apple tree in summer" (*CE* 2: 280). Later, she would imagine in *Three Guineas* a "poor college," which "would have nothing to offer" so that "competition would be abolished. Life would be open and easy. People who love learning for itself would gladly come there." It "would be a place where society was free; not parcelled out into the miserable distinctions of rich and poor, of clever and stupid; but where all the different degrees and kinds of mind, body and soul merit co-operated," much like the freer society she envisioned in the late 1930s where "the professions in future will be practised so that they will lead to a different song and a different conclusion" (*TG* 181). Looking at her views across her entire career, the overall goal of her critique seemed not to be for the purpose of undermining university education in English as such, but for it to be based, as Cuddy-Keane has argued, on a more encompassing, democratic methodology.

The Professional Writer, the Amateur Writer and Money

Being a professional writer herself, most of whose money was made at the height of her career as a highly esteemed novelist, one might expect Woolf's criticism of the exclusivity of literature to be more tempered. But

Woolf often portrayed the writing profession as one of the most accessible and least exclusive of all professions. "[W]hen I came to write," she says in "Professions for Women,"[23] "there were very few material obstacles in my way. Writing was a reputable and harmless occupation. The family peace was not broken by the scratching of a pen.... The cheapness of writing paper is, of course, the reason why women have succeeded as writers before they have succeeded in the other professions" (*CE* 2: 284). In *Three Guineas*, she writes that "the only profession which does not seem to have fought a fierce battle during the nineteenth century is the profession of literature. All the other professions, according to the testimony of biography, seem to be as bloodthirsty as the profession of arms itself" (188). "[R]eading and writing," she points out, "have been, since the eighteenth century at least, so universally taught in our class, that it was impossible for any body of men to corner the necessary knowledge or to refuse admittance" (214–15). To Woolf, the accessibility of the writing profession was something to be valued and preserved.

T. S. Eliot had a very different view of what the writing profession should be like.[24] An article entitled "Professionalism in Art" which appeared in *The Times Literary Supplement* on 31 January 1918 attracted Eliot's fierce criticism. In it, Arthur Clutton-Brock writes: "Professionalism is a dull, ugly word: but it means dull, ugly things, a perversion of the higher activities of man, of art, literature, religion and philosophy." He sees professionalism as "mechanical invention," which "makes the technique of art too difficult, and so destroys the artist's energy and joy in his practice of it." Clutton-Brock concludes: "In art there is always humility, in professionalism pride. And it is this pride that makes art more ugly and tiresome than any other work of man."[25] In his response in the *Egoist*, Eliot writes that Clutton-Brock's attitude exemplifies "the British worship of inspiration, which in literature is merely an avoidance of comparison with foreign literatures, a dodging of standards." He criticises Clutton-Brock for "identify[ing] technique with what may be learned from a manual of prosody. This is making technique easy.... Surely professionalism in art is hard work on style with singleness of purpose." Clearly thinking that Clutton-Brock is contrasting the professional with the amateur, Eliot writes:

> The opposite of the professional is not the dilettante, the elegant amateur, the dabbler who in fact only attests the existence of the specialist. The opposite of the professional, the enemy, is the man of mixed motives. Conspicuously the Victorian epoch is anti-professional; Carlyle as an historian, Ruskin as an economist; Thackeray who could write such good prose

as the Steyne episode, and considered himself a kindly but penetrating satirist; George Eliot who could write *Amos Barton* and steadily degenerate. Decadence in art is caused by mixed motives. The art of the Victorians is spoiled by mixed motives.[26]

Eliot takes issue not with amateurs, whom he thinks need not be taken seriously, but with people who purport to be experts in multiple areas, and allow all these to influence their writing: "we must learn to take literature *seriously*."[27] Literature must stand on its own, as an autonomous profession, with its own standards, conducts and rewards.

In this exchange, the tensions set up between amateurism and professionalism, which exemplify the tensions between the two antonymous terms at the time in art and literature, justify a brief return to their basic meanings, and the use of some examples of their occurrences as documented by the *OED*. "Amateur," as I mentioned in the Introduction, is derived from the Latin verb *amare*, to love. It is a relatively new word in the English language, with the first documented use by the *OED* in 1784. Its first meaning in the *OED* is someone who loves or has a taste for something. Its second is someone who engages in an activity as a pastime. This second meaning is first exemplified in 1786, and, in an example from Abraham Rees's *The Cyclopædia or Universal Dictionary of Arts* (1803), contrasted with moneymaking: "*Amateur*, in the Arts, is a foreign term introduced and now passing current amongst us, to denote a person understanding, and loving or practising the polite arts of painting, sculpture, or architecture, without any regard to pecuniary advantage."[28] The word's antithetical relationship with "professional" also means that it is sometimes, as the dictionary points out, "used disparagingly," as Eliot does here. In 1807, for example, a review of the book *On the Hindoo Systems of Astronomy* (1805) says:

> The author of the paper ... should therefore have thought well before he hazarded an assertion that was to charge with ignorance or presumption such men as Cassini and Bailly, who had explained the astronomy of the East; it was not likely that an *amateur*, however distinguished, should convict these astronomers of gross ignorance, or find it so easy to *do away* their opinions, in a matter that concerned their own profession, – a science which, day and night, had been for many years the subject of their study.[29]

That amateurs practise something for love rather than money, therefore, means that their work and skills are not only unpaid for, but also not subject to measurable requirements and public scrutiny, making the quality uncertain.

Just as the word "amateur" is inextricably linked to money, so of course is its perceived antonym "professional." The *OED* separately lists the noun form of "professional" as referring to someone who performs a paid occupation, and someone who does work in a profession demanding specialist knowledge, training and skills. [30] The earliest instance it identifies of the word used as a noun in the first sense is in 1811, in Jane Austen's *Letters*: "There is to be some very good Music, 5 professionals, … besides Amateurs."[31] The first instance of the second sense is in Charles Dickens's *Dombey and Son* (1848). Dickens describes "the family practitioner opening the room door for that distinguished professional, and following him out, with most obsequious politeness," where the "distinguished professional" is "Doctor Parker Peps, one of the Court Physicians, and a man of immense reputation for assisting at the increase of great families."[32] It is in this second sense in which Eliot uses the word in his essay.

Eliot complains that Clutton-Brock is not defining professionalism properly, saying that "[w]e cannot be absolutely sure, after reading the article several times, what is actually the definition of the professional; the professional is not contrasted with anything definite; and the writer engages our sympathy by charging the worst lines of Milton and Wordsworth to professionalism."[33] However, Eliot's own explanation of the word is limited to descriptions of the attitude one has when one is a professional ("hard work on style with singleness of purpose" [34]), and notably does not consider its socioeconomic basis, omitting any mention of its inevitable ties to money. This is very different from Woolf's consideration of the word. To Woolf, as we saw in Chapter 1, and which Collier has also pointed out,[35] money was a key characteristic of the professions, and this may be why she had a very different view of the nineteenth century from Eliot, seeing it as the start of professionalism in literature and criticism because of its mixture of organisations, social status and money. The examples from the *OED* would seem to coincide with such a view.

But in the early twentieth century, the unprofessional qualities of the writing profession which Woolf had identified were making money earned from writing problematic.[36] Its openness, which Woolf admired, was also a potential danger. Since anyone who could write could enter the profession, and since there was no official body to enforce professional standards that were largely indefinable, whatever writers did was left much to their own discretion, causing what Woolf calls in *Three Guineas* "brain prostitution" in "the brain-selling trade" (219). What she was referring to were those writers who wrote solely with financial concerns in mind. In contrast, in established professions such as medicine, the wealth of a professional was often seen as proportional to his ability. In *Mrs Dalloway*, for example, "the very large fee which Sir William very properly charged for his advice" seems to merely increase his reputation "of lightning skill and almost infallible accuracy in diagnosis" (103–04). The difficulty of imposing external professional standards, therefore, was what made money earned in writing problematic.

Woolf herself was at times afraid of the implications of financial success. She declared, for instance, that "I will very much dislike the popular success of Flush" (*D* 4: 181). A review which later appeared of the novel – stating that "the deadly facility of [*Flush*] combined with its popular success mean ... the end of Mrs Woolf as a live force" and that "[w]e must mourn the passing of a potentially great writer who perished for lack of an intelligent audience" (*D* 4: 186) – seemed to confirm her fears: that success in financial terms could be correlated to a failure in artistic terms.

The purpose here is not to belabour the points generations of scholars have made about the anti-commercialist impulses latent in modernist literature, and the subsequent critical responses, mentioned in the Introduction, which see this as another form of commercialisation. Instead, I wish to reinterpret the implications of money earned from writing for Woolf from the perspective of the relationship between amateurism and professionalism, on which money issues put much pressure. On the one hand, an "amateur" could be seen as merely a "dabbler" who did not warrant attention; yet on the other hand, to be an "amateur" could clearly be appealing precisely because of its dissociation from money. Thus where amateurism provides a retreat from accusations of commercialism, it might also come with the stigma of dilettantism. In contrast, a professional identity is generally implicated in money issues, unless one ignores its close association with money entirely, as Eliot did in his essay.

At first glance, Woolf would seem to prefer positioning herself on the side of the amateur. In a letter to Harmon H. Goldstone, who wanted to write a book about Woolf and was asking her for suggestions on the outline he had written, Woolf writes that "I have had an independent income ever since I was of age; and have never had to write for money or to pursue any profession" (*L* 5: 91). This statement combined both fact and fiction. Woolf had inherited money from relatives, which invested amounted to an annual income of less than £400.[37] Upon marrying Leonard Woolf, her plans, as she wrote to Madge Vaughan, were to "take a small house and try to live cheaply, so as not to have to make money" (*L* 1: 503). Statistics of income levels at the time show that this was far from unfeasible. The average salary for the "higher professions," which comprise lawyers, doctors and dentists,[38] was £372 from 1922–24, increasing to £392 in 1935–36.[39] But in the late 1910s and most of the 1920s the Woolfs needed £400 to £500 more than that per year.[40] This was due to a combination of necessity and lifestyle choices. For instance, Woolf's medical bills in 1915 – when, according to Leonard Woolf, her "mental breakdown was at its worst" – were over £500 because of continuous attendance by nurses for months and constant visits by Harley Street specialists.[41] In 1919, as another example of their spending, the Woolfs bought Monk's House in Rodmell as a summer house for £700 (*D* 1: 286–88).

Woolf did not earn any income from her books until 1919, and even then her books did not start yielding substantial money until the mid-1920s.[42] This meant that writing articles was how Woolf topped up her income, something she alternately resented for pulling her away from fiction-writing, and was fascinated with because the money she earned gave her a sense of solidity and independence.[43] But she could not allow someone who might be writing a book on her to think that money had exerted an influence on her writing. In "Professions for Women," Woolf relates the term "professional" to material concerns, and distances herself rhetorically from both by telling her audience what she did with the first income she received from her writing: "But to show you how little I deserve to be called a professional woman, how little I know of the struggles and difficulties of such lives, I have to admit that instead of spending that sum upon bread and butter, rent, shoes and stockings, or butcher's bills, I went out and bought a cat – a beautiful cat, a Persian cat, which very soon involved me in bitter disputes with my neighbours" (*CE* 2: 284–85). Woolf's emphasis is on the redundancy of this additional spending power to her. The Persian cat, although bought with money from a professional activity, is a symbol of leisure used by Woolf to assert her position outside the politics of professionalism, and in exchanging the money for the impractical cat, she seems to deny in herself the fierce competition for money that she saw as characterising the professions.[44]

Woolf's vision of an art driven primarily by the variety and vibrancy which amateurism could provide can be glimpsed in what she says in 1927 in the BBC broadcast "Are Too Many Books Written and Published?," in which she argues against the topic in a pre-scripted debate with Leonard Woolf. Although, as Cuddy-Keane points out, the format prevents us from taking the views expressed as those of the speaker,[45] I wish to draw attention to one particular point which Woolf raises to show how important the concept of amateurism could be for literary activities. The revised typescript for the broadcast reads:

> As a reader, I deplore the fact that I am catered for almost wholly by professional writers.... Even today, when reading and writing are so much more practised than they have ever been before, the writing of books is far too much in the hands of a small <class of> professional ~~class~~ <writers>. For my own part, I should ... <put ... a tax on every book after a writer> <has written> 30 books. On the other hand, I should of <fer> a prize to induce people who had never written a book to write one.... Above all things the reader wants variety; he wants books written by all sorts of people; by tramps and duchesses; by plumbers and Prime Ministers.[46]

The relationship between literature and professionalism is contradictory: For the former, variety and novelty keep the field alive, whereas for the latter, traditions and standards emphasise similarity and conformity. Woolf is saying that the nature of the market for writing and the services which writers render mean that demand cannot be satisfied by professional writers alone; individual amateurs will always be needed.

After this broadcast, Woolf would in her next two novels create protagonists who were literary amateurs in specific ways. In *Orlando*, the eponymous protagonist is an aristocrat who spends his/her life writing the poem The Oak Tree, which does not make any money until it earns a prize of two guineas at the very end of the novel. In *The Waves*, all three soliloquising male protagonists (leaving out the silent Percival) are self-professed writers, but none are professional writers in the sense of this work making them a living. Louis, a financially successful businessman, even self-consciously confines his poetry and poetry-writing to his attic. The moneylessness of writing, however, detracts little from its importance, expressed through the intensely personal soliloquies which interweave questions of how to express oneself through writing with issues of ontological being.

The author who seemed to have exemplified the amateur figure for Woolf in real life was Samuel Butler.[47] In writing about him in "A Man with a View,"[48] she concurs with critic John F. Harris, whom she quotes and who writes of Butler that "to the end he remained an amateur – the last of the courageous amateurs – by which we mean a non-professional worker in the various departments that interested him, as well as a lover."[49] Harris records how Butler himself viewed the distinction between amateurs and professionals in art. Butler says:

> There is no excuse for amateur work being bad. Amateurs often excuse their shortcomings on the ground that they are not professionals, the

professional could plead with greater justice that he is not an amateur. The professional had not, he might well say, the leisure and freedom from money anxieties which will let him devote himself to his art in singleness of heart, telling of things as he sees them without fear of what men will say unto him; he must think not of what appears to him right and lovable, but of what his patrons will think and of what the critics will tell his patrons to say they think; he has got to square everyone all round and will assuredly fail to make his way unless he does this; if, then, he betrays his trust he does so under temptation.[50]

Woolf knew only too well the influence that the patron could exert on the professional writer, saying in "The Patron and the Crocus" (1924) that "since the patron is not merely the paymaster, but also in a subtle and insidious way the instigator and inspirer of what is written, it is of the utmost importance that he should be a desirable man" (*CE* 2: 149). She says of Butler that "[t]o have by nature a point of view, to stick to it, to follow it where it leads, is the rarest of possessions" (*E* 2: 38).[51] Here Woolf highlights what were to her some of the key attributes of the professional:

> The Victorian age, to hazard another generalization, was the age of the professional man. The biographies of the time have a depressing similarity; very much overworked, very serious, very joyless, the eminent men appear to us to be, and already strangely formal and remote from us in their likes and dislikes. (*E* 2: 35–36)

This was why, whereas Butler's contemporaries "were imprisoned," Butler was "free," having "achieved a freedom of soul which he expressed in one book after another":

> He had to preserve that kind of honesty, originality, or sensibility which asserts itself ... , and asks, "Now why am I doing this? Is it because other people do it? Is it right? Do I enjoy doing it?" and is always preventing its possessor from falling into step with the throng. In Butler's day, at any rate, such a disposition was fatal to success.... But his triumph lay not in being a failure, but in achieving the kind of success he thought worth while, in being the master of his life, and in selecting the right things to do with it. (*E* 2: 36)

Professionalism, in contrast, necessitates the abidance by external standards, whether commercial or institutional, which can become disconnected from the self, from personal joys and individual perceptions of value.

In this sense, Woolf's response to professionalism can be partially linked to John Ruskin's exhortation for the pursuit of the human, the individual and the unique in the art. Woolf described Ruskin, as she did Butler, as an amateur – in Ruskin's case as a "wealthy and cultivated amateur, full of fire and generosity and brilliance, who would give all he possesses of wealth and brilliance to be taken seriously, but who is fated to remain for ever an outsider" (*CE* 1: 206). In the second volume of his essay *The Stones of Venice* (1853), Ruskin writes: "Men were not intended to work with the accuracy of tools, to be precise and perfect in all their actions. If you will have that precision out of them, ... you must unhumanize them." Disparaging the industrialisation of society, he says that

> [i]t is verily this degradation of the operative into a machine, which ... is leading the mass of the nations everywhere into vain, incoherent, destructive struggling for a freedom of which they cannot explain the nature to themselves.... It is not that men are ill fed, but that they have no pleasure in the work by which they make their bread, and therefore look to wealth as the only means of pleasure.[52]

But although Woolf's concerns about modern professional society – of it having become too "serious" and "joyless" (*E* 2: 36) – share similarities with Ruskin's concerns, her response to Ruskin's writing shows how differently each approached such social issues, and how different her idea of good writing was. Woolf read Ruskin's work and admired his zeal for social reform, or what she calls "a force which is not to be suppressed by a whole pyramid of faults," and "a spirit of enthusiasm which compels those who are without it either to attack or to applaud," because "beneath its influence they cannot remain merely passive" (*CE* 1: 207). Nevertheless, she thought his writing overly didactic, and considered only his last autobiographical work, *Praeterita* (1885–89), a masterpiece, because by that stage he "ceased to preach or to teach or to scourge." Ruskin's fervour to reform society in accordance to his views caused "his aesthetics" to be "wrong," and she writes that "[i]t is hard not to regret that so much of his force went into satire and attempts at reformation for which, as he knew well, he was not well-equipped by nature" (*CE* 1: 207). Woolf saw the disadvantages of Ruskin's amateur position, and the dangers of being too obstinate in the pursuit of one's personal beliefs. Thus she says that "for years after most men are forced to match themselves with the real world 'he was living in a world of his own,' ... and losing the chance of gaining that experience with practical life, that self-control, and that development of reason which he more than most men required" (*CE* 1: 206). The "amateur," for Woolf, was a lonely figure; the "professional man" of the "Victorian age," despite his "overworked" state, and "very serious, very joyless" pursuits (*E* 2: 35–36), at least interacted in demonstrable ways with the outside world, receiving recognition for his work. Clearly a balance needed to be struck between "falling into step with the throng" by overworking oneself with the goal to become one of the "eminent men" (*E* 2: 36) of the age, and relentlessly pursuing one's individuality to the extent of isolation and despair like Ruskin.

We can take a closer look at one of Butler's novels, *The Way of All Flesh* (1903), which Woolf read and reviewed for *The Times Literary Supplement* in 1919, to explore her views of the amateur figure who pursues literary activities. In the book, which is one of Butler's most autobiographical, Ernest, the protagonist, blunders through life in his youth, and becomes, in rapid succession, a clergyman, a tradesman and finally a gentleman writer with a substantial private income. In the novel, Butler often exposes the hypocrisy of professional language: For example, after Ernest becomes a clergyman, he is deceived by Pryer, a colleague, who has specious visions of each priest in the country becoming "a professional adviser,"[53] and who argues for a more scientific approach, one modelled on medical studies, in religious activities in the pursuit of "greater knowledge of spiritual pathology." He persuades Ernest to give him money to set up a "College of Spiritual Pathology"[54] for the purpose, but is finally exposed as a swindler who has run away with Ernest's capital. The novel's stance against overzealous professionalism is reflected in Ernest's final philosophy of life, which he arrives at after all his misadventures: that people should "striv[e] to be as lukewarm as possible." In an attitude which shares some similarities with that of Woolf, the problem for Ernest does not lie in joining the professions per se: as he says, "[w]e should be churchmen, but somewhat lukewarm churchmen." Propounding his views using his collection of essays, which he has written but which he pretends were written by different people, Ernest thinks that people "become persecutors as a matter of course as soon as we begin to feel very strongly upon any subject; we ought not therefore to do this; we ought not to feel very strongly even upon that institution which was dearer to the writer than any other – the Church of England."[55] Even when people belong to a certain profession, their attitude should be relatively casual and noncommittal: they should not take the ideals of that profession too seriously. This means that Ernest, as a writer, does not abide by any standards or requirements set by the public or the publishing trade, to his godfather Overton's exasperation. Overton complains that "I want him to write like other people, and not to offend so many readers," and points out that "[w]ith the public generally he is not a favourite."[56] Ernest's books do not sell well, and he lets it be so: It would be taking things too seriously if he wished to aspire to money-making success as the standard of the value of his writing. Fortunately, he is in a financial position to be able to disregard money matters; as he says,

"I have too much money to want more, and if the books have any stuff in them it will work by and by."[57]

At first glance, this would seem to be the ideal situation for Woolf, who says that "[t]he great desirable is not to have to earn money by writing" (*D* 5: 91). Woolf's diary suggests that the changes she proposed to the writing profession were informed by her ideal of being "a dreamy amateur":

> I think I must read Ibsen & Shakespeare & Racine. And I will write something about them; for that is the best spur, my mind being what it is; then I read with fury & exactness.... But no: I am surprised & a little disquieted by the remorseless severity of my mind: that it never stops reading & writing; makes me write on Geraldine Jewsbury, on Hardy, on Women – is too professional, too little any longer a dreamy amateur." (*D* 3: 210)[58]

It is not difficult to see why the concept of the amateur was so attractive to Woolf, even as it could be "used disparagingly."[59] The figure of the artist who practised art for art's sake and who wrote without being tainted by the corrupting influence of money was the counter-image to professionalism which Woolf desired not only for herself, but also for other writers. But when Woolf says that "[t]he great desirable is not to have to earn money by writing" (*D* 5: 91), the superlative sense of the words "great desirable" show both the supremacy of the notion and its unattainability. Woolf knew that only people with no financial concerns could afford to be full-time amateurs, and even she did not qualify as one of them.

But even if Woolf could afford to be such a wealthy amateur, I contend that she would not actually have wanted to be one. The material basis which the female narrator argues is necessary for artistic creation in *A Room*, namely an own room and five hundred pounds of independent income a year, is vital because it removes one from bitterness and undue external influences: "Intellectual freedom depends upon material things. Poetry depends upon intellectual freedom" (97). But it is also merely the foundational stage, one where Woolf herself would not have wanted to remain. Woolf did not wish to be seen as a mere dilettante: She writes in her diary that "writing must be formal. The art must be respected. This struck me reading some of my notes here, for if one lets the mind run loose it becomes egotistic; personal, which I detest" (*D* 2: 321). Earning money, in some ways, meant public recognition and a common judgment of her writing as worthy, and she derived a great sense of satisfaction from it. In April 1929, she remarks contentedly on her earnings: "I think with pride that 7 people depend, largely, upon my hand writing on a sheet of paper. That is of course a great solace & pride to me. Its not scribbling; its keeping 7 people fed & housed" (*D* 3: 221). The power which money gave her also meant that she could have more of a sense of control and authority over her own life. The attraction she felt towards a pure amateur identity was one held by someone who had to struggle with anxieties about public recognition and opinion, and who resented the influences of commercialism and professionalism in writing. But although such an identity might in theory liberate her, and spare her both from having to consider what her audience would think of her works and what social and financial rewards she could expect, it would have been an empty identity for a writer who attached so much importance to other people's opinions of her work. "One wants," Woolf wrote in her diary in April 1921, "to be kept up to the mark; that people should be interested, & watch one's work" (D 2: 106–07).[60] Both the real and the symbolic rewards that her "professional" writing yielded meant to Woolf that when she spoke, her voice was heard.

Some aspects of Butler's amateurishness, therefore, left Woolf dissatisfied. No matter how much she recommended amateur values, she recoiled from the amateur figure as an ideal. Although she praises *The Way of All Flesh* for being "a novel which differs from most professional novels by being more original, more interesting, and more alive," she also says that "[t]here is a sense, after all, in which it is a limitation to be an amateur; and Butler, it seems to us, failed to be a great novelist because his novel writing was his hobby" (E 3: 59). There is something lacking in the way the book "bears in every part of it the mark of being a home-made hobby rather than the product of high professional skill," in which "[a]ll his convictions and prejudices have been found room for; he has never had the public in his mind's eye." In his very disregard of what people may think of his work, he has become too self-focused, with "didactic passages" which "constantly block the course of the story, or intrude between us and the characters" (E 3: 58). Amateur work might, as Butler claimed, have "no excuse" for "being bad,"[61] but Woolf thought that writing just for oneself could limit artistic expression in other ways than being a professional writer did. The criterion which she had for good writing, that it should necessarily be interconnected with other people, caused her, despite her criticism of professionalism, to be wary of the other extreme, no matter how painful at times the criticism from her audience could be to her.

Therefore, even in instances where the concept of the "amateur" is romanticised and praised, there is often at least a suggestion of disparagement, whether because of inferior skill, insufficient attention to artistic methods, inconsistencies or frivolity. This deficiency in purposeful method and determined resolve left her alternately delighted and exasperated. In "On Re-Reading Novels" (1922), she writes:

> Let us look at [the novel] in Richardson's hands, and watch it changing and developing as Thackeray applies it, and Dickens and Tolstoy and Meredith and Flaubert and the rest. Then let us see how in the end Henry James, endowed not with greater genius but with greater knowledge and craftsmanship, surmounts in *The Ambassadors* problems which baffled Richardson in *Clarissa*.... At every angle someone rises to protest that novels are the outburst of spontaneous inspiration, and that Henry James lost as much by his devotion to art as he gained. We will not silence that protest, for it is the voice of an immediate joy in reading without which second readings would be impossible, for there would be no first. And yet the conclusion seems to us undeniable, Henry James achieved what Richardson attempted. "The only real *scholar* in the art" beats the amateurs. The late-comer improves upon the pioneers. More is implied than we can even attempt to state.
>
> For from that vantage ground the art of fiction can be seen, not clearly indeed, but in a new proportion. We may speak of infancy, of youth, and of maturity. We may say that Scott is childish and Flaubert by comparison a grown man. We may go on to say that the vigour and splendour of youth almost outweigh the more deliberate virtues of maturity. (*CE* 2: 128–29)

The earlier writers are "amateurs," because their novels are more the products of "spontaneous inspiration." Henry James, with his careful and rigorous focus on novelistic method, is able to achieve more than these forerunners. "Craftsmanship" is a potentially ambiguous term, used at times by her close friend Roger Fry to refer to unimaginative, mechanical art,[62] but here it seems to be evaluated positively by Woolf, suggesting that it is a skill which is not merely formulaic and mimetic, and which requires both deliberation and creativity. It is, more specifically, unlike the mechanistic way of writing which Woolf criticises in a diary entry in 1918, when she talks about an acquaintance called Mills Whitham, who was a writer: "Whitham's elaborately literary get up is a fair index of his mind. He is what the self-taught working man thinks genius should be; & yet so unassuming & homely that its more amusing than repulsive. His passion for writing is the passion of the amateur – or rather of the person who's got it up from a text book" (*D* 1: 113). Writing about him again in a letter to Clive Bell in 1919, she says that "he has just produced his 21st imitation of Tess of the D'Urbervilles" (*L* 2: 403).

Yet after her assertion of triumph for James's meticulousness, Woolf cannot help but express her approbation for these "amateur" writers' refreshing "vigour and splendor." Unlike in other professions, which operate more formulaically, where work for a large part consists in applying expertise so that the same duties can be performed repeatedly, and which allow comparatively little space for innovation and newness, originality and creativity are at the heart of writing.

To draw a provisional conclusion, therefore, we have seen how both amateurism and professionalism have their advantages and drawbacks. Amateurism, on the positive side, means that one writes out of love, and not for money, and that one is therefore free to pursue whatever avenue and methods one wishes. On the negative side, it can mean writing mostly for oneself; fickleness in subject and method; or even a lack of concern for form and method altogether. Professionalism, on the negative side, means creating art for the sake of money, with its concomitant concerns of pandering to one's audience and selling out; and the establishment of literary institutions which encourage concerns about money, status and power in a pursuit that should be "disinterested" (*TG* 218). Thus, like amateurism, it can indicate ignorance of writing as art. But on the positive side, it can also mean writing not just for oneself – so that the creation achieves "disinterestedness" (*TG* 218) precisely because it is not "egotistic" (*D* 2: 321) – and having an audience. And, seemingly in contradiction to its possible sense of mere commercialism, it can also be taken to mean a conscientious and scrupulous attention to aesthetics, the kind which James devoted to his fiction, and the specific attitude to fiction which Eliot was inclined to describe as professionalism.

Admittedly, Woolf, in her writing, most often associated the word "professional" not with this sense, but with money-making commercialism. Nor, although she contrasts him with "amateurs," and describes him as a "scholar," does she explicitly call James "professional" in his methods. But she was obviously aware of the antonymic affiliation between "professional" and "amateur," as when she describes her own writing mind as "too professional, too little any longer a dreamy amateur"(*D* 3: 210).[63] Also, the sense of the word "professionalism" which Eliot focused on was commonly used for writing in her time, and she herself used this meaning when she described Butler's work as wanting because it lacked "high professional skill" (*E* 3: 58). Because of the constantly interacting multiple significances of the words, Woolf, although using these concepts, was not able consistently to evaluate amateurism or professionalism in art as either positive or negative. But this did not stop her from continuing on positioning her considerations of how writing should be relative to these concepts.

Even towards more specifically commercial professionalism Woolf did not – and perhaps could not be expected to – express consistent approbation or deprecation in her own life as a professional writer. Her own career shows continuing tensions between individual creativity, exclusivity and freedom for fewer financial rewards on the one hand, and writing more articles for newspapers and magazines on the other, which to her were secondary in importance to creative writing, and which she clearly associated with moneymaking. In her diaries, she treats her articles as her currency, as commodities worth and to be sold for certain amounts of money, as when she writes: "I hope to settle in & write one nice little discreet article for £25 each month; & so live; without stress; & so read – what I want to read" (*D* 3: 177); and "[a]nother £350, & repairs – more articles" (*D* 3: 255). This type of commercial professional writing often had an ambiguous influence on her: its rewards needed to be seen as mere by-products of her writing, but at the same time meant recognition, which was vital to her self-image as a public writer, and meant more money than she needed to live comfortably, which she was fascinated by. As Hermione Lee points out, in the second half of the 1920s, as Woolf became a more famous and esteemed novelist, she found that she could demand much higher fees for her articles than before, and started writing "more and more for the big, distinguished American magazines and papers."[64] Because of her fame, her articles benefited from what Harold Perkin calls "an artificial scarcity," where there is higher payment for better professional control over the market.[65] She made good use of the greater bargaining power afforded her by her increased professional status. In July 1927, she writes in her diary that she plans to tell Bruce Richmond, the editor of *The Times Literary Supplement*, that "I can't always refuse £60 in America for the Times' £10" (*D* 3: 149). And in June 1928, Woolf politely negotiates with Helen McAfee, the editor of the *Yale Review*, for a fee raise: "I have now made an arrangement with Curtis Brown for articles in various American papers. As I don't write many, I want of course to place my work as profitably as I can – but I will of course quite understand if the Yale Review is not able to offer more than the twenty pounds which I think it paid me before" (*L* 3: 511). But although she was amused and pleased at this new bargaining power, in June 1929 there is a slight discomfort in Woolf's tone when she writes that "[n]ow I am overpaid I think for my little articles" (*D* 3: 237). In the 1930s, Woolf's reviewing activity decreased from its peak in the late 1920s,[66] and in June 1937, she seems finally to wish to put an end to this excessive moneymaking: "But here my gorge rises. No I will not write for the larger paying magazines: in fact, couldn't. In this way I put 3 Guineas daily into practice" (*D* 5: 96). But she did in fact continue to write "for the larger paying magazines": after this entry, she wrote for such big American magazines as *Harper's Bazaar*, *The Yale Review*, *The Atlantic Monthly*, and *The New Republic*.[67] Ultimately, the dilemmas which both professionalism and amateurism posed caused conflicts that Woolf could not, for all her thinking, eradicate from her own life as a writer.

Woolf's choice, as Collier has argued and which this section has expanded on differently, was to navigate herself on the continuum between professionalism and amateurism, refusing to be located purely in either position. Either would have been too limiting for an occupation which Woolf thought should be both driven by one's personal vision and also taken seriously by others. Among existing professions, writing seemed particularly subversive of the professional-amateur dichotomy, and Woolf made conscious use of this to envision it as an activity which should have attributes of both positions, constantly using these two reference points to negotiate the conditions for writing.

This instability could in fact be desirable, as Woolf's work with the Hogarth Press demonstrates, which, as Laura Marcus has written, allowed Woolf herself "a way of negotiating the terms of literary publicity, and a space somewhere between the private, the coterie, and the public sphere."[68] The press started off hand-printing on a hand press, but the Woolfs began using commercial printers from 1919 onwards. Elizabeth Willson Gordon – in a revision of the common narrative of the press which foregrounds how liberating it was for Woolf (she could now publish her own works, and choose what works by other writers to publish), and the accompanying view that it became almost accidentally commercially successful in spite of its non-commerciality – has shown how the various seemingly opposing strategies of the press as "commercial/artistic, professional/amateur, traditional/avant-garde, elitist/democratic"[69] enabled it to position itself as both artistic and commercial, both exclusive and profitable, both "niche" and a hobby.[70] The Woolfs consistently professed the "disinterestedness" of the press in their stated goals, yet also consistently profited from this, in what might be read as a careful and calculated marketing strategy.[71] For instance, in the press circular to celebrate its fifth anniversary, the Woolfs write: "We aimed in the first place at producing works of genuine merit which, for reasons well known and difficult to gainsay, could scarcely hope to secure publication through ordinary channels. In the second place we were resolved to produce no book merely with a view to pecuniary profit."[72] This can be read as an advertisement aimed at both elitism and at maximum profit. But the profits the Woolfs did make, with the help from such publicity, was not necessarily incongruous with their intention to publish writing of genuine merit. As Gordon writes, "[p]erhaps it is better to say that the apparent contradictions are actually supplementary.... Both Leonard and Virginia could use multiple discourses and types of appeal. The press, like much of Virginia Woolf's writing, refused to be fixed or pinned, and used productive negotiations."[73] "[T]he ambiguity," Gordon points out, "is useful."[74] It helped create a new configuration of artistic work, one which allowed Woolf to reconcile the demands of money with artistic standards and love for her art.

An additional way for the two positions of professionalism and amateurism to be reconciled would be to incorporate both into a more fundamental sense of the term "professional," so that it means an activity one "professes" oneself to because it is intrinsically meaningful. This sense, as Chapter 3 argues, is what Woolf attempted to realise in the characterisation of her two women artists, Lily Briscoe in *To the Lighthouse* and Miss La Trobe in *Between the Acts*. But before moving on to this, we should first look at the position of women writers in such debates, whom Woolf saw as vital for the future development of the profession of literature.

Women's Difference

Arabella Kenealy, a woman writer who was Woolf's contemporary, and who believed firmly in female difference and in the domestic sphere as the site of women's true profession, complains in *Feminism and Sex-Extinction* (1920) that "[t]he woman point-of-view and method are regarded, for the most part, ... as mark of the amateur – the model aimed at being the eternal masculine in mode and trend."[75] Women's work, she thinks, should instead be seen as equally important, although distinct from men's work. Woolf's politics were very different from Kenealy's, but she also believed in female difference, particularly in fiction, and thought that women should not blindly emulate male models of writing. In her essay "Women and Fiction,"[76] she argues that "the very form of the sentence does not fit her" as it has been "made by men; it is too loose, too heavy, too pompous for a woman's use," therefore necessitating "altering and adapting the current sentence until she writes one that takes the natural shape of her thought without crushing or distorting it" (*CE* 2: 145). Such female uniqueness could offer different types of creative expression to the art of writing. But the charge of trivial amateurism similarly weighed on her argument. She writes:

> [W]hen a woman comes to write a novel, she will find that she is perpetually wishing to alter the established values – to make serious what appears insignificant to a man, and trivial what is to him important. And for that,

of course, she will be criticized; for the critic of the opposite sex will be genuinely puzzled and surprised by an attempt to alter the current scale of values, and will see in it not merely a difference of view, but a view that is weak, or trivial, or sentimental, because it differs from his own. But here, too, women are coming to be more independent of opinion. They are beginning to respect their own sense of values. (*CE* 2: 146)

Katherine Mullin has seen women writers' treatment of the so-called trivial at the beginning of the twentieth century as part of their own version of modernist innovation, an exploration of "what might be a fit topic for modernism." She points out that such labelling of women's writing aligned it with "'insubstantial' and evanescent popular literature and culture," in contrast to the male modernist, who is viewed as being "objective, ironic, in control of his aesthetic means," and creating "serious and durable art forms."[77] But to call women's modernist writing "trivial" does not just construct and portray it as low and mass, and male modernist writing as high, serious and durable.[78] It is also linked to the assertion of professional values in an age in which they had come to represent values which some modernist writers such as T. S. Eliot and Ezra Point at times wished to claim for their writing.[79] Professionalism, with its concept of a higher calling, its ideals of social service and contribution, its emphasis on objective and stringent criteria and qualifications, and its fundamental principle of closure to outsiders, was seen as the antithesis of the "trivial" and the amateurish. Woolf herself constantly played with the ideas of the "insignificant" and the "trivial" to dismantle the boundaries between professional and non-professional domains. Marriage, she claims in *Three Guineas*, should be a profession like any other. Professional standards, such as those of medical diagnosis in *Mrs Dalloway*, can be as random as pure subjective opinion. The long series of titles which come after a male professional name, "O.M., K.C.B., LL.D., D.C.L., P.C., etc." (*TG* 208–09), are listed in a way that makes them slightly ridiculous, as trivial perhaps as male professional dress. The difference in "the values of a woman" (*CE* 2: 146) is crucial precisely because it offers an alternative to male professionalism, destabilising a one-sided view of what is "important."

Having seemingly defended women's difference from charges of mere triviality, Woolf peculiarly continues in the same essay with a detraction of it:

> In the past, the virtue of women's writing often lay in its divine spontaneity.... It was untaught; it was from the heart. But it was also, and much more often, chattering and garrulous – mere talk spilt over paper.... In future, ... literature will become for women, as for men,

an art to be studied. Women's gift will be trained and strengthened. The novel will cease to be the dumping-ground for the personal emotions. It will become, more than at present, a work of art like any other, and its resources and its limitations will be explored.

From this it is a short step to the practice of the sophisticated arts, hitherto so little practised by women – to the writing of essays and criticism, of history and biography. (*CE* 2: 148)

Woolf seems to suggest that there are objective standards for writing which can be taught, which should not change "women's gift" but strengthen it. However, in her desire for women's writing to be created seriously and taken seriously, she is also espousing certain professional qualities in the present which it has historically lacked. This meant that she was caught between hailing women's difference as something unique and precious to be protected, and knowing that it would be unappreciated until women could make their writing conform more to existing standards of art. Too much of such imposition, however, could lead to complete assimilation instead of a celebration of this difference. Women's difference in writing is therefore simultaneously asserted and critiqued in the same essay: It should be valued, but it should also be changed. One possible way to make sense of this apparent conflict is by understanding how Woolf saw neither solely amateurism (when one wrote whatever one wanted), nor solely professionalism (with its commercial and institutional concerns) as the path for development for writing, whether by women or men. Here, she sought to undermine the boundaries she saw between institutional writing, which was dominated by men, and women's writing. But an understanding of women's difference could ensure that this would not be a process of pure assimilation or amalgamation. Both women writers and their male colleagues could improve by learning from each other, where women would be educated more formally in the art of writing, and male institutions, including those of writing, would be less exclusive and less power- and status-driven.

Woolf's criticism of the novel as women's "dumping-ground for the personal emotions" echoes that by nineteenth-century writers such as George Eliot, whose essay "Silly Novels by Lady Novelists" (1856) harshly criticises "lady novelists" of "the *oracular* species," whose novels are "intended to expound the writer's religious, philosophical, or moral theories."[80] Eliot instead argues for a different ideal of the woman writer:

A really cultured woman, like a really cultured man, is all the simpler and the less obtrusive for her knowledge; ... she does not make it a pedestal from which she flatters herself that she commands a complete view of men and things.... In conversation she is the least formidable of women, because she understands you, without wanting to make you aware that you *can't* understand her. She does not give you information, which is the raw material of culture, – she gives you sympathy, which is its subtlest essence.[81]

"Sympathy" was the initial title of Woolf's short story "An Unwritten Novel," in which the narrator travels on a train and describes and tries to understand – as both a human being and a character – a woman who is sitting opposite, suggesting that Woolf felt "sympathy" to be a vital ingredient to successful fictional writing. This short story was an important exercise for Woolf, who hoped that the form, extended to novel-length, would be able to "get closer & yet keep form & speed, & enclose everything, everything" (*D* 2: 13). She was to repeat the method in "Mr Bennett and Mrs Brown,"[82] in which she argues that in order to understand and "describe beautifully if possible, truthfully at any rate, our Mrs. Brown" in a way that does her complexity, and the complexity of life, justice, writers must "come down off their plinths and pedestals," "never to desert [her]" (*CE* 1: 336–37). A good novelist, therefore, should be sympathetic, touching common ground with others and attaining the human affinity with them necessary to recreate real, individual and psychologically complex characters, instead of using writing only as a "dumping-ground" (*CE* 2: 148) for personal views and political diatribes.

Later, in *Three Guineas*, such ethical standards for women's writing become even more important. Sympathy should not take the form of "forced fraternity" (232–33), through a subservience to, for example, "the tired professional man demanding sympathy and resisting competition" (257) or though using "immense stores of charm, of sympathy, to persuade young men that to fight was heroic" (160), but should be a "human sympathy" (232–33) which allows them to observe other people, feel their affinity with them and use their intelligence to create works which "tell the truth" so that "we should not believe in war, and we should believe in art" (222). Chapter 1 argued that Woolf thought that doctors needed more sympathy. Here, it seems writers also needed sympathy as both an ethical and an aesthetic requirement, and the best writers to set the example were the women writers Woolf appeals to in *Three Guineas*, who had enough personal income to do what they wanted, and had the flexibility to exercise sympathy on their own terms.

However, without these ideal financial circumstances, such a positive development of writing could become hampered by money concerns. In *Orlando*, Greene criticises the contamination of literary standards by the commercialism rife in the book trade: "'The truth of it is,' he said, pouring himself a glass of wine, 'that all our young writers are in the pay of booksellers. They turn out any trash that serves to pay their tailor's bills'" (193). Woolf, in the essay "Oliver Goldsmith" (1934), traces the change in the patronage of literature back to the eighteenth century, and summarises Goldsmith's views: "Now in the mid-eighteenth century young men of brains were thrown to the mercy of the booksellers.... Men of original-ity and spirit became docile drudges, voluminous hacks" (*CE* 1: 107). The commercialisation of writing had a profound influence on women writers: "Hundreds of women began as the eighteenth century drew on to add to their pin money, or to come to the rescue of their families by making translations or writing the innumerable bad novels which have ceased to be recorded even in textbooks" (*AROO* 59). Many critics have discussed what they see as the contradiction of women's novels in the eighteenth and nineteenth centuries being on the one hand financially successful and, in the sense of yielding money, professional, but on the other hand being seen as transient and making no valuable contribution to culture, of being amateurish in standards despite the money they made. Jane Moore, for example, argues that in the eighteenth century, the view of "the increasing feminization of literature" emerged, noting that Alexander Pope portrays in *The Dunciad* (1728) "a picture of a woman as the corruptor of male poetic standards," writing for "the denizens of Grub Street who privilege commercial concerns above literary value."[83] But Penny Boumelha, in considering both the real and the fictional woman writer at the end of the nineteenth century, writes that although there was "the association of femininity with trash," including "commerce," "the marketplace, alienated labour, and inferior aesthetic values," these came also with "professionali-sation, career, financial independence, and the opportunity to manifest talent."[84]

Woolf herself relates such commercialisation to professionalism only when describing commercial writing activities by women in the twentieth century who busily perform professional activities. They are "at the desk writing those books, lectures and articles by which culture is prostituted and intellectual liberty is sold into slavery," and "accept any of those bau-bles and labels by which brain merit is advertised and certified – medals, honours, degrees" (*TG* 219). Writing, then, failed in divesting itself from its commercial side by processes and tokens of professionalism by which it is "certified," which are instead reduced to being described as "prostitu-tion" (*TG* 219) by Woolf.

Her use of the word "prostitution" for what she calls the "brain-selling trade" (*TG* 217–19) is not only highly gendered, but also has the connotation of being the "oldest profession"[85] for women. As different needs of society have led to the establishment of different professions, this one "profession" has remained – socially marginalised yet at the same time meeting the needs of men. Although Woolf reserves some of her most bitter criticism for these women writers, in considering the immediate historical context of the word "prostitution," the metaphor can perhaps be better understood as an attempt to highlight how these women writers were not simply perpetuators of vice, but were as much victims of participation in professional society in the twentieth century.

Woolf, in its use, was building on the political rhetoric against prostitution in the nineteenth century. In *Three Guineas*, for example, she praises Josephine Butler, who "led the campaign against the Contagious Diseases Act to victory," and the women who helped her in her campaign against them, for "the purity of their motives" (*TG* 201). The acts were passed in the nineteenth century to target prostitution and combat the spread of sexually transmitted diseases in military towns. Their establishment allowed police in designated cities to put any woman they thought might be a prostitute onto a roster, which they presented to a magistrate who could order her to be medically examined at designated hospitals, where, if it was found that she had a contagious disease, she could be detained for compulsory treatment.[86] In each of the acts of 1864, 1866 and 1869, areas in which the legislation applied were extended, and the length of maximum detainment was increased from three to six and finally nine months.[87] Many who protested against the acts at the time saw them as highly ineffective legislation which punished the wrong party. Butler was one of the leaders of the Ladies' National Association for the Repeal of the Contagious Diseases Acts, which in 1869 published a Ladies' Protest in the *Daily News*, arguing that the acts "punish the sex who are the victims of vice and leave unpunished the sex who are the main causes both of the vice and its dreaded consequences."[88] Her fight can be seen not just as a fight for the fair treatment of women, but also as a fight against social institutions which penalised women for engaging in a "profession" the demand for which came from men.

The metaphor of "prostitution" in *Three Guineas* links this situation in the nineteenth century with that found in the twentieth century, when both the demands of the market and of the publishing trade, and the professionalisation of literature, could be seen as the perpetuators of "intellectual harlotry" (*TG* 224). Woolf thus felt it necessary in *Three Guineas* to delimit the group of women to whom the guidelines she suggested for countering "prostitution" applied: They had to be in a good enough financial position to have the freedom to write what they wanted. In her argument that "[j]ust as for many centuries … it was thought vile for a woman to sell her body without love, … so it is wrong, you will agree, to sell your mind without love" (*TG* 218), two parallel ideas can be identified: the importance of shifting the position of writing closer to the amateur value of "love," and of moving it away from being a mere commercial profession, with "money," "power," "advertisement," publicity" and "vanity motive[s]" (221), which she abstracts into "prostitution" to leave no ambiguity as to its deleterious qualities. Writing could then become a more personally rewarding and economically "disinterested pursuit of reading and writing the English language" (216). Woolf's choice of metaphor was therefore a calculated one, able to vividly express what, as the result of the professionalisation of literature, was at stake in the late 1930s: "culture" and "intellectual liberty" (216).

If, however, part of professional rhetoric is the claim that professions are removed from commercial concerns, where the aim of the provision of service is primarily out of a sense of vocation and duty rather than for financial rewards, this sense of "professionalism" enables us to look at Woolf's discussion of writing from a new angle. The ethical and aesthetic requirement of sympathetic connection in writing, and the appeal in *Three Guineas* for women writers not to prostitute their writing, could be seen as a partial reversal to specific professional ideals, perhaps as an idiosyncratic type of professional rhetoric in itself: Woolf calls for responsibility on the part of women writers, asking them to counter the commercialism in which writing had become mired, and to focus not on moneymaking but on writing what they wanted to write. This seems to suggest that, for Woolf, ideals in and of themselves, professional or otherwise, were not necessarily harmful; the moment they become so is when they are used disingenuously, as the figure of Bradshaw in *Mrs Dalloway* so potently and dangerously does, as a mask to gain respect, power and self-protection, denying that money and status are their primary concerns, while using this cover to gain exactly these.

But at the same time, in an ironic twist, the claim to removal from the marketplace was not just made by professional ideals, but also by amateurism, with its qualities of "honesty, originality, or sensibility" (*E* 2: 36).[89] This potential similarity between amateur and professional ideals in art poses a conflict which is difficult to reconcile entirely. To draw an example from *Three Guineas*, Woolf asks:

> Is it not possible that if we knew the truth about war, the glory of war would be scotched and crushed … ; and if we knew the truth about art … , the enjoyment and practice of art would become so desirable that by

> comparison the pursuit of war would be a tedious game for elderly
> dilettantes in search of a mildly sanitary amusement – the tossing of bombs
> instead of balls over frontiers instead of nets? (222)

Here she compares warfare to games, seeing it as an amateurish and trivial activity rather than as a profession which warrants respect. But at the same time, using such words as "enjoyment" to describe the activity of writing almost equates it to an amateur activity, which risks diminishing its importance. In order for there to be no tension between the respect and seriousness which should be accorded to writing as a profession and the "enjoyment" which it should afford, there must be a change in the term "profession" itself. Instead of excessively institutionalising literary activity, where readers are shut "in a lecture room, rank with the fumes of stale print, listening to a gentleman who is forced to lecture or to write every Wednesday, every Sunday, about Milton or about Keats," the importance of the practice of art should also derive from its spontaneity and freedom, where "the lilac shakes its branches in the garden free, and the gulls, swirling and swooping, suggest with wild laughter that such stale fish might with advantage be tossed to them" (*TG* 225). The inherent contradictions of a vision of art as vitally important to civilisation yet remaining free and enjoyable remained fundamentally unsolved, perhaps impossible to achieve in a world in which, stressing economic efficiency and productivity, "enjoyable" and "desirable" had become synonymous with amateurish. The instability of meanings in the words professionalism and amateurism, and the dynamics between them, made it impossible for Woolf exclusively to use either as a model for the future direction for writing. However, as this chapter has shown, although Woolf was never entirely satisfied with either term or their implications, the two concepts were points of triangulation for her thinking on how writing should be.

In addition, in the real world, the number of women writers who fulfilled Woolf's financial stipulations was, as she herself acknowledges, very low. She asks: "how many of them are there? Dare we assume in the face of Whitaker, of the laws of property, of the wills in the newspapers, of facts in short, that 1,000, 500, or even 250 will answer when thus addressed?" (*TG* 218). Having the financially independent daughter of an educated man remind the narrator not to "dream dreams about ideal worlds behind the stars," but to "consider actual facts in the actual world" (223), Woolf would have realised only too well that ultimately, there could be few final solutions to the dilemmas which money and standards posed for writing, few perfect conditions under which writing could be produced, few ideal rules to apply.

Having a private income on which to rely was not just an elusive goal for most, it could also in itself never be entirely disinterested. Woolf did not discuss this directly, but she was not unaware of the issue. The shift in the sources of her narrators' money from *A Room* to *Three Guineas* demonstrates its increased problematisation. In *A Room*, the narrator's legacy is from her aunt, and although the female source of the inheritance relieves it from immediate implications of patriarchy, the regular income is probably the result of the investment of existing capital, which brings with it an additional set of moral issues. According to Lee, Virginia and Leonard Woolf's investments yielded from £310 in 1924 to £802 in 1939. Nor was the narrator's inheritance entirely fictional: Woolf received £2,500 when her aunt died in 1909, bringing her total inherited capital to over £9,000 in 1912, which was invested and yielded slightly less than £400 a year.[90] Lee comments that such capital meant that Woolf, "like Forster and Strachey and others of her English friends, and unlike incomers such as T. S. Eliot and Katherine Mansfield," was a rentier, deriving income from invested money.[91] Despite these problems, the narrator's focus is on the enormous sense of liberation that the money gives her rather than its moral implications, which she hints at but does not address directly.[92] *Three Guineas*, the very title of which foregrounds the concerns about money in the book, has a narrator who lives under different circumstances, who, despite all the disparities in education which distinguish her from the barrister she addresses, and despite her own argument for the "daughters of educated men who have enough to live upon" (218–19) as the only group in society able to address the question of war disinterestedly, admits that she is part of the "paid-for culture" (216) when she writes in reply to his letter that "we both earn our livings" (118). In between these two narrators, both thematically and chronologically, is the narrator in the essay "Professions for Women," a woman writer who earns her own money but still has "a certain sum of money – will we say five hundred pounds a year?" left by "some excellent ancestors" (*CE* 2: 285–86).

In moving from the rentier narrators of *A Room* and "Professions for Women" to the money-earning narrator in *Three Guineas*, Woolf was perhaps responding, in her own way, to the problems raised by the previous narrators' complicity, and placing her later narrator in a better position to engage with the ambiguity of money as a powerful, multi-faceted and dangerous instrument which should be used carefully. Her status as someone who is not above the struggle to make a living makes her vulnerable, like almost everyone else, to the instability of money. This, however, also endows her later narrator's guineas, used to influence the policies of the societies she donates to, with additional worth and authority: "since guineas are rare and guineas are valuable you will listen to the terms we wish to impose" (*TG* 182). The abundant ten-shilling notes automatically bred by the purse of the narrator in *A Room*, or the money used to buy Persian cats by the narrator in "Professions for Women," are in their detachment from the real world perhaps also less persuasive.

Even if financial independence were attained and its moral implications ignored, and even if writers told the "truth" as they saw it, the danger is of becoming a mere amateur like Ernest in *The Way of All Flesh*, isolated in his views, his hope to inspire next generations if not this one far from certain. Throughout her career, therefore, Woolf circles such problems, offering tentative solutions, but always returning to qualify and problematise these. She would herself dispute her late model in *Three Guineas* of the financially and artistically independent woman writer with the more ambiguous and impecunious figure of Miss La Trobe, who will be discussed in Chapter 3.

The goals of this chapter have been firstly to explore Woolf's views of professionalism in literature; secondly to problematise a facile conclusion that she evaluated it wholly negatively; and thirdly to suggest that although she used notions of amateurism and professionalism in exploring the idea of a rewarding profession of writing, it proved impossible, and indeed undesirable, to reconcile material concerns with a single coherent vision. As its beginning specified, the chapter has mainly focused on the commercial and institutional facets of professionalism. Yet there were alternative ways of interpreting professionalism extant in Woolf's time, which I have already hinted at, such as conceiving of it as the meaningful pursuit of a line of work for its own sake and personal fulfilment. Chapter 3 will use these to move beyond existing interpretations of Lily Briscoe and Miss La Trobe, arguing that they embody different senses of the word "professionalism" which Woolf wanted to imbue art and writing with. This, however, also comes at a great cost to them.

Reconfiguring Professionalism: Lily Briscoe and Miss La Trobe

Critical descriptions of Lily Briscoe in *To the Lighthouse* and Miss La Trobe in *Between the Acts* in the social terminology of professionalism and amateurism has resulted in them being variously identified as professionals *and* as amateurs. On the one hand, neither of these two women artists in Woolf's fiction enjoys the kind of critical renown and financial success which Woolf had by the time she was writing *To the Lighthouse*, as Alison Booth has pointed out.[1] They seem so remote from social standards of achievement that Bridget Elliott and Jo-Ann Wallace have called them "amateurs and spinsters, 'outsiders' who are tolerated by the communities on whose edges they live, and who seem to regard their unmarried status and their financial disinterestedness as essential to their art."[2] At first glance, the label of amateur, which has been applied by numerous critics over the past few decades,[3] seems appropriate: Lily and La Trobe work not for money, one of the key rewards of professional work, but for the sake of the work itself, and receive little recognition for their art from their community. On the other hand, in seeming contradiction to these views, they have also been declared "professionals" by others because of their obvious dedication to their work. Eileen Sypher, for instance, has called Lily a "professional, unmarried woman"[4]; Makiko Minow-Pinkney points out that Lily needs to kill the Angel in the House to "establish her own identity as a new woman, professional, unmarried, independent"[5]; and Sally Greene considers La Trobe "the only professional artist" in *Between the Acts*.[6]

This chapter both qualifies and combines these two directions of evaluation. The two women artists cannot be described as professionals in an unquestioning, unproblematic manner. But neither can they be construed solely as amateurs whose lack of professional status expresses Woolf's ambivalence towards professionalism.[7] Further exploring Booth's suggestion that Woolf imagines "a different model of success without need of patriarchal laurels,"[8] this chapter argues that through them, Woolf mapped out a new type of artistic "professionalism" which contains salubrious values of existing modes of both professionalism and amateurism, one which is rid both of charges of disingenuous self-interest, and of dilettantism and artistic carelessness. It thus continues from the varying configurations of the notion of professionalism in the previous chapter. There, it was pointed out that characteristics of self-interest which Woolf attributed to professionalism, including institutionalisation, money and other social rewards, led to her aversion towards the concept in art. But it also showed that the notion for Woolf could mean a seriousness of purpose, and a deliberate attention to form and style, which were essential in her own career as a writer, and which approaches the more literal sense of "profession" (henceforth put in quotation marks in this chapter to isolate this meaning), as a "declaration of faith," "belief" or "principles."⁹ Although Lily and La Trobe are not professionals in the first sense, their art is something they profess their lives to: It is not a hobby which they do in their spare time, but work which they are ardently zealous about, and the formal execution of which is a painstakingly meticulous process which comes about only after careful deliberation. In some ways, therefore, Lily's and La Trobe's chosen vocations are no less their "professions" than Peggy's in *The Years*.

If it is possible to see in Lily and La Trobe an alternative mode of "professionalism," it also becomes possible to view Woolf's representations as her literary attempts to solve the contradictions which underlie the concept of "professionalism," which she never managed to resolve entirely in her own career as a writer: The tension between its claims of disinterest, and its inevitable entanglement with economic interest, whether this is in the form of money, social status or power. In removing the taint which economic self-interest can bring, Woolf retains in the two women artists, at the cost of their social isolation, a distilled form of "professionalism" which is based on what Jennifer Ruth has called the "disinterested" interest of aesthetics.¹⁰ This also allows us to reconfigure the relationship between the women artists and professionalism: the opposition between them and male professionals, whom Woolf suggestively names "the patriarchs, the professors" (34) in *A Room*, and "the Professors" (258) in *Three Guineas*, is not one of amateurism to professionalism per se, but of dissimilar manifestations of the notion of professionalism.

The chapter therefore pulls slightly back from Pamela Caughie's view that Woolf "creates no ultimate portrait of the woman artist because no one portrait will suffice," and "no successful woman artist because the standards for success change."¹¹ I agree with Caughie that Woolf did not offer a conclusive, fixed and universal ideal of the woman artist; that she was aiming at "flexibility" and "freedom," not just from patriarchy or even matriarchy, but from the very need to adhere to a tradition in the first place; and that her writing constantly undercuts "empirical stability" which tries to draw rigid distinctions.[12] But Woolf did, to some extent, envision ways of living and artistic creation by fashioning these two women artists, who were deliberately different from the trope of the socially successful woman artist which was readily available to her. And she did so, I contend, for the specific purpose of imagining an alternative "professionalism" with distinct characteristics, although, as the two women artists demonstrate, this "professionalism," applied in the real world, was far from ideal.

Navigating "Amateurism"

In Chapter 2, we saw how Woolf's work showed two different evaluations of money. On the one hand, in *A Room*, she says that "[m]oney dignifies what is frivolous if unpaid for" (59), that it is a valid form of recognition or critical approbation of one's work. On the other hand, it is also a symptom of the subjugation of women to commercial standards, which is why Woolf writes with some approval in the very same essay – in contrast to the attitude one would expect from an advocate for commercial female authorship – that "publicity in women is detestable. Anonymity runs in their blood. The desire to be veiled still possesses them" (46). She adds that "I often like women. I like their unconventionality. I like their subtlety. I like their anonymity" (100). However, lacking formal validating professional mechanisms and organisations, money earned from art was especially contentious, perching artistic endeavours dangerously between public acknowledgement and economic interest. Portraying a financially successful woman artist risked the perception of her work being produced mainly for the sake of money. To avoid such a portrayal was to eschew the suggestion that Lily and La Trobe might be working at their art for anything other than its own sake. A tension therefore underlies Woolf's choice of characterisation: The women artists' moneylessness is a pre-emptive gesture to avoid the stigma of money, and becomes an assertion of their artistic autonomy and freedom; but this comes at the cost of precisely the freedom, confidence and validation that income from one's own work could provide. That Woolf was aware of this but still made such a choice reflects the depth of the anxieties she felt about money concerns in art. Even in her own life, as Chapter 2 detailed, Woolf had difficulty reconciling artistic vocation with money.

Woolf's representations of Lily and La Trobe as located outside money economies lead to other compromises, which become evident when we analyse critics' usage of the laden word "amateur" to describe them. Because of the implicit presuppositions of the word "amateur" as a social category, and the complex ways Woolf herself viewed the term, its use should not be taken lightly. Penelope J. Corfield has shown that throughout the nineteenth century, amateur work became seen as an inferior type of effort. The notion of a profession was set apart as superior, involving specialist work which people viewed as "dignified, expert and socially admired." The word "amateurish," in contrast, became a derogatory term, suggesting "a dilettante approach and slapdash execution." She points out a journal in 1868 which states that "[a]mateurism is the curse of the nineteenth century."[13] For literature, the term "amateurism" similarly took on negative connotations. In 1894, Hubert Crackanthorpe, a writer Woolf mentions in *Roger Fry* (1941), complains about it in literature:

> True is it that the society lady, dazzled by the brilliancy of her own conversation, and the serious-minded spinster, bitten by some sociological theory, still decide in the old jaunty spirit, that fiction is the obvious medium through which to astonish or improve the world. Let us beware of the despotism of the intelligent amateur, and cease our toying with that quaint and winsome bogey of ours, the British Philistine, whilst the intelligent amateur, the deadliest of Art's enemies, is creeping up in our midst.
>
> For the familiarity of the man in the street with the material employed by the artist in fiction, will ever militate against the acquisition of a sound, fine, and genuine standard of workmanship. Unlike the musician, the painter, the sculptor, the architect, the artist in fiction enjoys no monopoly in his medium. The word and the phrase are, of necessity, the common property of everybody; the ordinary use of them demands no special training. Hence the popular mind, while willingly acknowledging in the creation of the sonata, the landscape, the statue, the building, in the case of the short story, or of the longer novel, declines to believe even in their existence, persuaded that in order to produce good fiction, an ingenious idea, or "plot," as it is termed, is the one thing needed. The rest is a mere matter of handwriting.[14]

What Crackanthorpe laments as the writer's lack of "monopoly in his medium" was for Woolf, as we saw in the previous chapter, cause for both celebration and fear. Significantly, Crackanthorpe's two examples of pernicious amateurs – "the society lady" and "the serious-minded spinster" – are both women. As Anne Stott writes, "the growth of male-only professions" in the nineteenth century meant "the relegation of women's work to the informal, the amateur, and the unpaid."[15] The fall of regard for amateurism thus paralleled its feminisation: It was used not just to describe women who did not earn money from their activities, but also to characterise women's activities as unserious and dilettante.

Such readings of the term spilled over into the twentieth century. We have seen this with regards to Kenealy's complaint in the previous chapter about the labelling of female work as amateurish. In another essay, published at the turn of the century, entitled "Women in Social Life" (1899), R. C. Phillimore writes that women

> must have the moral courage to face the fact that, so far, they have been Jacks-of-all-trades, and that in a complicated society where the doctrine of the expert is daily gaining ground, it is perfectly reasonable to distrust the amateur who claims to have a voice in affairs. And they must see that the best way the modern woman can help to solve the difficulty is to cease to be an amateur.[16]

They must therefore, Phillimore argues, all become more professional. The designation of amateurism, applied in opposition to professionalism and gendered female, could be a disavowal of the worth of women's work in a society which privileges the practices of institutional professional work.

Calling women "amateurs" in fields other than domesticity and maternity could also be an effective way to claim that these were their natural spheres of expertise. This is what A. Maude Royden, a contemporary feminist writer, used the idea of amateurism to argue, unlike Kenealy, who feared that characterising women's work as amateurish would mean that their work in the private sphere would not be taken seriously. Royden writes in an essay entitled "The Woman's Movement of the Future," part of a collection of essays which attempt to "frame, in spite of differences of opinion on minor points, a unified feminist policy, and to suggest, without laying down an absolutely definite programme, the lines on which feminism should develop"[17]:

> If I am right in believing that most women desire to have children, and that motherhood is to them an absorbing duty and not merely an episode, it follows that the average woman will generally be in other walks of life not an expert but an amateur. She will be an amateur in arts and professions, and expert in human life. This, again, is (I believe) a permanent difference between the average woman and the average man, due to their natural qualities and vocations.[18]

Woolf neatly sidesteps possible claims of marriage and motherhood as vocations for Lily and La Trobe in their characterisation: Neither is interested in these possible aspects of womanhood. This portrayal seems a necessary condition for greater artistic autonomy not just because marriage and motherhood would usurp the place in their lives reserved for artistic energies, but also because it reduces their perceived amateurism, a description which Woolf perhaps knew the women artists would not be able to avoid entirely. I began this chapter by pointing out that critics have described Lily and La Trobe as amateurs. However, the two women artists invite this description not just from critics of our own time, but also from Woolf's (near) contemporaries. *The History of the Novel in England* (1932), for example, describes Lily as "spinster and amateur artist, whose only achievement is a sweet yearning to appreciate the life and art in which she seems cast for the role of spectator."[19] And in 1946, in the American literary journal the *Sewanee Review*, Vivienne Koch, reviewing Joan Bennett's *Virginia Woolf: Her Art as a Novelist* (1945), calls La Trobe Woolf's "amateur playwright."[20] In the case of Peggy in *The Years*, who is more unequivocally a professional as a doctor, Woolf decided to approach characterisation in a very different way: Marriage, which Booth rightly points out is often represented in Woolf's novels "as a woman's estrangement from herself than as her proper vocation,"[21] instead becomes part of Peggy's yearning for a different, more fulfilling life. This is not because being a doctor is not her interest or vocation of choice, but rather because society does not seem to allow for a woman to venture outside of the "ruts" which professional success carves in one's life. Peggy's professional success therefore becomes a mental prison, so that even her thought patterns are bound by the fixed codes of her profession.

Lily Briscoe's "Professionalism"

Ruth writes in her analysis of professional values in Victorian novels that "the professional putatively boasts mental 'gifts' that anticipate his future ... but he simply becomes what he was always meant to be."[22] The idea of answering an inborn calling underlying the act of professing suggests that professionals are born with mental gifts which make them good candidates for certain types of brainwork, but only in the labour of trying to become a public professional, and of actually performing work which can be measured by existing standards, does such intrinsic ability become manifestly determinate. Characterising Lily as an unprofessional amateur threatens to ignore the tension within the concept of professionalism itself between the notions of innate ability and externally quantifiable aptitude: The first does not always lead to the second.

And in fact, in portraying Lily, Woolf did draw on ideas of personal interest, ability and calling. In the novel, Lily says that "she would always go on painting, because it interested her," and when she feels threatened by Charles Tansley's view that "[w]omen can't write, women can't paint," she thinks in self-defence: "there's my painting; I must move the tree to the middle; that matters – nothing else" (94). The ideology of separate spheres – the view that the professions comprise a male, public domain, and that home and maternity comprise female, private space – encourages her to diminish the importance of her painting, so that even when she herself describes her life, she demurely puts her painting last, appropriately qualified by a conditional clause: "there was her father; her home; even, had she dared to say it, her painting" (56). The suggestion is that she is made to trivialise her art by others, who want their priorities to be hers. Yet the narrative makes it clear that her painting is her life force, her "profession."

At the same time, Woolf contrasts Lily with male characters who rely more on externally measurable social standards of professional aptitude and success. Lily explains why she cannot make fashionable paintings in the style of a well-known artist called Paunceforte: "She would not have considered it honest to tamper with the bright violet and the staring white, since she saw them like that, fashionable though it was, since Mr. Paunceforte's visit, to see everything pale, elegant, semitransparent" (23). And in what we can contrast with descriptions of Mr Ramsay's intellectual labour, Lily's working method is described more in moments of realisation than as a linear progression: Her painting takes time to evolve slowly in her mind, and she only draws the line in the middle when, having "borne it in her mind all these years," "the solution had come to her" (161). Refusing to sacrifice any aspect of her vision, the advancement of her painting only comes when she is fully satisfied that it expresses what she sees in her mind's eye. Although Mr Ramsay's academic work is at times similarly described as not immediately productive, the terminology Woolf uses is very different: He is "plodding" at his work, which is metaphorically reduced to that of a graduated march through the alphabet (40).

A profession is underpinned by the concept of specialisation: One chooses to specialise in one occupation out of many. Yet the professions also often encourage additional, and sometimes excessively narrow, specialisation within one's own field, which leads to a limitation in one's subject matter and method. Lily suggests this when she uses the kitchen table as a symbol for Mr Ramsay's learning and efforts:

> The kitchen table was something visionary, austere, something bare, hard, not ornamental. There was no colour to it; it was all edges and angles; it was uncompromisingly plain. But Mr Ramsay kept always his eyes fixed

upon it, never allowed himself to be distracted or deluded, until his face became worn too and ascetic and partook of this unornamented beauty which so deeply impressed her. (169–170)

The kitchen table is Lily's way to transmigrate Mr Ramsay's specialisation into an everyday setting, where it becomes barren and spartan. We can compare this austerity with the vibrancy in her widely integrating and encompassing vision: "She saw the colour burning on a framework of steel; the light of a butterfly's wing lying upon the arches of a cathedral" (54).[23] Lily's art draws expansively from her surroundings, instead of narrowly progressing from and remaining within one specialised subtopic. It is verbalised as a question of "parts" and "how [t]o bring them together" (161), of "how to connect this mass on the right hand with that on the left"; as a consideration with "the unity of the whole" (60), rather than Mr Ramsay's fixed study of one object.[24] The problem is that such expansive creativity is hard to articulate within the narrow confines of codified professionalism. Woolf's solution in portraying Lily is to remove professional quantification, retaining only the parts of creative brainwork and zealous devotion and dedication by which her merit can find expression.

In so doing, Woolf removes the bureaucracy of professionalism, endowing Lily with a female disinterest which allows the expression of her skill and creativity without conforming to the external rules of artistic fashion, although the temptations of "aggression" or "conciliation" (AROO 67) in her environment are forces which she feels she continually has to repulse in order to retain artistic autonomy. Lily's identity as a painter becomes a "profession" which is the purer for the lack of any ulterior motives, yet she still "struggl[es] against terrific odds to maintain her courage; to say: 'But this is what I see; this is what I see,' and so to clasp some miserable remnant of her vision to her breast, which a thousand forces did their best to pluck from her" (TTL 24). This is what Woolf would refer to in A Room when she discusses the difficulties of writing for the woman in the nineteenth century, whose mind was often "slightly pulled from the straight, and made to alter its clear vision in deference to external authority" (67). Such unwavering dedication to one's "clear vision" takes "genius" (AROO 67), something beyond Paunceforte's reliable, formulaic productivity; but it also requires "integrity," a wholehearted "profession" to one's art in the literal sense of the word, so that one "hold[s] fast to the thing as [one sees] it without shrinking" (AROO 67–68).

"[T]o hold fast to the thing" is what Lily Briscoe's predecessor, Lily Everit in the short story "The Introduction" (1925), does not quite manage. Lily Everit's love of and studies in poetry become tainted when she meets another male scholar, Bob Brinsley, through introduction by Clarissa Dalloway with the phrase: "Both of you love Shelley" (*CSF* 188). Lily, however, thinks that "hers was not love compared with his" (188). She associates Brinsley's love with "the towers and civilisation" (188), "[c]hurches and parliaments, flats, even the telegraph wires" (187), so that the "three red stars" with which her professor had marked "her essay upon the character of Dean Swift" to indicate that it was "[f]irst rate" (184) "burnt quite bright again, only no longer clear and brilliant, but troubled and bloodstained as if this man, this great Mr Brinsley, had just by pulling the wings off a fly as he talked ... charged her light being with cloud" (188). It is not merely the imagined act of pulling wings off a fly which is chilling, but the manner in which Lily visualises the act being conducted: "He tore the wings off a fly, standing with his foot on the fender[,] his head thrown back, talking insolently about himself, arrogantly, but she didn't mind how insolent and arrogant he was to her, if only he had not been brutal to flies" (187).[25] Lily pictures him as wholly unsympathetic to a creature which she herself can immediately identify with, having just compared herself to a butterfly who has "come out of her chrysalis" (185). Lily's love and achievements are polluted not because they are incompatible with professionalism per se (her essay would have needed to conform to existing academic discourse to receive the mark it does from her professor), but with the type of violent, competitive, unsympathetic professionalism ensconced in and propagated by the institutions which immediately crop up in her mind's eye. In *To the Lighthouse*, Paunceforte is not portrayed as similarly vicious; nevertheless, he can be seen as a counter-model to Lily Briscoe. Allen McLaurin has called Paunceforte's method "professional artistry," where professionalism means "carefulness" and "lack of imagination."[26] He contrasts Paunceforte's aesthetics to those of both Woolf and Roger Fry,[27] whose aversion to "craftsmanship," he points out, originated "from the same feeling that any specialisation is a barrier to the free play of the artist's imagination."[28]

Like Woolf, Fry thought about the problems which the notion of professionalism posed to artistic production. In "The Grafton Gallery – I," published in the *Nation* on 19 November 1910, Fry writes:

> [M]any of the artists whose work is shown at the Grafton have already proved themselves accomplished masters in what is supposed to be the more difficult task of representation. That they have abandoned the advantage which that *professional skill* affords is surely rather a sign of the *sincerity* of their effort in another direction. No doubt the acrobatic feats of virtuosity always will appeal to our sense of wonder; but they are better reserved

for another stage. If only an artist has *genuine conviction*, he rarely lacks sufficient skill to give it expression. And as things are at present, with our gaping admiration for professional skill, we are in less danger of finding a *prophet* whose utterance is spoiled by imperfect articulation than of being drowned beneath floods of uninspired rhetoric. (89; emphasis added)

Fry sees what he calls "professional skill" as secondary to and insufficient by itself for genuine artistic work. He is therefore troubled by the trend he observes in society of emphasising specialist skill and knowledge, thinking these obstacles to art. This is contrasted with his idea of the artist as a "prophet," who has "sincerity" and holds "genuine conviction" towards work, which can in fact also be facets of professionalism, though Fry reserves the term for more formulaic skill.

Similar qualities in Lily, however, also come at the cost of a lack of social recognition, of the reliability and linearity of labour which characterise institutional or socially recognised professionalism. The details with which Woolf expresses Lily's artistic labour seek to address the potential drawbacks to the possibility of Lily being seen as lacking in "professional skill": She is careful to portray the artistic exploration and experimentation which Lily performs as serious, meticulous and deliberate, in contrast to the capriciousness and inconsiderateness of form which she thought characterised Samuel Butler's type of amateurism, as discussed in the previous chapter. Such concerns about the right aesthetics are a major part of Lily's artistic anxieties. She thinks, for instance:

> Then beneath the colour there was the shape. She could see it all so clearly, so commandingly, when she looked: it was when she took her brush in hand that the whole thing changed. It was in that moment's flight between the picture and her canvas that the demons set on her who often brought her to the verge of tears and made this passage from conception to work as dreadful as any down a dark passage for a child. (23)

McLaurin points out that Lily's problem with form mirrors Woolf's own in her fiction, and that Woolf, despite her dislike of types and attributes of professionalism, thought there must be some "'design' as well as 'vision'" in art.[29] Thus while Lily's art can be seen as contrary to Paunceforte's formulaic, unimaginative and financially successful professionalism, there is one alternative way in which it can be conceived of as "professional," in addition to her wholehearted dedication to it: because of Lily's attention to form and method, which distinguish her work from "amateurism" and its common associations with wilful dilettantism.

Fry, like Woolf, envisioned an art which escaped existing social models of not just professionalism, with its concern with replicable standards and money, but also of amateurism. Both were aware of the potential danger of being seen as lacking in specialised skill or "craftsmanship": the possibly derogatory charge of "amateurism," and of producing unserious, dilettante work which could be executed by anyone with some interest in the field. In his essay "Independent Gallery: Vanessa Bell and Othon Friesz," published in the *New Statesman* on 3 June 1922, Fry starts with the statement: "The first quality of Vanessa Bell's painting is its extreme *honesty*" (emphasis added).[30] Bell, he writes, "has no trace of what would ordinarily be called cleverness in a painter," that is, "the power to give an illusion of appearance by a brilliant shorthand turn of the brush." Bell "follows her own vision unhesitatingly and confidingly, without troubling at all whither it may lead her." [31] Instead of making the mistake of "artistic insincerity," of chasing after "beautiful quality as an end in itself," hers is that of a singular pursuit of "trying to express an idea," making her "a very pure artist, uncontaminated with the pride of the craftsman."[32] Woolf characterised Lily in similar ways, writing that "[s]he would not have considered it *honest* to tamper with the bright violet and the staring white, since she saw them like that" (*TTL* 23; emphasis added). But Fry also realises the charges of dilettantism his comments might invite, and immediately qualifies them: "To say that Vanessa Bell is not clever may perhaps give a wrong impression, for she is a very accomplished artist; there is nothing amateurish or haphazard about her work."[33] The implicit association between unspecialised method and amateurism is something he felt he needed to invalidate overtly.

A claim to dilettante amateurism would run counter to Fry's belief in the need for genuine and serious dedication to one's artistic work, one which Lily shares. Lily reflects on the problems she has in addressing Mr Ramsay's demands on her for sympathy now that Mrs Ramsay is dead, which prevent her from engaging with her work: "Here was Lily, at forty-four, wasting her time, unable to do a thing, standing there, playing at painting, playing at the one thing one did not play at, and it was all Mrs. Ramsay's fault. She was dead" (163–64). Her sense of artistic urgency derives from a fear of her art as mere dilettante play: "One can't waste one's time at forty-four, she thought. She hated playing at painting. A brush, the one dependable thing in a world of strife, ruin, chaos – that one should not play with, knowingly even: she detested it" (164). Instead, painting is what she wants to be able to "profess" her life and efforts to. What both Fry and Woolf tried to do, therefore, was to conceive of an artistic professionalism which defied both economic and institutionalised professionalism, and amateurism.

The contrast which Lily provides to male professional characters can thus more usefully be seen as that of an individual realisation of an artistic vocation to well-established professional institutionalism, rather than categorically of amateurism to professionalism as such. Although choosing not to conform to social expectations or to external standards of art, Lily refuses to disavow the seriousness of her work, and remains faithful to her vision. If the concept of "professionalism" is taken in its literal sense – as one's sincere and wholehearted dedication to a particular area of work which is personally meaningful – then Lily honours these specific senses of the word, and arguably achieves "professional" disinterest, objectivity and impersonality in her work more successfully than Mr Ramsay and Charles. When Lily talks to William about her painting, for instance, she transcends her individual identity and her sex to become what Woolf would later call androgynous in *A Room*:

> She took up once more her old painting position with the dim eyes and the absentminded manner, subduing all her impressions as a woman to something much more general; becoming once more under the power of that vision which she had seen clearly once and must now grope for among hedges and houses and mothers and children – her picture. It was a question, she remembered, how to connect this mass on the right hand with that on the left. She might do it by bringing the line of the branch across so; or break the vacancy in the foreground by an object (James perhaps) so. But the danger was that by doing that the unity of the whole might be broken. She stopped; she did not want to bore him; she took the canvas lightly off the easel. (59–60)

Unlike Mr Ramsay and Charles, Lily's mind thrives on disinterestedness, on the loss of "consciousness of outer things, and her name and her personality and her appearance" (174). This allows her mind to "throw[] up from its depths, scenes, and names, and sayings, and memories and ideas" (174), which act as a source of inspiration for her painting. On the other hand, institutionalised professionalism, although arising out of the need to set objective standards for an area of work, often created aspirants focused on self-centred material or social pursuits. Woolf's ironic descriptions of Mr Ramsay's and Charles's labours suggest that their type of professional work is insincere, through which she casts doubt on whether they should be considered as valid. As mentioned, she calls Mr Ramsay's work "plodding" (40); and she puts Charles's academic efforts in quotation marks, problematising his idea of "work": "He was always carrying a book about under his arm – a purple book. He 'worked.' He sat, she remembered, working in a blaze of sun. At dinner he would sit right in the middle of the view" (174). Charles seeks rewards of prestige and recognition rather than the pursuit of knowledge itself: of Mrs Ramsay, he admits that "[h]e would like her to see him, gowned and hooded, walking in a procession. A fellowship, a professorship, – he felt capable of anything" (15). Mrs Ramsay likewise observes that Charles "wanted to assert himself, and so it would always be with him till he got his Professorship or married his wife, and so need not be always saying, 'I – I – I'" (115).

In contrast, Lily strives towards a generality and impersonality in her art which is at the same time also premised on the experiential and subjective "I." Randi Koppen and Jack Stewart have both recently emphasised that Fry was not simply a rigid formalist who separated artistic form and life,[34] or an artist who thought of life as something to be transmuted away in the process of its transformation into art,[35] but that he believed that "under certain conditions the rhythms of life and of art may coincide" (*RF* 214),[36] and that art could be simultaneously "a conversion/turn away from life *and* . . . experientially grounded."[37] This interrelation between life and aesthetics shows itself in Lily's art, in which the experiential combines with formal concerns of pattern, design and order.[38] Her painting communicates this interaction between the subjective and the objective, so that in it, Mrs Ramsay and her son James can become sublimated into a "triangular purple shape" while retaining a vital connection to Lily's personal experience, or, as William Bankes thinks, "reduced . . . to a purple shadow without irreverence" (59). The resultant vibrant yet formally methodical whole runs counter to the tenets of a codified professionalism of invariable form, and is in contrast to Paunceforte's art, which uses fixed interpretive acts to create the "fashionable" (23) no matter what he is painting. In Paunceforte's art, form does not change according to the variations of life, experience and feeling: Form stands on its own, untouched and disconnected from the experiential, so that art becomes a mechanical construct rather than grounded in subjectivity. The final coherency and wholeness of Lily's paintings suggest a symbolic reconciliation of the conflicts between her art and her life as expressed throughout the novel, from which a different "professionalism" emerges from that of Paunceforte – one which attempts to bridge the outer and inner worlds. The ideal "professional," arguably a status which Lily does not fully attain, becomes neither a self-isolated amateur, unsuccessful in communicating with the outer world, nor someone fully conforming to external codes and practices with little space for self-expression.

The financial success that Woolf denies Lily, which critics have made much of, is granted the other artist in the novel, the poet Augustus Carmichael. Yet the narrative does not portray this as a vindication of

Carmichael's poetry. His success is described almost as an afterthought in the section "Time Passes," seemingly the result of fortunate circumstance rather than as a necessary outcome of his work: It is "unexpected," and is because of the war, which "had revived [people's] interest in poetry" (146). Lily herself provides a slightly deprecatory, and perhaps biased, view of Carmichael as an artist, thinking that "[s]he had never read a line of his poetry. She thought that she knew how it went though, slowly and sono-rously. It was seasoned and mellow. It was about the desert and the camel. It was about the palm tree and the sunset. It was extremely impersonal; it said something about death; it said very little about love" (211).[39] His success is real, but at the same time seems secondary to Lily's achieve-ments, which are vindicated by the narrative itself. That Lily's work does not receive recognition by the public does not detract from the triumph accorded her at the end of the novel, at the crowning moment of achieve-ment when she sees her next step: "With a sudden intensity, as if she saw it clear for a second, she drew a line there, in the centre. It was done; it was finished. Yes, she thought, laying down her brush in extreme fatigue, I have had my vision" (226). Woolf, in *To the Lighthouse*, suggests not only that artistic accomplishment does not necessarily come with commercial or critical success, but also that whether or not an area of work is one's "profession" may depend on more than formal recognition of one's work, whether in the form of money, social status or other rewards accorded by professional institutions.

Professionalism and Female Disinterest

Scholarship on Woolf has made much of the restrictions which patriar-chal society and values placed on women writers, and with good reason: Woolf devotes large parts of *A Room* to such issues, and felt that she had to kill the "Angel in the House" (*CE* 2: 285) to start finding her own voice in writing. Lily and Miss La Trobe constantly experience the anxieties induced by a mismatch between social expectations and their devotion to their vocation. Yet they do not simply discard patriarchal or domestic ide-als after initially rejecting them; the novels suggest that they channel these energies elsewhere. For instance, after Mrs Ramsay's death, Mr Ramsay's requests for female "sympathy," an attribute of the Ramsays' patriarchal relationship, is tyrannical to Lily, "weigh[ing] her down" and "ma[king] it difficult for her to paint" (185). But Mr Ramsay is, in fact, also part of her artistic method: Lily thinks she needs to "achieve that razor edge of bal-ance between two opposite forces; Mr Ramsay and the picture; which was necessary. There was something perhaps wrong with the design?" (209). He is here a point of artistic triangulation for Lily, as necessary for her painting as Mrs Ramsay, who is her model. In *Between the Acts*, what La Trobe lacks in literal sexual fertility in the domestic sphere is recompensed by the metaphors of procreation used to describe her next artistic conception. After the village play, La Trobe significantly retreats not to her home but to the public house. Although this is not a happy picture, induced by "the horror and the terror of being alone," it is within the "shelter; voices; oblivion" provided by this setting that she "heard the first words" of her next play. Here, "[t]he mud became fertile. Words rose above the intolerably laden dumb oxen plodding through the mud" (125).

Without losing sight of Woolf's criticisms of patriarchy and its ideology of separate spheres, this section explores the elements in the ideology of the "private house" (*TG* 207) which Woolf found worth celebrating. Such an approach is in line with Steve Ellis's recent revision of existing readings of Woolf as solidly anti-Victorian, which, as Ellis points out, have been used to support the portrait of a radically feminist and democratic Woolf. Ellis instead highlights Woolf's problematic "Post-Victorianism" which was rife with ambiguities and contradictions: Woolf both continued to be profoundly influenced by the Victorian age in which she was born, and simultaneously reacted against its traditions and values throughout her life. Acknowledging Lily's rejection of some Victorian traditions, he reminds us that there are components from the Victorian period which can be used to counterbalance "the rationality and categorisation of the modern attitude."[40] Lily should therefore be seen as negotiating herself between the past and the present, a woman artist who is a "site of antithesis," whose painting incorporates both "masculine intelligence" and "feminine subtlety."[41] Relating this view back to professionalism, I wish to argue that Woolf used some Victorian values to fashion Lily's and La Trobe's versions of disinterested "professionalism." Such remoulding and reappropriation of Victorian values appear in both *A Room* and *Three Guineas*. In *A Room*, as I pointed out earlier in this chapter, Woolf writes both critically and admiringly that

> it was the relic of the sense of chastity that dictated anonymity to women even so late as the nineteenth century.... Thus they did homage to the convention, which if not implanted by the other sex was liberally encouraged by them ... , that publicity in women is detestable. Anonymity runs in their blood.... They are not even now as concerned about the health of their fame as men are, and, speaking generally, will pass a tombstone or a signpost without feeling an irresistible desire to cut their names on it. (46)

And in *Three Guineas*, she discusses how "disinterested culture and intellectual liberty" (217) can be best protected by financially independent women writers because, as women, they have been taught in "the traditions of the private house, that ancestral memory which lies behind the present moment," so that they are able "to transmute the old ideal of bodily chastity into the new ideal of mental chastity – to hold that if it was wrong to sell the body for money it is much more wrong to sell the mind for money, since the mind, people say, is nobler than the body" (207). Lily and La Trobe continue the economic disinterestedness bred from being "greatly fortified in resisting the seductions of the most powerful of all seducers – money" (207), applying their resistance to vocations of their choice. In other words, in representing the two women artists, Woolf is drawing upon the ideology of the private house in the nineteenth century, but fashioning it for vocations of women's choice in the twentieth century.

Two famous examples of nineteenth-century writers who emphasised the importance of women's "disinterested kindness"[42] and whose views can be compared and contrasted with Woolf's are Sarah Stickney Ellis and Samuel Smiles. Ellis writes in *The Women of England* (1839) that "the *true English woman*" spreads happiness "without appearing conspicuously as the agent in its diffusion," "from the unseen, but active principle of disinterested love," "applying the magical key of sympathy to all [that those around her] suffer or enjoy, to all they fear or hope."[43] Samuel Smiles's *Self-Help* (1859) similarly depicted the domestic sphere, presided over by the woman, as located outside of the economically interested public world. He writes that "the best philanthropy comes from the fireside.... From this little central spot, the human sympathies may extend in an ever widening circle, until the world is embraced; for though true philanthropy, like charity, begins at home, assuredly it does not end there."[44] In *A Room*, Woolf describes a comparable scenario, of the woman to the man

> as some stimulus, some renewal of creative power which is in the gift only of the opposite sex to bestow. He would open the door of drawing-room or nursery ... and find her among her children perhaps, or with a piece of embroidery on her knee – at any rate, the centre of some different order and system of life, and the contrast between this world and his own, which might be the law courts or the House of Commons, would at once refresh and invigorate; and there would follow, even in the simplest talk, such a natural difference of opinion that the dried ideas in him would be fertilized anew. (78)

Woolf's views serve two purposes: as criticism of the ideology of separate spheres, but also to highlight the importance of differences between the sexes which are inspiring and worth keeping. More specifically, she writes in the essay that since women's "creative power differs greatly from the creative power of men," "it would be a thousand pities if it were hindered or wasted, for it was won by centuries of the most drastic discipline, and there is nothing to take its place" (*AROO* 79). In conceiving of a "professionalism" – and in the case of the two women artists specifically an artistic "professionalism" – based on the values of disinterest of nineteenth-century domestic ideals, Woolf was inspired by female values deriving from the tradition of the "private house," but for very different reasons from such nineteenth-century writers as Ellis and Smiles.

I would not be the first to point out an overlap between professional and nineteenth-century domestic ideology. Mary Poovey has highlighted the similarities between domestic work of middle-class women and professional work in the nineteenth century: Both were, or claimed, disinterestedness; and both were seen as at some remove from direct economic interest. The male professional in nineteenth-century fiction both utilises such ideology, and at the same time attempts to disavow the connection between his work and that by women through emphasising the distinction between the competitive public sphere that his work belonged to and the private sphere which was the domain of the woman.[45] Interestingly, such reassertions were made by women who wished to break out of the private sphere as well. Dorice Williams Elliott has called this "an internal contradiction within domestic ideology,"[46] which combines underlining the importance of the private sphere with ambitions for the public sphere. For instance, sympathy in the form of women's philanthropy can be seen as both a negative vessel which restricted women's freedom, and as a kind of "empowerment" to break out of traditional roles. Women used such domestic ideology – which characterised them as having such feminine qualities as being "emotional, nurturing, kind, and sympathetic" – to justify their taking up philanthropic duties. This both reinforced traditional values and allowed women to have ambitions and opportunities beyond the strictly defined domestic sphere.[47] Elliott argues that this resulted gradually in the metaphorical nature of the branding of philanthropy as a "profession" for women in the early nineteenth century becoming more literal towards the middle of the century. For example, writer and philanthropist Hannah More writes in her novel *Coelebs in Search of a Wife* (1808) that "I have often heard it regretted that ladies have no stated employment, no profession. It is a mistake. Charity is the calling of a lady; the care of the poor is her profession."[48] In comparison, in an 1856 lecture on female philanthropy, Anna Jameson says much more assertively: "Why should not charity be a profession in our sex, just in so far (and no farther) as religion is a profession in yours!"[49] Although here Jameson seems to be drawing more upon the sense of the word "profession" as a calling or vocation outside of money economies, women's use of such terminology to describe female philanthropic work can be seen as an attempt to endow it with the same standing as men's work.[50] This, however, posed a challenge for male professionals, who needed to emphasise that their work in the social sphere was professional whereas women's philanthropy was amateurish.[51] Women, in turn, felt the need to undercut their own position in order to efface this potential threat to professional men.[52]

Woolf, in representing the two women artists, reclaims some of the economic disinterestedness that derived from women's domestic tradition and from the concept of amateurism – without, in fact, portraying them as domestic or amateurish, two historically interrelated concepts. But even while avoiding these labels, the danger of financial detachment and neutrality was that they might reinforce the view of women and women writers as different, as "outsider[s]" (*TG* 233) who would always remain external to mainstream society, and who could best help it by staying so. In the nineteenth century, this had already become problematic: Smiles's views, for example, could be used as justification for excluding women from professional life. Harriet Taylor Mill had already addressed this issue before the publication of Smiles's famous book. In her essay *Enfranchisement of Women* (1851), Mill writes:

> The third objection to the admission of women to political or professional life, its alleged hardening tendency, belongs to an age now past.... There are still, however, persons who say that the world and its avocations render men selfish and unfeeling; that the struggles, rivalries, and collisions of business and of politics make them harsh and unamiable; that if half the species must unavoidably be given up to these things, it is the more necessary that the other half should be kept free from them; that to preserve women from the bad influences of the world is the only chance of preventing men from being wholly given up to them.
>
> There would have been plausibility in this argument when the world was still in the age of violence, when life was full of physical conflict.... Women, like priests, by being exempted from such responsibilities, and from some part of the accompanying dangers, may have been enabled to exercise a beneficial influence. But in the present condition of human life we do not know where those hardening influences are to be found, to which men are subject and from which women are at present exempt.... [T]he enmities of the present day arise not from great things but small, ... and if there are hatred, malice, and all uncharitableness, they are to be found among women fully as much as among men. In the present state of

civilisation, the notion of guarding women from the hardening influences of the world, could only be realised by secluding them from society altogether.[53]

In rejecting the claim that women naturally possessed more traditionally feminine qualities such as charitableness, Mill also rejects the claim for the preservation of such values for the social good, or what Amanda Anderson refers to as the view of the redemptive possibilities of the private sphere to remedy "the negative moral implications of self-interestedness."[54] This is unlike Smiles and Woolf, who, in acknowledging the existence of a special feminine space which is beneficial to the outside world, were in effect arguing for its protection and preservation. Where Smiles's view was in accordance with Victorian ideals of domesticity, however, Woolf's aim was not to encourage women to remain at the fireside, excluded from the professions; rather, she was concerned with the need for the existence of feminine space within the professions themselves. This was a difficult balance to strike: Woolf's espousal of women's difference at times sat uneasily with her criticism – especially in *Three Guineas* – of views that women were unsuited to the professions.

Another quandary was that the notion of the "private house" was not always purely disinterested, and could itself become a tyrannical device, a measure of control which the woman uses to assert her power, much as the professional man could with his status as a contributor to the public sphere. David Bradshaw, for instance, has suggested that Mrs Ramsay's philanthropy in *To the Lighthouse* could indicate her desire for control over others, giving us a portrait of her "as a woman who likes to 'dominate' and who gets a kick out of being 'masterful.'"[55] Drawing on values of the "private house" was therefore far from unproblematic. Woolf's portrayals attempt to work around such constraints, so that Lily's and La Trobe's "professionalism" both disavow and endorse ideals of the "private house," drawing upon its economic disinterestedness, but discarding the idea of the single fate of marriage and maternity for women. This latent conflict, however, erupts in the characterisation of Peggy in *The Years*, who is forced to choose success in her profession over possibilities for maternity and motherhood, which she also desires.

Miss La Trobe and Standards

In "Anon," a draft essay Woolf planned to include in a book on the history of English literature called "Reading at Random," and which she started work on in September 1940,[56] the modern artist, in search for professional prestige, is "asking for recognition, and bitterly conscious of his relation [to] the world, of the worlds scorn" (391). "Anon" purposefully starts at a time before this change occurred, when art was disinterested, had "an impersonality, a generality," and "allowed us to know nothing of the writer" (397). The eponymous premodern artist Anon originates from a time when the distinction between professional and amateur artists did not yet exist, when the artist was not wholly in possession of art because it was participatory in nature, with the audience playing a crucial part in artistic creation. Woolf writes:

> The voice that broke the silence of the forest was the voice of Anon. Some one heard the song and remembered it for it was later written down, beautifully, on parchment. Thus the singer had his audience, but the audience was so little interested in his name that he never thought to give it. The audience was itself the singer; "Terly, terlow" they sang; and "By, by lullay" filling in the pauses, helping out with a chorus. Every body shared in the emotion of Anons song, and supplied the story.... He is the common voice singing out of doors. (382)

"Anon," Woolf says, "was not responsible. He was not self conscious.... No one tries to stamp his own name, to discover his own experience, in his work" (397). He shares with the modern women artists Lily and La Trobe a lack of interest in public laurels. His work is a "profession" of skill, imagination and personal interest, but not yet a profession in the modern sense, with social rewards.

Like Lily, La Trobe struggles with a crisis of form in conceiving of and enacting her pageant, of how to join pieces together to create a whole; but unlike Lily, her struggle is also with her audience, who, like Anon's, are inextricably interweaved in *Between the Acts* with her artistic form, so that audience members are as much the actors of the performance as the performers themselves. In that her "profession" does depend on social recognition distinguishes her from Lily, who, although uncomfortable with her social position, can retreat back into herself more easily. This makes Anon more pertinent to understanding La Trobe's artistic dilemmas throughout the novel.

Yet the times are also no longer Anon's times, and La Trobe's intense labour contrasts with the effortless cohesion between Anon and his audience. When La Trobe, for example, engineers a break into the pageant in order "to expose them, ... to douche them, with present-time reality," the audience ends up impatient, "slipping the noose" (*BA* 74). The metaphor suggests that their participation is no longer spontaneous, and that they constantly need to be ensnared and controlled, to be held together as part of the form of the pageant. In this instance La Trobe is saved by a sudden downpour, rescuing her momentarily by providing natural cohesion which fills the gap where the modern audience fails to, until the pageant can get to work again. But the anxiety that "[e]very moment the audience [would] slip[] the noose; split up into scraps and fragments" (74) haunts La Trobe throughout the play. Ultimately, La Trobe's relationship with her audience is not satisfactory: She yearns for "a play without an audience" (107) so she can stop being their "slave" (127). Standing in front of and "facing the audience" (107) nervously, instead of being one of them like Anon, the distinction between the two parties in modern times is only too apparent.

La Trobe's outsiderness lends itself to many interpretations, and critics have used it to support their argument for various political positions by Woolf, such as her pacifism and feminism, and her views of how art can participate in such issues. Woolf scholarship since the 1990s has tended to evaluate the artistic and political opportunities which La Trobe's otherness provides positively, without discounting the bleak backdrop of fascism and war. As a few prominent recent examples, Gill Plain has read La Trobe's "breakdown of identity" (she is a lesbian, a newcomer, and very little part of traditional patriarchy) as a particularly potent subversion of patriarchal order by undermining "a simple male/female division."[57] Christine Froula considers La Trobe's outsiderness necessary for creating "her radically dialogic art,"[58] in order to "rewrite[e] history,"[59] and "'to re-create the world' for an audience that longs for 'a new plot.'"[60] Melba Cuddy-Keane sees La Trobe not as a satire of the traditional notion of a successful leader, but as "an amiable comic figure" who helps reshape this notion.[61] And Patricia Cramer understands La Trobe as "the behind-the-scenes goddess/artist," a "prompter of matriarchal memory" and "forgotten origins," especially in the "women in patriarchy" in the novel, who "are diminished goddesses" and need to remember "their lost grandeur."[62] Without reverting back to the overly simplistic accounts which Froula argues against, which "discount[] [La Trobe] as a failed artist, an ineffectual village eccentric, even a parody of the fascist group leader" (297), I wish to problematise La Trobe's social status as an artist further, to explore the contradictions inherent in her professional identity based on the various configurations of the word "profession" which have been (de)constructed in this book so far. I consider her outsiderness as an expression of the type of "professionalism" which Woolf sought to create, while at the same time showing the problems in Woolf's vision that remained unresolved. Such a view is based on the belief that Woolf was still working, in this very last novel, on her career-long project of remoulding the professional system, to which I will return in the final chapter.

La Trobe desperately attempts to achieve a meaningful connection with her audience through her work despite being an outsider in the community. Two interrelated types of social contracts would be available for this: first, a professional relationship, where the artist is seen as rendering others a professional service; and second, an economic pact, where the audience pays the artist for his or her work. But the states of both are precarious in the novel, as the status of the artist was uncertain at the end of the 1930s. Carr-Saunders and Wilson explain the difference between authors or artists and other professionals as due to "the absence of any technique which can be made the basis of a formal course of instruction," although they argue that "the author, the composer, and the playwright are regarded as belonging to the class of intellectual workers and therefore as coming within the professional world" (271). The scarcity of objective standards in the creative arts, which sets it apart from the more standardisable professions, is a necessary condition, yet also makes it a potentially and frighteningly lonesome pursuit. Common standards, no matter how arbitrary and relative, are a means to guarantee understanding, and could be beneficial in times when the value of art was increasingly unstable in society, since "[a]rt is the first luxury to be discarded in times of stress; the artist is the first of the workers to suffer" (*CE* 2: 231).

Arguably the best way to achieve the communal response La Trobe desires in the modern context is by conforming to more commonly accepted codes of evaluation, for instance to the audience's expectations of a village pageant. Her refusal to abide by these means great difficulty in evoking the participation she desires, leading to the villagers' discomfort at the fixity of reference and the lack of any ultimate code with which to decipher the precise significance of the experimental pageant. The gap between La Trobe's individual artistic vision and her audience's understandings is therefore also the conflict between art as a personal "profession," a sincere pursuit to which one professes one's life to and which requires creativity and artistic individuality; and as a social profession, abiding by common standards and technique, and conforming to ready modes of evaluation with quantifiable results.

Apart from the innovativeness of her play, the minimal economic pact La Trobe has with her audience – who do not pay her but rather the fund for renovating the church to see her play – aggravates her difficulties in maintaining a relationship with them. Ironically, her economic disinterestedness works against it: In modern times, becoming a more economically interested artist, which indicates a more quantifiable social agreement between oneself and one's audience, might be the easiest way to connect with one's audience. Some incongruity results between the artistically serious impulse of the play (which is based on La Trobe's "professional" devotion to aesthetic meticulousness) and the economic production and execution of it (the villagers are amateurs, and the props are cheaply made). La Trobe's artistic endeavours and "professional" frustration seem out of all proportion to what the play means in socioeconomic terms: It is merely a village pageant. By being more "professional" – that is, by remaining economically disinterested from the results of her labour, and doing the work for the sake of the expression of her artistic vision – La Trobe baffles most of her audience, and in so doing paradoxically deprives herself from the more widespread commercial, professional and social recognition she could attain as a playwright. "Professing" oneself to one's art, Woolf seems to suggest, might mean to forego social professional rewards, and to relinquish possibilities for serious evaluation of one's art. After the pageant, in a typically ambiguous moment, La Trobe's triumph is both asserted and undercut:

> The bells had stopped; the audience had gone; also the actors. She could straighten her back. She could open her arms. She could say to the world, You have taken my gift! Glory possessed her – for one moment. But what had she given? A cloud that melted into the other clouds on the horizon. It was in the giving that the triumph was. And the triumph faded. Her gift meant nothing. If they had understood her meaning; if they had known their parts; if the pearls had been real and the funds illimitable – it would have been a better gift. Now it had gone to join the others. (124)

La Trobe has succeeded in bestowing her gift. But what the value of the gift is remains uncertain, and even she struggles to translate it into something more concrete, solid and enduring, both due to the nature of writing and directing as creative work, and because the aesthetics of the pageant purposely tempt yet defy traditions, codes, definition and conclusion.

As the political outlook in the late 1930s reached its nadir, art which did not abide by common tradition might not only seem to fail in holding the chaos and the disintegration of the times at bay, but was also in danger of being more readily dismissed. The question was whether to abide by accepted traditions for a ready but possibly facile communal response, at the price of one's own personal artistic standards which, if adhered to, in turn risked utter isolation. Storm Jameson, Woolf's contemporary and a fellow writer, expresses the hazards of the writer's relationship with his or her audience in such times:

> In an age when values are disintegrating, or when any number of special-ised values (the values of bankers, soldiers, politicians, etc.) are competing madly for place, the novelist is forced out of his proper growth. Either he will waste his energies in contriving his own system of values ... with the danger of cutting himself off from the majority who neither share nor like his values ... or accept disorder and disintegration, and swearing that all is for the best, write books to amuse and distract the populace.[63]

Though not a novelist, La Trobe's battle against "disorder and disintegra-tion" is indeed a fight for her "own system of values." But this "system" is far from stable: the execution of La Trobe's stage directions is disorderly, controlled not just by her, but also dependent on environmental contin-gency and her amateur actors and props. In addition, although merely "to amuse and distract the populace" implies "disorder and disintegration," it at least means some connection with one's audience, some form of order in one's acknowledgement by others. The dichotomy between order and disorder which Jameson presents is destabilised in *Between the Acts*: There is no reliable method via which La Trobe can keep the fragmentation which she is so frightened will undermine her art at bay.

   Therefore, La Trobe's attempts to forge her own standards and her own "professionalism" instead of entirely conforming to or following existing codes of practice and evaluation are perilous. Her decision to build on yet also subvert the pageant tradition requires additional courage and sac-rifice in the time she is working in, with the prospect of another world war looming: Despite the potential liberation in discarding accepted codes, an absence of these evokes terrifying emptiness and meaningless-ness. Woolf herself, in an environment which was pervaded by mounting anxiety about the potentially ruinous impact of politics and economy on individual lives, felt increasingly anxious about her ability to reach out and connect to her audience. In "The Artist and Politics,"[64] she writes of the artist that "intellectually also he depends upon society. Society is not only his paymaster but his patron. If the patron becomes too busy or too distracted to exercise his critical faculty, the artist will work in a vacuum and his art will suffer and perhaps perish from lack of understanding" (*CE* 2: 231). Writers, as Woolf knew, could not work in a complete vac-uum, but the war threatened to remove the standards which had formed her own working environment for so many years. In her diary in June 1940, she writes: "Those familiar circumvolutions – those standards – which have for so many years given back an echo and so thickened my identity are all wide and wild as the desert now. I mean, there is no 'autumn,' no winter. We pour to the edge of a precipice ... and then? I can't conceive that there will be a 27th June 1941" (*D* 5: 299). The fluidity of an empty world in which everything is possible is no longer liberating, but paralysing. A month later, she writes: "All the walls, the protecting and reflecting walls, wear so terribly thin in this war. There's no standard to write for: no public to echo back; even the 'tradition' has become transparent. Hence a certain energy and recklessness – part good part bad I daresay. But it's the only line to take. And perhaps the walls, if violently beaten against, will finally contain me" (*D* 5: 304). The final image is pregnant with paradoxical impulses: She is both wishing for "walls" to "finally contain" her and shelter her, so that she can feel more secure, and at the same time she is resisting this imprisonment, wanting the walls "violently beaten against" as if in a bid for total freedom. The conflict La Trobe faces – between the certainty which comes with the existence and abidance by communal standards, and the unconstraint and abandon which comes with the lack of these – was thus one which Woolf herself was forced to confront.

The result is a pageant which contains contradictory impulses: It celebrates instability and tries to liberate, but simultaneously fears instability and tries to fix. La Trobe understands that the villagers are both "too close; but not close enough" (41): they need the joint event of the village pageant, the result of La Trobe's vision, to bring them together, but need it also to separate them through its stimulation of multiplicity and different interpretations. Despite the pageant acting as a gathering force, its form, with its many intended and unintended breaks, disjointed progression, and disrupted speeches and dialogue, disassembles simultaneously as it assembles. As examples of these contrasting forces, the great effort La Trobe makes to control and direct her audience to compensate for working outside of existing codes leads to a dictatorial and didactic streak, ironically resulting in the dangers of fixity and immutability of meaning rather than the polyphony of Anon's premodern participatory art, when "Every body shared in the emotion of Anons song, and supplied the story" (382). Yet at the same time, La Trobe incorporates formal devices into her play which shatter a facile oneness and prevent her audience from turning into a homogeneous mob, such as the disintegration of familiar tunes and rhythms from the gramophone player, and the reflection of the audience in shards of mirrors at the end of the pageant, both of which will be discussed in Chapter 5. Just as the lack of fixed social professional identity and role allows her the freedom to create a multifarious art, so she celebrates being able to stir people's "unacted part" (92), attempting to offer the audience the possibility of transgressing their existing fixed identity.

Even the financial value of the play – the amount of money that has been donated to the village church – remains unable to be fixed. This comes to an ostensibly exact "sum of thirty-six pounds ten shillings and eightpence" (114), and seems the one aspect which is certain in Mr Streatfield's futile attempt at summing up the pageant. But the method of appraising money itself, the central marker of value in modern society, had been rendered unstable because of the cessation of the gold standard in 1931, which had effectively defined what money was in society. Abandoned, it meant that money, physically just scraps of paper, had no intrinsic value but what was nominally inscribed into it by economic forces. Without it, the real value of this numerically precise sum may fluctuate wildly beyond average rates of inflation, and with the onset of another war, could be expected to.

The gold standard policy in the interwar years received a huge amount of attention at the time, and references to the continuous fiddling with the value, and thus the meaning, of money filled the newspapers in the 1930s.[65] The theme is taken up in *Between the Acts*, when Bart reads about the pegging down of the franc in the newspaper (11, 128). One possible source for this is an article entitled "The Daladier Franc," which appeared in *The Times* in May 1938. It reported that Edouard Daladier, prime minister of France, had announced the devaluation and stabilisation of the franc to a level "on which it can be effectively defended," with the goal to peg it to the pound at a fixed exchange level, in response to attacks on the franc which had rendered the currency and the financial system in France unstable.[66] The ambiguity of the status of writing as a profession without fixed external standards – an uncertainty which La Trobe must face and which is both liberating and terrifying – is embedded into and amplified by such other uncertainties of the times. How, for instance, could one ask to evaluate art when one could not even reliably evaluate money?

Here, as in *To the Lighthouse*, greater financial stability is yet again granted to a man with artistic impulses – in this case William Dodge, whom Mrs Manresa introduces as "an artist," an identity denied by Dodge himself, who instead responds that he is "a clerk in an office" in, Isa thinks he says, "Education or Somerset House" (26). Isa observes that he is "of course a gentleman; witness socks and trousers; brainy – tie spotted, waistcoat undone; urban, professional, that is putty coloured, unwholesome; very nervous, exhibiting a twitch at this sudden introduction" (25). Woolf allows us glimpses of the artist in the homosexual William. He imagines Isa artistically: "She was handsome. He wanted to see her, not against the tea urn, but with her glass green eyes and thick body, the neck was broad as a pillar, against an arum lily or a vine" (64). Yet when William is caught by Bart staring at a picture of a lady, and Bart says that he is "an artist," William again "denied it, for the second time in half an hour, or so Isa noted" (32). Giles's contempt for William is expressed in language which, in his derision of William as homosexual, contains charges of effeminacy, amateurism and dilettantism all at once:

> A toady; a lickspittle; not a downright plain man of his senses; but a teaser and twitcher; a fingerer of sensations; picking and choosing; dillying and dallying; not a man to have straightforward love for a woman – his head was close to Isa's head – but simply a – At this word, which he could not speak in public, he pursed his lips. (38)

His anger at William is mixed up with, and allows him a channel for, his silent "rage with old fogies who sat and looked at views over coffee and cream when the whole of Europe – over there – was bristling like.... He had no command of metaphor" (34). William later wishes to confess to Lucy that he has been forced to enter into a profession, abiding by more ready social standards and means of making his living so that he can provide for his family and comply ostensibly to mainstream sexuality: "'At school they held me under a bucket of dirty water, Mrs. Swithin; when I looked up, the world was dirty, Mrs. Swithin; so I married; but my child's not my child, Mrs. Swithin. I'm a half-man, Mrs. Swithin; a flickering, mind-divided little snake in the grass, Mrs. Swithin; as Giles saw; but you've healed me....' So he wished to say; but said nothing" (46). The suggestion is that his profession is an act of asserting his masculinity in a society in which this is the accepted mode of living for a man of his class, an act of hiding and compensating for his artistic impulses and his homosexuality, which the narrative interrelates. William is thus trapped within his own unfulfilled desires while twisted into conformity, making him possibly even more wretched than the lonesome La Trobe. When Mrs Manresa claims that "He's an artist," Isa immediately imagines him as having a "knot which had tied itself so tightly, almost to the extent of squinting, certainly of twitching, in his face" (25–26). If the difficulty for women artists like La Trobe was in carving out an alternative space for themselves beyond existing artistic standards and codes, and beyond existing social models of professionalism, then the difficulty for men like William Dodge, who felt they could not even give impulse to alternatives such as artistic work or homosexual desires because of fixed professional models for men of their class, was no less dire. The question of if and how the professions could lead to a better life, "a state of being, in which there was real laughter, real happiness, and this fractured world was whole; whole, vast, and free" (*Y* 285), is one which Part II will continue to explore.

In this chapter, I have argued that Woolf's representation of the two women artists drew upon the category of "profession," yet also unsettled and transcended the prevalent social model by removing jeopardising commercialism. Dissatisfied with the options which contemporary professionalism offered women artists, Woolf tried to forge a new version, in which we have traced influences from two sources: more literal interpretations of a disinterested "professionalism," where one professes oneself dedicatedly to a meaningful and fulfilling intellectual and/or aesthetic pursuit; and some of the values of selflessness in "the private house" (*TG* 133) in which women were confined in earlier centuries. Through the defiance of predetermined socioeconomic narratives of professionalism, Woolf was able to conceive of more dynamic women artists who explore alternatives to these prevailing fixed models, and who carve out their own artistic space in society. And through these fictional women artists, Woolf reinvented a different type of artistic "professionalism," a disinterested vocational model which, put in the context of the early twentieth century, unfortunately came at the cost of isolation from the larger public community.

PART II

Literary Aesthetics, the Professions and the Specialisation of Society

Translating the Fact of the Professions into the Fiction of Vision: The Years and Three Guineas

But what other way of life, save this of striving to be important is open? ... Every profession fostered it. Specialists, men. The traitors are the successful, the specialists, the professional successes, who put a ring round the mind & impede its natural expansion.

– "HY" 7: 9

[I]f people are highly successful in their professions they are failures as human beings.

– "HTG" 60

While writing *The Pargiters*, the book that eventually split into *The Years* and *Three Guineas*, Woolf remarks in December 1932 that it "releases such a torrent of fact as I did not know I had in me. I must have been observing & collecting these 20 years" (*D* 4: 133). The Introduction explained the background, for instance, of some of her involvements with the Fabians in the 1910s, whose views may have influenced the two works. Like the Fabians, Woolf was to focus in *Three Guineas* on the professional in her vision of a better society. And both Woolf and the Fabians were informed by an aversion to excessive wealth and potentially destructive competition: They all identified commercial traits in the professions which made them too competitive and individualistic, and made professionals little more than slaves for money and status. In *Three Guineas*, Woolf cites from various biographical writings of successful professional men to demonstrate that they become mere "cripple[s] in a cave" (197). From *Sir Ernest Wild* (1935), Robert J. Blackham's biography of a barrister, she quotes: "He went to his chambers about half-past nine.... He took briefs home with him ... so that he was lucky if he got to bed about one or two o'clock in the morning." From *The Life of Charles Gore* (1935), G. L. Prestige's biography of a bishop, she quotes: "This is an awful mind-and-soul-destroying life. I really do not know how to live it. The arrears of important work accumulate and crush" (195). Bernard Shaw, in a Fabian Tract published in 1909, similarly writes:

> In the professions the beginners are forty; there is no security; health is impossible without the constitution of a thousand horses; work never ceases except during sleep and the holidays which follow the usual brea[k] down two or three times a year; shirking or taking things easily means ruin; the possibilities of failure are infinite; and the successful professional man is wretched, anxious, debt-crippled, and humbled beyond almost any other unfortunate who has mistaken his vocation.[1]

The civil service, in contrast – called "that part of Socialism which already exists" – is described as the ideal profession, well-structured and organised, and with the least opportunity of exploitation: "In the Civil Service there is status; there is pay from the time you begin work; there are short hours and at least the possibility of good health; there is security; there is a pension; and there is early marriage without imprudence or misalliance."[2] Importantly for Shaw, it also ensured that there would be no exploitation of an unknowing public, as civil servants were hired "at moderate salaries," in contrast to "exceptional payments made to men whose pre-eminence exists only in the imaginative ignorance of the public."[3] Shaw differentiates between state-organised and private practice professions to criticise the latter for not being centrally organised enough to ensure that it is not subject to excesses. Like Shaw, Woolf attempted to imagine a new professional system which would ensure that people could "join the professions and yet remain uncontaminated by them" (*TG* 208).

But unlike the Fabians' vision of "an elite of unassuming experts who could make no claim to superior social status,"[4] and for further organisation of the professions to guarantee "an appropriate Standard of Life" and "the most efficient service,"[5] Woolf thought the very concept of an elite would inevitably lead to superior social status, marked off by "dressing differently, or by adding titles before, or letters after ... names," which in turn would lead to "competition and jealousy" (*TG* 138). What was needed in the new system was less elitism, not more. The short story "A Society" (1921), written a few years after her initial acquaintance with the Fabians, already expresses many of the views she would later voice at greater length in *Three Guineas*. In it, a group of women form a society to question the workings of the world. One comes to the conclusion that "it's intellect ... that's at the bottom of it" (*CSF* 135). A boy, she says, "becomes a barrister, a civil servant, a general, an author, a professor. Every day he goes to an office. Every year he produces a book. He maintains a whole family by the products of his brain – poor devil!" His prizes are "stars of all shapes, ribbons of all shades, and incomes of all sizes," but at the sacrifice of making the women in his life "uncomfortable," to whom "he condescends" and "dares not tell the truth," and who "perish beneath the fruits of [his] unbridled activity" (*CSF* 135). Here, the humorous solution she proposes so that "the object of life," namely "good people and good books" (134), is attained and preserved is to "devise a method by which men may bear children," so that he is provided with "some innocent occupation" (135). The improbability of ever effecting such a change in biology does not so much mitigate the severity of Woolf's critique in this story, as it shows the immensity of the problems that the existing professional system posed, which Woolf knew only too well was inextricably intertwined with the fabric of modern British society. In *Three Guineas*, the solution is qualified by the necessity of providing realisable remedies: It becomes instead the exhortation to belong to the professions yet to remain as detached from their negotiation tactics and bureaucracy as possible. As mentioned in Chapter 1, women who wanted to enter the professions were to practise "poverty, chastity, derision": to make no more money than was strictly necessary, to refuse to sell their brains for money, and to ridicule fame and praise (*TG* 203–05). The exclusiveness that the Webbs saw as necessary to allow professional expertise to act as a medium for a better-run society were to Woolf not the solution to but the source of oppression. As Jessica Berman has argued, the nationalism and imperialism that the Fabians increasingly promoted and endorsed were to Woolf too close to the system of patriarchy that had historically meant the suppression of women.[6] Likewise, the thin line between protection and exclusion in the professions proved problematic to Woolf. The associations which the Webbs viewed as "indispensable as a defensive force"[7] to protect professionals against the forces of the marketplace were to Woolf too analogous to the type of bureaucratic exclusion that women had been subjected to throughout history. "The traitors are the successful, the specialists, the professional successes, who put a ring round the mind & impede its natural expansion" ("HY" 7: 9), Woolf writes of such successful professional monopoly, suggesting that such specialisation is unnatural, an artificial process that optimises the chances of material success, but sacrifices a unity that is integral to the well-being of the mind. This prevented her from endorsing existing practices in professional associations in her own suggestions as to how the professions should be changed, and drove her to make her criticism of the professions the core of *Three Guineas*.

Woolf's argument against the extant form of the professions was revolutionary at the time in that it was also an argument against war. The emergence of fascism and the threat of war in the 1930s gave an urgency to showing the masculine aggression latent in the professions, which had long occupied her, at its worst and most destructive. The professions, which operated under "the desire to hall-mark the competent"[8] and the quest for "a public recognition of status,"[9] in her opinion functioned on the same belligerent impulses on which war was instigated and operated: They "rouse competition and jealousy – emotions which ... have their share in encouraging a disposition towards war" (*TG* 138). Their common root lay "in the conglomeration of people into societies that releases what is most selfish and violent, least rational and humane," and which created "a monstrous male, loud of voice, hard of fist, childishly intent upon scoring the floor of the earth with chalk marks, within whose mystic boundaries human beings are penned, rigidly, separately, artificially" (*TG* 230–31). In expressing her disparagement in this manner, Woolf was more explicit than she had ever been about thoughts she had harboured, and which had influenced her writing, for years. She knew that her arguments were daring, and expected "considerable hostility" to her views (*D* 5: 84). But the crisis leading up to the war was a danger which she felt she had to address. She could afford to be critical: Her reputation as an established novelist and her financial independence accorded her a greater sense of freedom than ever before, so that she could say on 12 April 1938, less than two months before the publication date of *Three Guineas*, that she had "a quiet composed feeling; as if I had said my say: take it or leave it; I'm quit of that; free for fresh adventures – at the age of 56" (*D* 5: 133).

As we have seen, Woolf's opinion of the existing professional system was intricately linked to her feminism, which is why her view of the professions has often been subjugated in analyses of *Three Guineas*, mentioned in passing to complement a larger picture of her politics rather than as a topic that merits individual analysis to see its relationship with Woolf's overall way of thinking. This is perhaps not surprising considering that Woolf herself, as we have seen throughout this book, seemed to equate the professional system in her time with oppressive masculinity. Women who have managed to enter the professions, she points out in *Three Guineas*, are not earning the same salary as men; men have continuously attempted to exclude women from professional ranks. Entry to the professions may make women identical to the successful professional men in the biographies from which she quotes, and take away those feminine values that are worthy of emulation. But the professions, as this book has shown, were a much larger concern for Woolf, and by examining parts of *The Years*, I wish to show that they became views on which Woolf based her thoughts for a new type of society, a "new world" in which "we will be free" (*Y* 217).

In addition, problems arise when *Three Guineas* is taken as Woolf's last word on the issues raised in it, while the novel *The Years*, with its ellipses and omissions, is dismissed as incomplete in comparison.[10] For example, Grace Radin, whose meticulous and extensive work on the holograph has been indispensable to this chapter, sees the elimination of details throughout the rewriting of *The Years* as resulting in a loss of clarity and a loss of complexity in the characters, and Woolf's moderation of the original political content as causing a break in the link between *The Years* and *Three Guineas*.[11] But this assumes that *The Years* was merely the creative expression of the ideology in *Three Guineas*, and overlooks the possible intentions behind the very vagueness of the published version. Similarly, Gill Plain calls *The Years* "a novel of symptoms," writing that it "is a warning against the cancer of war, but it has no resources to fight that cancer." In contrast, she thinks that *Three Guineas* "prescribes a drastic cure instead of surveying the symptoms of decay with the detached and witty eye of the observer."[12] But the essay form, to a certain extent, commits the writer to providing answers, and omission itself can sometimes be a more expressive tool. If, as Hermione Lee writes, "the structure of the novel itself makes a gesture against totalitarianism,"[13] it would be useful to focus on one major type of totalitarianism the two works engage with – the professional system – and compare the two different forms of the novel and the essay. Bearing in mind that the boundary between these two genres was porous for Woolf in general, and for these two works in particular,[14] the elusive fictional form of *The Years* may have allowed expressive means that the ostensible essay form of *Three Guineas*, with its more dialogic structure, could accommodate less. This chapter will argue that the vision in *The Years*, continuously hinted at but never fully divulged in the published version, is possibly even more sweeping and radical than the solutions provided in *Three Guineas*.

The Years

The soul shrivels; the soul screws itself up into a horrid little ... he stopped, unable to find a word – [...] There are no words for what I mean! Nicholas exclaimed. None whatever!

– "HY" 5: 113

We'll break down the professions. [...] We'll make a new society – a civilized society – a society where you've got to mix all the professions – not excell [*sic*] in one.

– "HY" 7: 111

In a letter written in February 1933 to novelist and critic Winifred Holtby – who had in the previous year published one of the first books about

her – Woolf refers to their discussion on the professions in a previous
meeting, and her plans to rewrite "a paper on professions that she had
read a 'year or two ago' in which 'I want to keep rather more closely to
facts than usual.'"15 In fact, as early as 25 May 1932, Woolf had, as the
Introduction pointed out, called the work that was eventually to split into
The Years and *Three Guineas* (1938) "my book on professions" (*D* 4: 102).
Later on, in 1935, the essay, now separate from the novel, is again called "my
book on Professions" (*D* 4: 314) and "my Professions book" (*D* 4: 323).

The Years was originally conceived as part of "an Essay-Novel, called the
Pargiters" on the professions, which would "take in everything, sex, education, life, &c" (*D* 4: 129) and "give the whole of the present society –
nothing less: facts, as well as the vision. And to combine them both"
(*D* 4: 15). As the work progressed, however, Woolf found the separation of
the essay and novel parts into alternating chapters increasingly incompatible.
In February 1933, she decides on "leaving out the interchapters – compact-
ing them in the text" (*D* 4: 146). But even after this decision, Woolf struggled with how much she could be outspoken about and what she should
add, excise or leave unstated. From the time in September 1934 that Woolf
declared that "[t]he last words of the nameless book [*The Years*] were written
10 minutes ago" (*D* 4: 245), the book was to undergo a gruelling revision
process of over two years until its eventual publication in March 1937.16

Anna Snaith has argued that Woolf's decision to excise the essays shows
that she no longer needed the novel/essay genre divide: She was able to
incorporate fact into the novel part itself, and combine the two into one
form. Woolf's revisions, Snaith writes, show a "rejection of direct quotation" rather than a rejection of fact.17 Indeed, a removal of direct quotation may have liberated Woolf, and allowed her to explore professionalism
in a less prescriptive and restrictive way. I will examine some parts in the
holograph of *The Years* to see what was omitted, in order to compare it
with the published version and explore how omission may have served the
novel's needs better than explicitness. Here, the focus will be on certain
scenes in the last chapter which deal extensively with the question of what
role the professions should play in a person's life.

The Years traces the development of the Pargiter family across half a
century, from the 1880s to the 1930s. Through the passing of the years, the
book describes the family against a background of shifting social conditions. But if *The Years* can be read as a historical novel, it is also one which
deals with one of the most pervasive historical developments at the time –
that of professionalisation. When Nicholas, a family friend who lectures
for a living, says in the holograph that "[t]he nineteenth century was the

age of the specialist" ("HY" 5: 111), his words anticipate Woolf's present struggle with the ramifications of this process.

One of the central characters in the novel is Eleanor, the eldest daughter of Sir Digby Pargiter, who has three sisters and three brothers. In the 1880 chapter, the deprived conditions of the Pargiter girls – Eleanor, Delia, Rose and Milly, who receive no formal education – contrast with the public school education given to the boys, Morris, Edward and Martin. The situation in the 1880s in turn contrasts with increased educational and professional opportunities for women in the 1930s, exemplified in Eleanor's niece Peggy, the woman doctor I have continuously referred to throughout this book. Yet Woolf detailed such so-called liberations with unease. A newspaper cutting dated 1931 that Woolf pasted in her notebook to serve as background material for *The Pargiters* argues:

> [Women] behaved as if they could only express their freedom properly by imitating men; and so they rushed to offices, not always for need of wages, in the belief that to strap-hang in the Underground Railway every day on an adventure to type tedious letters ... was a more fulfilling occupation than the care of a home and the conception and nurturing and training of children. That delusion is rapidly being dispelled, and women are discovering that their enfranchisement will only be worth while if it enables them to increase in femininity.[18]

These views are echoed in the holograph. Talking to Peggy about the social conditions when she was young, a now elderly Eleanor paradoxically finds in the oppressiveness of women's social condition in previous decades much to be grateful for: "After all, I cant be too thankful in a way. isn't it Call it 'suppressed' – yes; but there's your father in the law courts, day after day; yes ... I don't know that I think they've solved the question" ("HY" 6: 96).

The narrative focus in the last chapter, which describes the 1930s, is on North and Peggy Pargiter, brother and sister. Both represent new forces at work in society. Peggy is a successful professional woman in the historically male-dominated field of medicine. In contrast, North, who in the holograph is called George, has just come back to England after years of being a farmer in Africa. He has been a practical producer of some of the most basic necessities of life. His contribution to society contrasts with Peggy's in its directness, yet it is also because of its very practicality and physical substantiality that farming is an occupation without the social prestige of the professions. Not having undergone professionalisation, it seems an occupation to make "enough money to live upon" (*TG* 205) without having the additional professional motives that come with the complexity of organisation and negotiation, such as the "money motive, power motive,

advertisement motive, publicity motive, vanity motive" (*TG* 221). But the
portrayal of farming as an alternative to the professions is complicated by
the context of North's farming. North keeps silent about the ramifications
of imperialism in Africa in which he has taken part, but Woolf would not
have been unaware of them. As Kathy J. Phillips points out,[19] Leonard
Woolf's *Empire and Commerce in Africa* (1920) shows some of the possible implications of North's work as a farmer in Africa, which include
taking some of the best farmland from native Africans and forcing them
against their will to work on farms of white settlers through punitive legislation and taxation.[20] Even Kitty's romanticising of farming outside of the
context of Africa in *The Pargiters* is portrayed as overly simplistic: "Why
should she not become a farmer? That was her dream. She would have to
marry, she supposed, in order to become a farmer – & her parents wd.
never let her marry a farmer" (105). Kitty sees farming as a way to escape
from her class and its responsibilities: "the life of a farmer was infinitely
preferable to the life of a don's wife at Oxford" (*P* 117). But her naïve and
class-insulated mindset is heedless of the realities of farming life. It is in
effect only able to play a limited role as an alternative to the professions
for the class of people that the Pargiters and their relatives represent, and
Eleanor perhaps hints at this when she tells North: "We shan't let you go
back … to that horrid farm" (*Y* 224).

North's return to England means that he must adapt to his new environment, in which being a professional is the ideal of the well-to-do middle-class male. At the party hosted by their aunt Delia, North's future is
discussed by his aunts Eleanor and Maggie. Money is the focal point in
their conversation, seen as determining what possibilities there are for
his life. Yet when Maggie is asked by Eleanor to work out the sums that
North will need to live in England, she ends up drawing something else
on the paper: "North glanced over [Maggie's] shoulder. Was she solving
the problem before her – was she considering his life, his needs? No. She
was drawing, apparently a caricature – he looked – of a big man opposite
in a white waistcoat. It was a farce. It made him feel slightly ridiculous"
(*Y* 280). In the same scene in the holograph, all three characters, especially
Maggie, are much more outspoken, both about the realities of money and
the limitations of discussing money alone. Maggie, quiet and merely suggestive in the published version, is assertive and incisive in the holograph.
But even here Maggie's mind is similarly preoccupied with other matters:

> Well George?" she [Maggie] said, <What> ~~Where do you want to live?~~ Rent.
> Rates. Food Clothing. ~~Travel. Books.~~ […] She was only using the surface
> of her mind, he saw. She was using another of these emergency outlets like

her politeness to the Gibbses; ~~in fact~~, she was thinking of something else. He changed his position so that she should not look at him, comparing him with a picture. ("HY" 7: 91)

What Maggie is thinking about becomes clear when she gives George/North explicit advice: "[']Dont go into a profession George' she added. [']~~Thats whats been the ruin of your our generation Eleanor~~' she added. All these elderly people sitting in offices. Thats whats been the downfall of the Pargiters" ("HY" 7: 92). Maggie, when she draws the caricature in the published version, is drawing the man she can see George/North becoming. What is discussed is the budget, but what occupies her mind is the image of North becoming yet another successful professional man. George/North's fear of being fixed by Maggie's gaze is the fear of being fixed to this rigid way of life, where the "picture" in the holograph that he is so afraid of being compared to corresponds to the caricature of the "big man opposite in a white waistcoat" (*Y* 280) in the published version. He is apprehensive of this possible future: a well-off, well-fed, well-attired man in a professional position that maps his life out for him and robs him of his agency. Later on, George/North will explicitly reflect on his own situation, and despair of his options: "how easy for a man to skip into the rut & follow it: the hammered road, the glittering prize; the obituary notice; the round; the gradual anaesthetic; the deadening, dulling; always striving for something not worth it; [...] he was bound to do the same" ("HY" 7: 147).

In *Three Guineas*, Woolf advises women who wished to enter the professions not to lose those virtues that historical tradition and circumstance had taught them, which could counter male aggression and thus help prevent war, and which include "not to be recognized; not to be egotistical; to do the work for the sake of doing the work" (201). This does not apply to George/North here, for the simple reason that he is not a woman. Maggie's advice is from one human being to another, and instead of telling him, as the narrator in *Three Guineas* tells women, to enter the professions with conditions attached, she implores him to stay out of them altogether in order to retain his individuality and freedom. Woolf's redemption of the professional system by imbuing it with feminine values in *Three Guineas* seems merely a compromise of the all-encompassing vision in *The Years* of freedom from it for those who could afford to escape it. Not just a feminist concern, the professional system was a source of oppression from which Woolf tried to find a way out rhetorically, but instead could only find in her way more questions, more challenges. In a typical moment in the characters' discussions and thoughts on how to live, George/North boils the topic down to the question of money: "[']But one has to make one's living my dear aunt' said George. What chance is there for being creative if one has to make ones living?" ("HY" 7: 94). And in a typical response, Maggie answers the question with further questions that themselves remain unanswered: "How much does one want to live on? What is worth living? Where does living cease? Where does it begin?" ("HY" 7: 95). The circuitous questioning shows Woolf's mind at work, searching for an ideal that would solve all social ills, yet unable to find it. Unsatisfied with the current system, unsatisfied with the system of bureaucracy proposed by the Fabians, and unsatisfied with the constant reality of money that interfered with her vision of freedom, Woolf felt committed to providing solutions to questions she could not really answer. The form of *The Years*, with its pattern of questions, equivocations, ellipses and truncations, was perhaps both the only way and the best way to express an unknown "new world" in which people are "free" and "live adventurously, wholly, not like cripples in a cave" (*Y* 217). The measures she proposed in *Three Guineas*, a book she called her "war pamphlet" (*L* 6: 159), were specific measures for a specific context. But where *Three Guineas* was restricted by the framework of existing society to produce constructive criticism to apply to that society, the fictional form of *The Years* afforded her the possibility of hinting at, if not expressing, what would otherwise, in an essay form, be too unrealistic to turn into practice.

Peggy is North's counterpart of a different sex and in a different occupational context. She represents the fruits of decades of feminist labour, a successful professional who has not only gained her financial independence, but who is also praised by her former teacher as "[m]y most brilliant pupil" (*Y* 265). However, as Chapter 1 pointed out, Peggy is painfully self-aware of the inadequacies in such a professional identity. In her suppressed desire to have children is her wish to have a private identity outside of the professional sphere. But the "groove" (*Y* 259) that she is in is inexorable and does not allow for side-tracks to alternative and unexplored areas in life. The equality that feminists have fought such bitter battles for has been achieved in Peggy, but even the pleasure that she derives from her teacher's praise is overshadowed by the immense alienation she feels in her role as a professional woman, a position which she has worked hard for but which seems ill-fitting and unsatisfactory. Peggy can be seen as Woolf's commentary on a society that allowed women either success in work or success in motherhood, but not both. It was a split felt personally by Woolf, who constantly compared herself to her sister Vanessa Bell, each having had one thing but not the other: "I put my life blood into writing," she writes in her diary, "& she had children" (*D* 5: 120).

In one of the most important moments in *The Years*, the writing of which excited Woolf so much that she described her own reactions as "my cheeks burn[ing]; my hands trembl[ing]" (*D* 4: 241),[21] Peggy tries to verbalise a vision "about a world in which people were whole, in which people were free" (*Y* 285). "[H]ere you all are – talking about North –" Peggy says, "How he's to live, where he's to live.... But what's the use, what's the point of saying that?" She then predicts that he will marry, have children and earn money by writing books, and says: "You'll write one little book, and then another little book ... instead of living ... living differently, differently" (*Y* 286). The description of Peggy's ensuing feelings about what she has just done seem to describe Woolf's own struggle to articulate the ideas she wanted to express:

> She stopped. There was the vision still, but she had not grasped it. She had broken off only a little fragment of what she meant to say, and she had made her brother angry. Yet there it hung before her, the thing she had seen, the thing she had not said. But as she fell back with a jerk against the wall, she felt relieved of some oppression; her heart thumped; the veins on her forehead stood out. She had not said it, but she had tried to say it. Now she could rest; now she could think herself away under the shadow of their ridicule, which had no power to hurt her, into the country. (*Y* 286)

Peggy has failed in the communication of her meaning. But like Woolf, who evaluates *The Years* as "a failure," but then immediately says that "its failure is deliberate" (*D* 5: 65), Peggy's failure is necessary because it refers to another world that does not yet exist and which ultimately no one can have complete knowledge of. The alternative that Woolf had in mind can be glimpsed in the holograph version, in which Peggy's speech extends for much longer than in the published version. Peggy bursts out:

> Why dont we get together, Eleanor – we young women, we working, professional women – & say, By God, we wont have it. We'll break down the professions. We wont take honours. We wont make money. We'll make a new society – a civilized society – a society where you've got to mix all the professions – not excell [*sic*] in one. Thats the only way you can learn anything about medicine – by learning about economics ... art. ("HY" 7: 111)

Peggy, while waiting for her listeners' reaction, thinks that

> they must form a new society: grounded upon anonymity, doing things for the sake of doing them; ... refusing titles, honours, refusing all competition, preserving the old tradition of her sex – love, charity; never praise famous women; never accepting praises, or honour; giving not taking. ("HY" 7: 112)

These were all themes that would return in *Three Guineas*. But *Three Guineas* could not cater to everyone: Members of the "Outsiders' Society" had to be "educated men's daughters working in their own class" (*TG* 232) because Woolf's rhetoric depended on such a class of women, who were in the financial and intellectual position to both exert influence and yet not be influenced by the corrupting and competitive environment of the existing professions. The source of this financial independence is not discussed in *Three Guineas*, but in the holograph of *The Years*, Woolf shows herself to be aware of the irony of the position of women who were financially and intellectually immune to professional corruption. Maggie attributes a female source to her and her sister Elvira's money by claiming that "our great grandmother gave her body to the French duke in the year 1812, & left us enough jewels to live on." But at the same time, this amount of money that would have granted them immunity from the professions and the market economy is being eroded by taxes to pay for the war: "But how we're going to live when the moneys all spent, paying for Johnnies pop guns" ("HY" 5: 101). By claiming that the origin of their inherited money is from their great grandmother's historical sacrifice, Woolf sought to avoid the negative implications of female financial independence outside the professions derived from a male source. But even she herself was sceptical of the realities of such independence. Later on, George/North removes all traces of female origins from Elvira's meagre allowance: "in all likelihood they were nothing more romantic than a few thousand inherited from her father" ("HY" 7: 8). Thus the "intellectual liberty" of "those daughters of educated men who have enough to live upon" (*TG* 218–19) may derive from their fathers and grandfathers, and could paradoxically be seen as a perpetuation of "the patriarchal system" (*TG* 199) from which Woolf wanted women to escape.

That she realised this weakness but chose not to address it could be attributed to the comparative inflexibility of the argument in *Three Guineas*. This can be contrasted with the potential function, in the published version of *The Years*, of the "little fragment" that Peggy has broken off from the whole of her vision, which can by its very incompleteness act as the master key to opening up various personal visions of "living differently" in different readers of different backgrounds, although, as we will see in the last section of this chapter, *The Years* could not escape all ideological frameworks. John Maynard Keynes, for instance, thought *The Years* "very moving[;] more tender than any of [Woolf's] books; did not puzzle him like The Waves; symbolism not a worry; very beautiful; & no more said than was needed" (*D* 5: 78). He did not extend this admiration to *Three Guineas*.

After it was published, Woolf writes in her diary: "Maynard sends for us on Wednesday; is said by Lydia to be very critical of 3 Gs" (*D* 5: 163). After the visit, she writes: "Maynard never said a word. Some were unsaid" (*D* 5: 163). *The Years*, in merely touching on the problems of the professions, was able to inspire Keynes sufficiently for him to think of it as "beautiful." In contrast, *Three Guineas* antagonised him into passive hostility.

In the eighth volume of the holograph for *The Years*, which she started writing on 27 September 1934, Woolf filled ten additional pages that she grouped under the heading "Revisions." Eight of these ten pages add to the "Present Day" chapter. Here George/North continues Peggy's previous outburst about what should be done to change society. Eleanor asks Peggy to make a speech, thinking that "[a]fter all, Peggy, a doctor, in the thirties, stood for a new generation" ("HY" 8: 14). Peggy refuses, saying that she has made a speech already. George/North then takes over from Peggy, recapitulating Peggy's outburst in his own words: "Yes, she said we were all wrong to have professions. She said we <'re> ~~were~~ humbugs. She said we made too much money. She ~~said~~ We're specialists: we're one sided: we're played out; we're men machines for making money" ("HY" 8: 14). George/North then admits: "And I think there's a lot of truth in what you said" (15). George/North cannot see any hope in the men around him, young or old: "all these young men" he looked ~~vaguely~~ comprehensively at the groups of politicians, theyre not going to live differently. Life's too easy as it is. And the older men; (he thought of Edward: he turned away from him) Theyre settled in; they've got their jobs" (15). He then appeals directly to women to change society: "my idea is, you women – well why d'you copy men? Why dont you create a new society? Its up to you … […] Its much easier for you –" (15–16). Then, "shift[ing] rather further from Edward," George delivers his verdict: "'Whats done for them' he indicated the people behind him, 'was property'" (16). George/North constantly distances himself from his uncle Edward, the professional academic, because he is afraid that proposing the establishment of a new order which supersedes figures like him will antagonise him. George/North's conclusion of the professional system here is similar to that in *Three Guineas*, where the endless pursuit of property and status in the professions creates cripples in caves and causes "intellectual harlotry" (*TG* 224). The advice that Woolf returns to in the holograph is for women to refuse the existing system and create a new society in which one has to "mix all the professions" and so "do away with specialists" ("HY" 7: 143). The closest that Woolf comes to saying the same in *Three Guineas* is when she suggests that the rebuilt women's college to which the narrator in *Three Guineas* is to contribute money should aim "not to segregate and specialize, but to combine. It should explore the ways in which mind and body can be made to co-operate; discover what new combinations make good wholes in human life" (155). But other solutions in *Three Guineas* seem almost a compromise. The narrator in *Three Guineas* uses the power of her guinea to tell the female treasurer of "a society to help the daughters of educated men to obtain employment in the professions" (163) that the society is to have her guinea only if the educated women will not make the endless pursuit of money and prestige that characterises the professions their goal as well. Having no power to revolutionise society, all women could do was to enter the existing system and resist the temptation of assimilation, with the hope that they might provide an example for others. The professions had entrenched themselves so deeply into society and into people's mentality that their existence seemed insuperable, and not even *Three Guineas* is able to satisfactorily answer George/North's question: "But how cd. they do away with specialists?" ("HY" 7: 143).

Woolf's attempt to imagine an ideal way of living was additionally complicated by her ambivalence towards the professions in her own life. Maggie's advice to George/North not to enter the professions was not advice that Woolf herself gave to her nephew Julian Bell in May 1937 when the opportunity arose: "Julian was bitter at dinner against the B[loomsbur]y habit of education. He had been taught no job; only a vague literary smattering. But I wanted you to go to the Bar, I said. Yes, but you didn't insist upon it to my mother, he remarked, rather forcibly. He now finds himself at 29 without any special training" (*D* 5: 86). The new form of education that she envisioned that would not "segregate and specialize, but to combine" proved impractical for Julian's needs, making him ill-equipped for the realities of life. The Bar, with its pursuit of status, prestige and money which corrupt and make a person a "cripple in a cave," was nevertheless a profession that Julian should enter. In addition, Woolf was aware of one of the most important reasons for professionalism: the objective guarantee of a certain level of competence. When the gravity of Rachel's fever in *The Voyage Out* is downplayed by her first doctor Rodriguez, and she dies due to delayed treatment, it is not medical incompetence that kills her, but Rodriguez's lack of solid medical credentials, "whose right to the title of doctor was not above suspicion" (300). Ultimately, the realities of life proved too much for her revolutionary vision. "I'm afraid of the didactic" (*D* 5: 145), Woolf writes in her diary in January 1933, a week before deciding to remove the novel-essay division. Woolf may in the end have been fearful of not just the didactic, but of the wrong didactic in a form of writing that she wanted to convey an unimpaired truth.

How far removed Woolf's priorities in the 1930s were from those of the Fabians can be seen in Beatrice Webb's response to *The Years* in 1937: "What a picture of decadence in the absence of any sense of obligation on the part of the family in the way of public work or personal conduct.... No stress is laid on the essential obligation of every individual to promote the welfare of the whole community."[22] What she read as a "picture of decadence" was Woolf's commentary on a world too caught up in forms of professional pursuits, and her attempt to inspire others to obtain freedom from the oppressive structural hierarchy of the professional system. The "obligation of every individual"[23] was not to contribute to the existing system, to "follow and repeat and score still deeper the old worn ruts" (*TG* 231) of society, but to create an alternative way of life. In the holograph, George/North asks Maggie to do more than just criticise: "Maggie laughs. Elvira laughs. But why cant you do something? [...] Why dont you create?" The answer that Maggie gives is hardly satisfying: "['] We are creating' said Maggie: [']Well, by living on one thousand a year instead of two. Well by saying What do I want to live on. This['] – she took the budget in her hand – [']is very creative. Anyhow you're not going to become a successful professional man, George. ~~I'm making out a budget on sensible lines~~. That's creating[']" ("HY" 7: 93). Eleanor continues: "[']Yes. And she made Renny give up his job [...]. Thats creating,'" to which Maggie adds: "Yes, if every woman said to the man she's going to marry, I'll divorce you if you make more than ~~2,000 a year~~ a thousand a year, if every woman said, I wont have you playing with pop guns" ("HY" 7: 93). The interference which Maggie and Eleanor propose here is what Woolf calls a woman's "indirect influence" in *Three Guineas*, which she criticises as "very low in power, very slow in action, and very painful in use" in comparison with the new "influence that is disinterested" because of the independence gained from "the right that was conferred upon us less than twenty years ago, in the year 1919, by an Act which unbarred the professions" (129–32). Women could hardly threaten men with divorce if they would not be able to provide for themselves. Caught in a rhetorical deadlock in the holograph, unlike in *Three Guineas* Woolf steadfastly refuses to promote women's entry into the professions. The absence of this advice in *The Years* makes her disapproval of the professional system resonate even more. "Keeping ~~his~~ appointments," George thinks of another man at the party, "but for *what good?* for no reason: treading out the old round; lured across the world by carrots" ("HY" 7: 147; Woolf's emphasis). Woolf had by that time grown highly suspicious of propaganda, of "innumerable labels" that "kill and restrict" (*TG* 266). By questioning the validity of certain types of professional service, *The Years* questions the very concepts of "obligation," "public work," and "welfare"[24] taken for granted by society and by the Fabians.

In a diary entry in March 1930, Woolf herself demonstrates a similar attitude in her own profession, which, as we have seen, she tried to sustain throughout her career, although not always successfully: "Yesterday I was offered £2,000 to write a life of Boswell by Doran Heinemann. L. [Leonard Woolf] is writing my polite refusal this moment. I have bought my freedom. A queer thought that I have actually paid for the power to go to Rodmell & only think of The Waves by refusing this offer. If I accepted I would buy houses, tables & go to Italy; not worth it" (*D* 3: 295). Buying her freedom was enough. Further rewards were "not worth it" because it was for things beyond "that modicum of health, leisure, knowledge and so on that is needed for the full development of body and mind" (*TG* 205).

At the heart of this is the idea of unnecessary excess, whether in terms of property, working hours or status, for instance "the glitter & the prizes & the things men set their hearts upon: houses & servants; & the fetters they lay on themselves; & the minute particles that they accumulate so zealously in heap after heap; & guard them with pop guns" ("HY" 7: 147). This is why she put so much importance on "not to be recognized; not to be egotistical; to do the work for the sake of doing the work" (*TG* 201), to "profess" oneself to a vocation for its own sake; and on the fact that the "Society of Outsiders" who would explore alternatives must be "anonymous and secret" (*TG* 235): Things should be done not for ostentatiously public rewards, but for private ones which can also carry over and contribute to public work. It is also why Woolf repeatedly advocated having basic necessities and comforts: These were for personal and private use, uncorrupted by the grotesque standards in the environment of the public sphere, with its huge buildings "of majestic masonry," with its "extremely ornate" clothes that are so removed from their "prime function" that they look "strange in the extreme" from the perspective of women "who see it from the threshold of the private house" and who contrast it with the "comparative simplicity" of men's dress at home (*TG* 133–37).

If productivity and the opposite of decadence are characterised by "leav[ing] the house at nine and com[ing] back to it at six," and by "do[ing] this daily from the age of twenty-one or so to the age of about sixty-five," then that, Woolf points out, "leaves very little time for fathers to know their children" and "very little time for friendship, travel or art"

(*TG* 194). These words were a warning against romanticising the professions and against the assumption that they were the only real way of contributing to society, one echoed by Ray Strachey in her essay "Changes in Employment," published by the Hogarth Press in *Our Freedom and Its Results* (1936):

> [T]he young women … who were obtaining the more solid education which the women's movement had won for them, grew very eager about it [the freedom to work]. Work, indeed, came to seem almost an end in itself to some of them and they attached a value to earning their own livings which that somewhat dreary necessity does not in reality possess.… They thought of work as a satisfaction of personal needs, an outlet for gifts and powers, a fulfillment of personal individuality.[25]

Both *The Years* and *Three Guineas* express Woolf's concern that newly educated women, eager to enter the professions, would not be able to draw the line where professional pursuits necessary to earn an independent income started to become "not worth it," becoming "highly successful in their professions" but "failures as human beings" ("HTG" 60).

Woolf writes, in the first essay of *The Pargiters*: "I prefer, where truth is important, to write fiction" (9). This suggests that she found only in the greater freedom of fiction a way to arrive closer at a truth that reality would not yet allow, and to liberate her vision of a freer society from immediate political and social restraints. It can be argued, as critics have, that in the indefiniteness of the published version of *The Years* Woolf's ideas remain unexpressed, lost in the blanks of the formal devices by which the novel hints but leaves unspoken, and to dismiss the novel at this. But Woolf herself had huge ambitions for the book: She had planned to include "millions of ideas but no preaching" (*D* 4: 152) in it, and as can be seen from the holograph, the sweeping vision of a society without specialisation underlies the published novel. Paradoxically, elusiveness may have seemed the only method that would not compromise the largeness of her vision, the only way of escaping the restrictions which threatened to drag it down to mundanity. Woolf was to call *The Years* "too ambitious" (*L* 6: 11) after its publication, which we can begin to understand better by seeing what is inscribed in the pregnant emptiness of the published version.

The Professional Classes and the Working Classes

"Isn't it much nicer," said Eleanor, taking her plate, "not having servants … "
"We have a woman to do the washing-up," said Maggie.
"And we are extremely dirty," said Renny.

– *Y* 207

In 1931, the Hogarth Press published *Life as We Have Known It*, a collection of autobiographical writings by working-class women of the Women's Co-operative Guild. Woolf wrote the introduction to the book, which took the form of a letter to Margaret Llewelyn Davies, who had been secretary to the guild from 1889 to 1921. As Mary M. Childers notes, instead of writing a preface addressing the broad readership of this collection of working-class women's memoirs, Woolf significantly chose to engage in correspondence with someone from her own class.[26] Her refusal to speak to and for the working-class woman informs the whole introduction, in which she writes of the division between the middle and the working classes that "the barrier is impassable" ("IL" xix). Her self-asserted indifference to the working-class woman's demands when she writes that these "leave me, in my own blood and bones, untouched" and that "[i]f every reform they demand was granted this very instant it would not touch one hair of my comfortable capitalistic head"[27] contrasts sharply with her close concern in *Three Guineas* with professional oppression that was very similar in nature. Woolf's examples of what the working-class woman was demanding – "divorce, education, the vote ... [,] higher wages and shorter hours"[28] – echo the middle-class woman's desire in *Three Guineas* for a proper education not corroded by "Arthur's Education Fund" (118), for "the right to vote" (130) which could contribute to an independent influence, and for a fruitful life in the professions different from that of successful professional men. Here, she attempts to minimise the importance of the working-class woman's concerns to her, even as she would later argue for the middle-class woman's concerns with respect to the professions in *Three Guineas*.

We can attribute such a discomfort with speaking on behalf of the working classes to Woolf's acute awareness of her lack of first-person experience. Nevertheless, when she does attempt to describe the working classes, although her portrayal of the working-class woman is not static, nor wholly derogatory, it is at times strikingly unsympathetic: She describes them as "indigenous and rooted to one spot," "common, grey, worn, obscure, docked of all splendours of association and romance."[29] Even when Woolf imagines a possible future intermingling between the two classes her tone is ambiguous: Such a mixing paradoxically both "exacerbated us" and ensured that "life will be richer and books more complex and society will pool its possessions instead of segregating them."[30] The metaphor Woolf uses to describe the assimilation of the working class into the middle class is one of violence and violation, not of peaceful integration: it is "this force of theirs, this smouldering heat ... with a hot and fearless flame, [which] is about to break through and melt us together."[31] The intensity of the image hints at an excess that Woolf felt she could not control, compelling her to create the rigid rhetorical opposition between "we" and "they" in the letter. Her later focus on the professions instead of other forms of oppression seems also to be partially motivated by this necessity for containment.

Absence is frequently as significant as presence in Woolf's writing, as I have shown in comparing Woolf to Davies in Chapter 1. In *Three Guineas*, Woolf's vision of freedom from patriarchy for those daughters of educated men who are not fortunate enough to have a private income is grounded in the possibility that exists for them to achieve basic material comfort by practising in the professions, but Woolf does not clarify what role the working classes should play in such a vision. Her extensive engagement with the problems of the professions in *The Years* and *Three Guineas* contrasts with the paucity of discussion of other types of oppression in society beyond the middle class. Such a position requires analysis because it is clear – however critics choose to interpret Woolf's attitude towards the working classes – that this absence and her perspective were deliberate decisions. Snaith mentions two letters which Woolf received from Agnes Smith, a reader of *Three Guineas*, who initially wrote to express her concern that Woolf only engaged with women from her own class in the work, but later accepted that Woolf had decided to limit her subject matter to issues which she was familiar with from personal experience. Snaith concludes that "Woolf's limitation of her subject matter is deliberate and carefully considered and is necessarily exclusive."[32]

Here, I wish to examine further reasons behind Woolf's position, and its implications for the message that she was trying to convey. In particular, I want to explore additional explanations for why Woolf chose to engage largely with professional oppression despite the fact that it could hardly be considered more oppressive than hardship in the working class or being unemployed. Such investigations would enable the diversity of the social background that forms the context of Woolf's writing to be taken into account. They would not detract from Woolf's importance as a writer but on the contrary make her, as Childers puts it, "a more vital figure."[33]

I am not suggesting that Woolf completely ignored other forms of oppression. She did not tackle the massive problems of the working classes and the unemployed in *Three Guineas*, and perhaps understandably so; but this did not prevent her from observing and portraying them, albeit in a restricted form, in *The Years*, where awareness of other forms of oppression beyond the professional system is present to a limited extent.[34] At Delia's party, Peggy hears the "far-away sounds" of "other worlds, indifferent to this world, of people toiling, grinding, in the heart of darkness, in the depths of night" (284). The excess of what is happening outside and the veiled threat of it passing into the comfort of the rooms recalls the fearful image of the "hot and fearless flame" in the introductory letter. Like the rhetorical opposition set up in the letter, the division between the middle and lower classes is preserved by the spatial separation set up by the rooms in which Delia's family party is being held, and what lies outside. The realisation that there is larger-scale suffering remains shielded by these strict barriers: There are hints of other types of affliction, but they are transmitted through sound and shrouded in "darkness," never seen and thus only partially represented, suggesting how little the disorder outside is visible and graspable by the people inside. In contrast, Peggy sees only too clearly what is wrong with the people inside the boundaries of Delia's rooms: "Had anyone in that room reached the perfect balance of having & living? Was there anyone whose capacities had been perfectly developed? neither overfed nor underfed? Not one of them. They were all crippled, deformed" ("HY" 7: 114). But although people inside may be "crippled, deformed," the harms inside can at least be articulated, unlike the chaos, disorder and darkness of suffering outside.

Woolf's ambivalence towards the working classes shows itself most clearly in the issue of servants, and in *The Years* and especially its holograph, the question revolves more specifically around whether or not to have them. As we have seen, having servants was viewed by Woolf as a status marker rewarded by professional pursuits: "houses & servants" are amongst "the things men set their hearts upon" when they "slip into the rut" ("HY" 7: 147). Thus when Maggie pinpoints the material excesses to be curbed, one of the things she singles out are servants: society would be better "[i]f every woman [...] had one servant & only 2 children" ("HY" 7: 93). This solution is similar to the solutions of joining the professions and earning only one thousand a year instead of two, or of abiding by the terms in *Three Guineas* which will allow women to "join the professions and yet remain uncontaminated by them" (208), in that it is a solution of limiting material wealth beyond the necessary. But it also seems merely the mitigation of the severity of, rather than a challenge to, the root of the problem. The crossing out – not only of the phrase but also of working-class concerns in her discussion of professional tyranny and hypocrisy – suggests that Woolf realised what an inclusion of working-class concerns in *The Years* and *Three Guineas* would entail: She would no longer be an outsider, as she could proclaim to be in relation to male professional privilege, but would be a perpetuator of a type of oppression that was very similar in nature to the tyranny she was criticising. Not entirely able to depart from viewing domestic servants as a professional marker of status, nor able to relinquish her own dependence on servants,[35] and even less able explicitly to propound having just one servant for basic material comfort, Woolf instead chose to encase her rhetoric firmly within the middle class.

There were other developments at the time which Woolf may have perceived as threatening to her position and that of other daughters of educated men. The auxiliary role of domestic service, first as a support to the domestic middle-class woman, then increasingly as a replacement in the domestic sphere of the professional woman,[36] could no longer be taken for granted: With the conditions of domestic service little improved,[37] there were fewer women who wanted to enter or return to domestic service after the war.[38] Indeed, the problem of the status of domestic work was sufficiently large in society for there to be calls for its professionalisation: In the 1920s and 1930s, the shortage of domestic workers was thought to be both attributable to and solvable by it. In December 1921, a meeting of the Girl's Friendly Society comes to the conclusion that "making domestic work a profession with training, qualifications, and status is in the interests of the community."[39] A domestic servant, Thirza Smith, sums up the problem: "girls did not look on the service as a profession or business, but simply as a means to live, and parents regarded it as an easy way to get a girl out to work without the trouble of having her trained."[40] And at the Domestic Service Inquiry at the Ministry of Labour in June 1923, the chairwoman of the Women's Subcommittee of a Local Employment Committee branch, Lady Matthews, "attributed the unpopularity of domestic service to the fact that it had never been recognized as a skilled profession."[41] If domestic service providers wished to gain respect from a more highly esteemed domestic service occupation, the middle-class service user desired the professional status of domestic servants for a very different reason. As Lady Matthews says, "We do not want to force girls into domestic service, but it should not be forgotten that the middle-class householder is going through a most trying time."[42] Professional status was thus paradoxically a way to elevate the esteem of domestic work, and a way to attract women into the occupation to retain the superior privileges of the middle class. Such efforts to improve the reputation of domestic service continued in the 1930s: *The Times* records in 1937 a competition organised to find "a better name than 'domestic servant'" to suit an occupation "which should be an honourable and self-respecting relationship between employer and employed."[43] The attempt at professionalisation was clearly not successful, even though, after years of effort, a National Union of Domestic Workers was finally established in 1938.[44] The jump to the status of a profession would have required not only the removal of the prejudice against domestic service as a lower-class occupation, but also the stigma of female amateurism in an occupation that had been historically dominated by women, and in which the nature of the work was considered fitting to the domestic role of women in society.

The issue surrounding servants that appeared in the 1920s and 1930s indicated new social forces at work. As Deirdre Beddoe points out, one writer in the *Woman's Leader* complains in 1920 that the servant class "has suddenly dwindled to astonishingly small numbers and has begun to demand unheard-of conditions."[45] These were part of the forces that Woolf had described as "a hot and fearless flame ... about to break through and melt us together" ("IL" xvi) in 1931 and that she in fact contributed constructively to through her own writing on the professions and her involvement with societies for working-class women such as the Woman's Co-operative Guild. But at the same time, in her own relatively privileged position, she could not help feeling apprehensive about these changes which threatened to undermine the hierarchy in which she was favourably situated.

"If every reform they demand was granted this very instant it would not matter to me a single jot," Woolf writes radically in an earlier version of the introductory letter.[46] Focusing on professional issues relevant only to the "daughters of educated men," she seems to have put these words into practice in *Three Guineas*; but at the same time, for all her harsh words, Woolf did seem to care about the damage such a system inflicted on working-class people. The holograph of *The Years* offers a glimpse of an attempt at drawing these bigger issues into the work, where she represents the oppression of the lower classes spatially closer than before. Elvira/Sara lives in relative poverty in a poor neighbourhood on a small private income. Although she has been to a job interview at a newspaper office, in the end she decides not to "[j]oin the patriarchy, sell my soul" ("HY" 6: 120) by writing articles for money. Refusing to "prostitute" (*TG* 224) her work, refusing to participate in the activities of the newspaper office that she visits in the holograph, she sacrifices the basic material comforts needed for the full flourishing of the soul because she refuses to sell out to professional journalism. Although Elvira/Sara's precarious socioeconomic condition may locate her as an outsider to the professional system, she still enjoys the services of one servant girl, Lydia, who cooks and cleans for the tenants of the building in which she lives. Despite this, Elvira/Sara seems closer than anyone else in the book to the issues which the working classes face, and gives haunting descriptions of the tyranny that servants endure: "And the human face. Lydias smacked by Mrs [illegible] that morning for eating the fat of the ham. Tears; gulping sobs, as she cleared away & her blouse torn; Heaven help us all, I said; the unemployed singing under the window, marching like geese in a row: then the bagpipes; hymns from the sodden & servile city" ("HY" 6: 117). The boundary between Elvira/Sara and the oppression outside is porous: The unemployed are "under the window," and the violence inflicted upon servants is in her very building.

In the 1920s, despite its aspirations to professional status, domestic service was still mainly considered as a low-skilled female occupation in the service of the middle-class professional man and his domestic wife.[47] Domestic servants are described by Lady Matthews as "women" who serve "men [who] leave before 8 o'clock in the morning for London," and who help "ladies ... trying to keep a fairly large house never meant for two pairs of hands."[48] But in the 1930s, servants slowly came to be valued by the small number of professional women for their mediating effect between the woman's professional world and the private world. "A woman could not serve her home and the office," said Sir Oswald Simpkin at a sitting of the Royal Commission on the Civil Service in December 1930, citing this as the reason against abolishing the marriage bar in the civil service.[49] In such a social context, Vera Brittain's autobiography, *Testament of Youth* (1933), which Virginia Woolf was reading in September 1933 "with extreme greed" (*D* 4: 177), asks: "Could marriage and motherhood be combined with real success in an art or profession? If it couldn't, which was to suffer – the profession or the human race?"[50] Brittain concludes that "[t]he reorganisation of society in such a fashion that its *best women* could be both mothers and professional workers seemed to be one of the most acute problems which my generation – and to a lesser but still important extent all subsequent generations – had now to face."[51] The beneficiaries of such a reorganisation would again be society's "best women," like the "daughters of educated men" in *Three Guineas*.

Brittain rightly saw that "[f]or a married woman without children there is only a psychological problem – a problem of prejudice – which can be overcome by determination," but that the practicalities of "the other problem – that of the woman with children – remains the most vital"[52] because it involved real time constraints. She was to depict the solution to this problem in a later novel. *Honourable Estate: A Novel of Transition* (1936) describes the fates of two generations as it moves from the 1890s to late 1929. Ruth Alleyndene, the female protagonist in the second generation, is able to balance a highly successful career as a politician with marriage and motherhood, succeeding to the position of one of the few female members of parliament[53] with the help of her domestic servants. For instance, after going on a speaking tour in America for a month, she comes back home to find that "incredible as it seemed, no catastrophe had occurred in her absence.... Miriam and Betty had carried on her household with exemplary competence; the twins, absorbed in the emotionless preoccupations of very young children, had not even missed her."[54] Brittain's eagerness in espousing married women's independence results in an overly rosy picture: She does not explore how children feel or how they are affected by absent parents. And towards the end of 1929, one of the last thoughts of Ellison Campbell, a famous dramatist in the novel who gave up finishing her education at Oxford and the chance of marriage to take care of her paralysed brother, reflect the changes that society had undergone since the 1890s: "Quite a number of young women seemed to imagine that it was possible to marry and have children and bring them up decently, and yet occupy a leading position in some art or profession. The idea of dedicating yourself, body and soul, to a chosen vocation, and counting everything well lost that was sacrificed for its sake, seemed to have gone altogether."[55] Woolf's writing, as we have seen, also engages with the dilemma of having a profession without sacrificing other aspects of one's existence, without being caught in a "groove" (*Y* 259). Woolf's view, however, was less optimistic. Here, Ellison's death seems symbolic of an old social order in which motherhood meant to a woman the abandonment of her professional career, and which female professionals such as Brittain hoped would become increasingly obsolete and be replaced by a new order in which women could both be full-time professionals and oversee the needs of the home. As Denis, Ruth's husband, reflects after the birth of their twins, "Whatever else we have to give up, we must have someone really competent to look after the twins so that she can go back to the office as soon as the nursing stage is over."[56]

Brittain was not the only woman writer to be concerned with this issue. Storm Jameson describes in an article entitled "Combining a Career with a Home" in 1926:

> [W]hen a woman with a professional or business career marries she is quite definitely expected to take on the additional job of making a home for her husband and perhaps their children.... Distractedly ... modern woman tries to do it. She runs her career, and makes hopeful gestures towards running her home too. It is usually a long time before she discovers that you cannot run a home on gestures.... Useless to protest against the injustice

of it, useless to say that people who have two centres to their lives are never really successful. She has got to be, or else be a failure in one or other of her jobs. Alternatively, she must arrange to be born all over again, as a man.[57]

Woolf's focus in *The Years* and *Three Guineas* is on professional specialisation. But, as Woolf knew from personal experience, there was specialisation in the domestic sphere as well. For the new professional woman to both have a successful career and be a successful mother, this specialisation – with some women relegated to domestic duties in order to free up time for other women who could spend it on intellectual or professional pursuits – became even more crucial. As Alison Light writes, few feminist and socialist activists were entirely egalitarian, and many thought of domestic chores as work to be done by others.[58] Light names Brittain as an example, noting that Brittain "depended utterly on two devoted servants."[59] Woolf herself, as we have seen, linked her success as a writer to not having children, in contrast to her sister; she also extended such a view to past woman writers, "the four great women novelists – Jane Austen, Emily Brontë, Charlotte Brontë, and George Eliot" of whom "not one had a child, and two were unmarried" (*CE* 2: 143). And when Nellie, Woolf's domestic servant in London, was hospitalised in May 1930, although Woolf still had the help of Mrs Mansfield, a charwoman, for basic cleaning, she complained in a letter to Quentin Bell in June 1930 that "I can't write when I must be planning dinner. How any woman with a family ever put pen to paper I cannot fathom. Always the bell rings and the baker calls" (*L* 4: 176).[60] As Light shows, domestic servants were essential to Woolf's professional career, and Woolf knew how important they would be for those of other daughters of educated men as well.

Woolf's unease with the dependence of her class – and potentially of a new professional class of women – on the working classes results in "the contradictory and complex feelings which beset the middle-class visitor when forced to sit out a Congress of working women in silence" ("IL" xxviii–xxix). In her own life, Woolf was uncomfortable with her own dependency on servants, which is perhaps why having servants was also seen by her as a type of oppression for the middle-class woman.[61] In the holograph, the sense of liberation expressed by Eleanor at managing without servants, which in the published version takes the form of the merely suggestive question "Isn't it much nicer ... not having servants ..." (*Y* 207), does not end in ellipses: "'Why did we ever have servants?' said Eleanor. When its so much nicer <doing without> ~~dining in the kitchen?~~' She told them about Crosby; about coming home at night to her own flat" ("HY" 5: 74). But although Eleanor may feel liberated at no longer having a live-in servant, she, as well as Maggie and Renny, are still being served: Eleanor herself still has, as Peggy reveals, "a woman in to wash up" ("HY" 6: 98), just as Woolf herself depended on servants throughout her life for basic household chores.

Peggy in *The Years*, a book strikingly similar to *Honourable Estate* in the social issues it touches upon, is not as lucky as Ruth Alleyndene, and feels forced to sacrifice marriage and children for a successful professional career. In portraying Peggy as one of the transition cases who is not able to bridge the divide between the professional sphere and the domestic sphere, Woolf paints a bleak picture of the professional woman. But although Woolf may not share Brittain's upbeat portrayal of this new type of woman in the 1930s, this also allows *The Years* a greater consideration of the complexity of the issue. Like Peggy, Woolf struggled to be inclusive: "She felt, or rather she saw, not a place, but a state of being, in which there was real laughter, real happiness, and this fractured world was whole; whole, vast, and free. But how could she say it?" (*Y* 285). The difficulty, or even impossibility, of including everyone in such a sweeping vision, combined with an underlying recognition that such freedom for some people must come at the expense of others, led Woolf to focus on professional tyranny. Although more democratic than *Three Guineas*, *The Years*, despite its freer creative form, likewise contained its compromises to this "whole, vast, and free" (*Y* 285) world.

CHAPTER 5

A Balancing Act: Between the Acts *and the Aesthetics of Specialisation*

As we have seen, in the holograph of *The Years*, Woolf writes: "But what other way of life, save this of striving to be important is open? [...] Every profession fostered it. Specialists, men. The traitors are the successful, the specialists, the professional successes, who put a ring round the mind & impede its natural expansion" ("HY" 7: 9) Two interrelated ideas can be observed from this. The first, which has been discussed in Chapters 3 and 4, is of the need for a reconfiguration of the notion of "profession," so that the sociopolitical meaning of "profession" can be reconciled with a more personal meaning of the word, of "professing" oneself to subjectively, as well as economically, worthwhile work. The second is the focus of this chapter: that excessive specialisation, which has led to the professions in modern society, is a force which runs counter to the "natural expansion" ("HY" 7: 9) of the mind, to the idea of an integral and integrating self that Woolf drew on when portraying Lily and La Trobe's artistic methods. One of the less desirable alternatives is an atavistic, liquid world without specialisation, which North briefly fantasises about before he modifies his vision:

> Why not down barriers and simplify? But a world, he thought, that was all one jelly, one mass, would be a rice pudding world.... To keep the emblems and tokens of North Pargiter ... but at the same time spread out ... myself and the world together. (*Y* 300)

The question is then how to balance specialisation in society and within the existing professions, so that the self can expand yet retain a meaningful, differential identity.

The answer we have observed is the radical yet constructive vision to ameliorate existing society by creating "a new society – a civilized society – a society where you've got to mix all the professions" ("HY" 7: 111). But latent in this vision are also a despair at the overspecialised state of modern society and an anarchic impulse for the destruction of the basis of modernity by completely "do[ing] away with specialists" ("HY" 7: 143).

Woolf's last novel, *Between the Acts* (1941), is both a thematic and aesthetic culmination of the conflict between these drives: to construction, for which the force of balanced specialisation, which is the foundation of human society, is necessary; and to destruction, either through the continuation of overspecialisation, or by discarding specialisation and the whole edifice of human civilisation and returning to the fluidity of the primordial.

These forces manifest themselves in the formal structure of *Between the Acts*. On the one hand, the novel is famously composed of scattered scraps of speech, thoughts, music and past literary works, "often shorn of context or contextual urgency,"[1] making up an unprecedented broken form in her fiction. Isa, for instance, is able to quote from one of Percy Bysshe Shelley's poems at one moment and switch to the more mundane topic of food the next: "'The moor is dark beneath the moon, rapid clouds have drunk the last pale beams of even ... I have ordered the fish,' she said aloud, turning, 'though whether it'll be fresh or not I can't promise'" (*BA* 14). Words are frequently inaudible during the village pageant which Miss La Trobe directs, breaking up actors' speeches and performances. The gramophone player fails to work properly, coming on and off throughout the play.

Yet at the same time, unity is often presented alongside, or even created out of, fragmentation in the novel. The literary allusions throughout, although they crop up seemingly randomly, assume a shared literary history and tradition. Pieces of language and sound are constantly recycled and repeated in different contexts. Snatches of tunes and nursery rhymes create a sense of affinity, resulting in "[m]uscles loosened; ice cracked" (*BA* 49). The gramophone sounds "chuff chuff chuff" throughout, "a noise a machine makes when something has gone wrong" (47–48), yet this apparent sign of chaos creates in its insistent repetition and regularity an order of its own, becoming, contrary to its original use, a marker of time: "Chuff, chuff, chuff went the machine in the bushes, accurately, insistently"; "Chuff, chuff, chuff went the machine. Time was passing" (90–91). The phrase "[d]ispersed are we" (117), played continuously in the intervals and at the end of the pageant, thematically signifies fragmentation, but formally creates the backbone of the pageant. The book seems to suggest the two are different sides of the same coin: after dispersal there can be assembly again, and after assembly, dispersal – which the structure of the pageant, with its many intervals, enacts.

This is what Patricia Laurence has called "[t]he structure of oppositions and the rhythm of alternation" in the book. It often divided critical scholarship. Laurence pointed out that critics had frequently focused either on the fragmentation or the unity of the novel, and failed to see that both are present and important.[2] Indeed, Woolf's vision of the novel was "a rambling capricious but somehow unified whole – the present state of my mind" (*D* 5: 135). Since then, many studies have attempted to provide accounts which consider both these forces in the novel. Michele Pridmore-Brown, for instance, has cogently argued that interruptions by static or noise in the gramophone's sounds counter totalitarianism by "short-circuiting the instantaneous connection among rhythm, emotion, and collective action."[3] Jane De Gay has written that the novel's "fragmentation of the literary past" undermines "conventional understandings of tradition," which can be used to fight fascism.[4] Such views pose formal fragmentation as a tool used by Woolf to break apart methods of cohesiveness in the novel, be they those of an unthinking collectivism or of literary tradition. Yet Joshua Esty has also pointed out that such communalism in the novel can clearly be seen in both positive and negative light. He writes that, for instance, while national tradition may encourage totalitarianism and mob mentality, it also offers "a meaningful shared history against the social fragmentation of the metropolis."[5] Esty concludes that Woolf intended the novel to convey "both antinationalist and nationalist sentiments, to reflect both authoritarian and antiauthoritarian possibilities in group ritual."[6] The challenge is thus to find a perspective that does not judge these varying forces as either damaging or beneficial: fragmentation and cohesiveness can be both dangerous and reassuring, both destructive and valuable. One example of an angle which is able to achieve this is that taken by Pridmore-Brown in the latter part of her article, where she incorporates the concept of wave-particle duality in physics in her reading of the novel to describe a state in which meaningful connectedness and individuality can coexist.[7] Another is Christine Froula showing how the sounds, voices and music at the pageant, instead of settling for either unity or discord, "strain apart, crash, solve, unite," addressing and creating an inclusive and multivocal "we" who are "the people, the demos, the community."[8]

This chapter shows how Woolf's concern with the directions professional society was taking civilisation in the late 1930s results in the structure of her final novel, which engages with the essence of professionalisation: the force of specialisation. It argues that the notion of specialisation – a means to describe the progression of humankind throughout history and a concept which can harbour both cohesiveness and disparity – contributes to the aesthetics of concurrent cohesion and fragmentation in *Between the Acts*. Through this, the novel reflects on the state of human society at a time when the world seemed on the brink of destruction. This, however, leads to no clearly argued and detailed political solutions to the dilemmas of human society of the type her husband Leonard Woolf provided, and which she herself attempted to offer, with some compromise, in *Three Guineas*. Like in *The Years*, the attempt at resolution is located in the very aesthetics of *Between the Acts*.

As Karl Marx argued in the nineteenth century that the division of labour had alienated workers from their work and its final product, so Aldous Huxley writes in *Beyond the Mexique Bay* (1934), which Woolf read in May 1934 (*L* 4: 306), that specialisation had created incomplete people in modern society who were incapable of being fully alive:

> Man's biological success was due to the fact that he never specialized. Unfitted by his physique to do any one thing to perfection, he was forced to develop the means of doing everything reasonably well. *Civilization reverses the evolutionary process. Generalized by nature, we impose upon ourselves, artificially, the narrowest specializations.* Primitives are men who have never succumbed to the suicidal ambition to resemble ants. Generalization – this is the great, the vitally important lesson they have to teach the specialists of the civilized world. The problem is to evolve a society that will retain all or most of the material and intellectual advantages resulting from specialization, while allowing its members to lead to the full the life of generalized human beings.[9]

Woolf subsequently invited Huxley to visit her, which he did in June (*D* 4: 222–23). At another dinner together in November 1935, she describes him as "g[etting] off on biology" (*D* 4: 351). Specialisation, described as a process which "reverses the evolutionary process," seems unnatural, and human civilisation has perhaps overspecialised, requiring reminders, such as those recurring in *Between the Acts*, of common origins in prehistory.

This is the framework which the chapter takes up: of specialisation as the historical bridge for the two extremes of unspecialised prehistory on the one hand and overspecialised professional society on the other. The first part of the chapter focuses on prehistory, which, as Beer has argued, allows Woolf both to build on and surpass her previous claims in *Three Guineas* on the link "between militarism and masculine education," in order "to emphasise the alternative insights offered by Darwin into kinship between past and present forms, the long pathways of descent, the lateral ties between humankind and other animals, the constancy of the primeval."[10] I argue that in expressing "the simultaneity of the prehistoric in our present moment,"[11] Woolf found solace not only in the continuity of the prehistoric into the here and now, but also enacted the retreat from overspecialisation necessary to reach a balance in modern life.

The second part of the chapter focuses on the ramifications of specialisation on the present, including both the fragmenting and the cohesive effects of money, the close accomplice of specialisation. Although this may seem a huge jump to make chronologically, Woolf herself continuously makes such alternations, spreading prehistory throughout the present in the novel, as Beer has highlighted.[12] Throughout human history, specialisation has served as a cohesive force, helping to build and sustain communities, cultures and civilisations. The nursery rhyme "Tinker, tailor, soldier, sailor, apothecary, ploughboy," which recurs thrice – when Mrs Manresa counts the stones from her cherry tart, when Bart follows suit and when he murmurs the rhyme in his sleep towards the end of the book – playfully suggests that the very foundation of society is made up of people dispersing into specific roles within particular occupations.[13] Yet now it also seems to be threatening to break people apart, to pull asunder. Money is a key tool which has facilitated specialisation throughout human history and which highlights people's interdependence. But in the novel, money also becomes a focus of both the potentially destructive force of specialisation and of the unthinking mentality of the "mob" (*PH* 91), its accumulation an ultimate and common goal to strive for. To achieve the right amount of specialisation and money is therefore crucial to thwarting the psychology of the herd and to mending the excessive fragmentation of modernity, both of which were leading the world to war.

Unspecialised Prehistory

In a passage in the earlier typescript of *Between the Acts*,[14] written in September 1938, Woolf describes the villagers streaming onto the lawn to see the pageant:

> Many were old; others in the prime of life. Some were lame. Yet there was a certain air.... [I]t was as though they were specialized. It was not a mob, a heterogeneous assembly, each clutching a shilling or a half crown, which would give them a right to enter. They were sure of places, even if they came late.
> Mr. J. F. Figgis, who had written the Guide Book in 1830, would have supplied the reason for that nameless common element; that dignity; that specialization. "The family of Dyce Odgers," he wrote, "whose present representative is Reginald Dyce Odgers of Dicker Hall, has been settled in the neighbourhood since the days of Henry the Eighth." ...
> It was true that these facts referred to the parents, grandparents, and in some cases to the great grandparents of those who were actually crossing the lawn.... But roughly speaking, had Mr. Figgis suddenly come to

> life and called the roll call of those names and flocks, half the ladies and
> gentlemen present would have said "Adsum".... And the consciousness
> that they would thus have answered ... gave their movements even now
> in 1938 ... a different motion or air from that ... in a London crowd ...
> <herded> in Oxford Street under the ruby light, <a dignity, a specialty.>
> (*PH* 91–92)

The nostalgic undertones in this passage would become part of what Alex
Zwerdling describes as "an acute longing for an earlier, more civilized
phase of English culture" in the face of "the barbaric present," one which
is "rural rather than industrial, feudal rather than democratic, simple
rather than complex, and above all, unified."[15] Here, the villagers' "specialized" state, derived from tradition and genealogy, creates both a degree of
certainty of identity and an interconnectedness Woolf thinks is lacking in
a modern-day "London crowd." This is not because there is no specialisation in the modern city, but rather because there is too much. Woolf tell-
ingly imagines such a city "mob" as "heterogeneous": people have become
so isolated from each other that they have lost their places in a meaningful
whole, and subsequently lost the fixed and various identities the villagers
seem to have.

Yet in the corresponding passage in the published version of the novel,
the villagers are not as harmoniously integrated as the draft would suggest. The explicit reference to the villagers' meaningful "specialization" is
removed, the past is made less unambiguously redemptive, and the possibility of fragmentation which modernity might bring more immediately
pressing:

> Roughly speaking, however, had Figgis been there in person and called a
> roll call, half the ladies and gentlemen present would have said: "*Adsum*;
> I'm here, in place of my grandfather or great-grandfather," as the case might
> be. At this very moment, half-past three on a June day in 1939 they greeted
> each other, and as they took their seats, finding if possible a seat next one
> another, they said: "That hideous new house at Pyes Corner! What an eye-
> sore! And those bungalows! – have you seen 'em?"
>
>   Again, had Figgis called the names of the villagers, they too would have
> answered.... True, there were absentees when Mr. Streatfield called his roll
> call in the church. The motor bike, the motor bus, and the movies – when
> Mr. Streatfield called his roll call, he laid the blame on them. (*BA* 47)

The reference to Figgis is not followed by the differentiation between the villagers and the "London crowd" as it is in the draft, but instead by markers of
change and modernity: new houses, new forms of transport which shorten
the protective distance between the countryside and the city, and new types
of entertainment. Although the places the villagers inhabit because of their

"specialization" may still give them "dignity," the countryside setting of the novel, and the characteristics it retains of older English community, now also seem threatened by the rupturing aspects of modernity.[16]

The implications of specialising differentiation in modern-day society have changed: where specialisation has been vital to the building of communities, of "civilization," throughout human history, it has possibly been taken to an excessive extent, with people in the present dispersed into shards with which it will be hard to build a lasting whole. The root of the word "special" from which specialisation is derived comes from the Latin word *species*, referring to form or appearance.[17] The theme of acting, of appearances, of superficial form, of pretence, of disingenuous professing, by people living in ill-fitting, incomplete or deceitful roles in society is present in all of Woolf's last three books. In *The Years*, the Pargiters' name suggests "to parget"; as Jane Marcus writes, it represents "perhaps a combination of whitewash and filth, a true 'whited sepulchre.'"[18] The name indicates that the Pargiters' superficial respectability is a façade, consisting of acts put on to cover their nature and inner desires. In *Three Guineas*, this takes the form of ostentatious and whitewashing pretence and acting in professional "pageantry" (239). In *Between the Acts*, there is the "pageant" itself, in which the actors take up different roles, and through which the audience of villagers are reminded at the end of the play, when the mirrors reflect them before they have "had time to assume," that they too are actors, who exist "only … in parts" (109). At this point, the anonymous voice addressing them asks: "*how's this wall, the great wall, which we call, perhaps miscall, civilization, to be built by … orts, scraps and fragments like ourselves?*" (111).

But the novel continuously reminds us that if we go back far enough, we find that we share common origins, that people used to be made up of one whole. Latin's *species*, from which "specialization" is derived, became the English word "species," one of its meanings a category of organisms sharing common distinguishing traits.[19] Charles Darwin's *On the Origin of Species* (1859) is perhaps the best known book which makes use of this sense of the word. It proposed that the differentiation of species was the result of the evolution of specialised functions in response to the demands of different environments. The significance of Darwin's work on the novel has been analysed by Beer, who, as I mentioned, has related its emphasis on the continuity of prehistory into the present, and the prehistoric roots which bind life together, to Darwin's thinking.[20] Here, another significance of Woolf's use of prehistory will be explored: prehistory as the time before specialisation.

If human history has been one of increasing specialisation, perhaps only in prehistoric and primeval mess can complete unity be glimpsed. In *Between the Acts*, the prehistoric is more present than in any of Woolf's other novels. The novel's frequent references to prehistory create an undercurrent of peculiar nostalgia for it as the source of mankind's common origins, when specialisation, as part of civilisation, had not yet occurred. As Lucy thinks, this was "when the entire continent, not then, she understood, divided by a channel, was all one; populated, she understood, by elephant-bodied, seal-necked, heaving, surging, slowly writhing, and, she supposed, barking monsters; the iguanodon, the mammoth, and the mastodon; from whom presumably, she thought, jerking the window open, we descend" (*BA* 8). Throughout the novel, the prehistoric can be glimpsed underneath the surface of the here and now: the bellowing of the cows is "the primeval voice sounding loud in the ear of the present moment" (85); "the great lady in the bath chair" (58), with her undefined age, is "the indigenous, the prehistoric" (121), so that "even her body, crippled by arthritis, resembled an uncouth, nocturnal animal, now nearly extinct" (58). Even the antics of the village "idiot" remind others of their origins, prompting Mrs Parker to ask Giles: "Surely, Mr. Oliver, we're more civilized?" (68).

Although specialisation has created welcome order out of the primeval soup, it has perhaps gone too far, and needs to be reset by reminders of bygone unity: "*Dispersed are we; who have come together. But,* the gramophone asserted, *let us retain whatever made that harmony*" (116). The use of rhyme in the novel is an effort to provide the most basic connections again.[21] As Beer argues, the novel's "semantic cacophony of rhyme" finds similarity via identical sounds in a shared language instead of "reasoned relationships."[22] Rhyme, for example, binds separate conversations into one mass: "So abrupt. And corrupt. Such an outrage; such an insult; And not plain. Very up to date, all the same. What is her game?" (*BA* 109). It seems a last attempt to find relations in a world split apart by overspecialisation, invoking memories of a common tradition. The loose connection of words with similar sounds, seen in such phrases as "[s]hall I ... go or stay? Slip out some other way?" (59), "Hadn't she, for twenty-five minutes, made them see? A vision imparted was relief from agony" (60), and "[s]he looks such a dear. Someone I know said his hair ... " (64), also gives them a playfulness which is more commonly seen in language used in childhood, for example in nursery rhymes, which, as Beer writes, hint at the "primitive" in their association with our childhood past, when boundaries between individuals, objects and concepts are blurred, their roles not yet demarcated by clear semantic limits.[23] The rhymes used here undo adult order by invoking the looser associations of childhood, as part of the return to the primitive in the whole novel.[24] This is both attractive and threatening, a balancing act between the awareness, suffering and commitment that come with knowledge, meaning and identity, and the escapism and potential nihilism of meaninglessness.

But although prehistory may be attractive for its vision of complete wholeness, in *Between the Acts*, Woolf does not claim it as a state to which to aspire. As Huxley writes, although people should learn to be more generalist, the goal should not be to regress to the state of "[p]rimitives," but "to evolve a society that will retain all or most of the material and intellectual advantages resulting from specialization, while allowing its members to lead to the full the life of generalized human beings."[25] The idea of the undifferentiated chaos of primeval mess rested uneasily with the prospect of the mess another world war was about to create. Moving towards this was for Woolf, as for many others, a horrifying thought, and the time when this novel was set, "on a June day in 1939" (*BA* 47), when Britain was on the brink of the Second World War, linked it uneasily to the vivid memories of the First World War. Trudi Tate has pointed out the association made in the First World War between primeval mess and tanks in the devastated landscape in various media, from newspapers to literary works. She writes that "the most advanced weapon of 1916 takes civilization into a new phase of modern technology at the same time as plunging it back into prehistory – an image both terrifying and pleasurable," and that *Between the Acts* includes this notion of simultaneous progress and regression.[26] The military tank, a product of specialised technology and a potent reminder of it, does not appear in *Between the Acts*. Instead, we have machines of which Woolf had firsthand observational experience: "Twelve aeroplanes in perfect formation like a flight of wild duck came overhead" (114). They appear while Mr Streatfield gives his speech at the end of the play, and become part of the play in the audience's mind: "The aeroplanes, I didn't like to say it, made one think ..."; "[t]hen when Mr. Streatfield said: One spirit animates the whole – the aeroplanes interrupted. That's the worst of playing out of doors.... Unless of course she meant that very thing ..." (118–19). If, as Huxley writes, "[c]ivilisation reverses the evolutionary process," then the danger at the time was that civilisation could ultimately, seemingly paradoxically, turn people back towards prehistory, towards the prehistoric mess of war.

Beer has pointed out the multiple significances of the aeroplane in
Woolf's work, for instance as a symbol of new possibilities, as the dis-
turber of geographical boundaries and as a war machine.[27] In *Between the
Acts*, its ambiguity derives from its symbolic status as the product of tech-
nological advances made possible by specialisation, its potential to bomb
the land back into prehistoric chaos and reverse all progress, and the possibility it provides to escape the present mess altogether. After the play, one
of the strands of conversation among the villagers is that "[i]f the worst
should come – let's hope it won't – they'd hire an aeroplane, so they said"
(*BA* 117). And when Isa thinks of "the infinitely quick vibrations of the
aeroplane propeller that she had seen once at dawn at Croydon," she
imagines it going "[f]aster, faster, faster, it whizzed, whirred, buzzed, till
all the flails became one flail and up soared the plane away and away" (12).
The place it goes to is "[w]here we know not, where we go not, neither
know nor care" (12). Like the tank in the First World War, the imagery
of the potency of the rotating propeller here is both exhilarating and terrifying. It suggests that the immense possibilities of the plane come hand
in hand with enormous danger. Bomber planes could destroy landscapes
and level homes in a matter of seconds, as Giles thinks while looking at
the view: "At any moment guns would rake that land into furrows; planes
splinter Bolney Minster into smithereens and blast the Folly" (34). Perhaps
only the primal imagery of prehistory was sufficient to evoke the dramatic
scenes of destruction in war.

Although imagining the primeval mud might be satisfying in certain ways, its absolute chaos threatens to replace the existing order with
nothingness. Complete unity would mean no differentiation whatsoever
would exist, rendering the world meaningless. Specialisation creates communal identity by creating ways to distinguish oneself from the rest. In
arguing this, I observe what Sam See has called the promise which Woolf
saw in "the transformative possibilities inherent in the atavistic human" in
the novel,[28] without considering this reversion to prehistory as ultimately
desirable, as something which must be taken to its extreme in order to
bring about its regenerative possibilities. In her diary in February 1940,
Woolf records the conversation at a dinner party with T.S. Eliot, Saxon
Sydney-Turner and Clive Bell:

> But our talk? – it was about Civilization. All the gents. against me. Said
> very likely, more likely than not, this war means that the barbarian will
> gradually freeze out culture. Nor have we improved. Tom & Saxon said the
> Greeks were more thoroughly civilized. The slave was not so much a slave

as ours are. Clive also pessimised – saw the light going out gradually. So I flung some rather crazy theories into the air. (*D* 5: 268)

I believe that Woolf retained a belief in what she calls "civilization" in the novel, a concept which defies firm definition but which remains vital to the hope for a capacity for renewal and a different future.

Woolf's more ambiguous application of the motif of prehistory differs slightly from Leonard's in his political writing. In *Quack, Quack!* (1937), Leonard describes the "instincts and emotions of barbarism" which allow "the politician who desires to [do so to] control large masses of men"[29] as "prehistoric savagery and quackery."[30] These, Leonard argued throughout the 1930s, must be countered by an international organisation like the League of Nations, which "regulat[es] the relations of states on a basis of compromise and co-operation."[31] I will refer again to the League in the next section of this chapter when relating specialisation in *Between the Acts* to the economics of war. The international community formed by the League would thwart not just the primal emotions which drive groups of humans, but also the ego of the single, charismatic politician who tried to take advantage of it. It would use, as Leonard puts it in *The War for Peace* (1940), "the power of the community" to "resist by communal force the use of force by an individual member of society," "the savage with a stone in his hand," so preventing "the anarchy of the man-ape."[32] In his book, "community" is the key concept which Leonard keeps returning to, one which encapsulates the meaningful balance between the extremes of formlessness and excessive egotism, both associated by him with the prehistoric. Though this is very similar to the vision underlying *Between the Acts*, in the novel, the prehistoric also becomes a powerful device for countering the overspecialisation of the present. Isa says in the earlier typescript: "to build a wall, we must ~~rebuild~~ <recollect> ourselves. Out of fragments" (*PH* 181). Here, besides the meaning of gathering ourselves from fragments, "recollect" perhaps also means to remember. Through recollecting, or remembering, our common origins in prehistory, we can recollect what has become overly fragmented, and build a lasting whole again.

The book ends with Lucy finishing "the end of the chapter": "'Prehistoric man,' she read, 'half-human, half-ape, roused himself from his semi-crouching position and raised great stones'" (129). This is the point at which mankind starts to build up civilisation using specialisation, when people must take up their different roles. Yet in the present, this has been taken so far that people are torn by "motives" which are "mixed" because they are always "after money" (*PH* 401). That is why the anonymous voice in the pageant, after asking how civilisation is to be built, ends by espousing things done for their own sake:

> there's something to be said: for our kindness to the cat; note too in today's paper "Dearly loved by his wife"; and the impulse which leads us – mark you, when no one's looking – to the window at midnight to smell the bean. Or the resolute refusal of some pimpled dirty little scrub in sandals to sell his soul. There is such a thing – you can't deny it. What? You can't descry it? All you can see of yourselves is scraps, orts and fragments? (BA 111–12; italics in the original)

These deeds mark a return to sincerity, which Woolf had been advocating for the professions and acts of professing. Specialisation, which had the potential both to encourage cooperation and interdependence, and to cause disharmony and conflict, seemed poised to do the latter, with disastrous results. By starting and ending with references to prehistory, the novel has come full cycle: as the day draws to an end and will soon be renewed, the question is perhaps also whether civilisation will be renewed from the metaphorical prehistory into which war was about to plunge Europe.

The next section moves away from Woolf's use of prehistory, to contextualise more solidly the novel's exploration of present-day (over)specialisation. As I explained, although this seems a huge chronological leap to make, prehistory is deliberately interspersed by Woolf into the present moment for the purpose of retreating from overspecialisation. As we will see, the question of specialisation was particularly significant in the 1930s, when political and economic instability forced wider society to re-evaluate its benefits and drawbacks.

Specialisation, Professionalisation and Money

> [M]oney, like dynamite and other tools used by men, can very greatly damage, as well as very greatly service, his society.
>
> – Norman Angell[33]

In the later typescript, written in the autumn of 1940,[34] Bart thinks, upon hearing that "[t]he profits [of the pageant] are to go towards the fund for installing electric light in the Church":

> All motives are mixed. Especially in England. Had it been so – say, in the middle ages? The monks – were they disinterested? He doubted it. Ourselves. The rise of the professional class. And so on. Aloud he said – he would have said, but was it worth it? – "The English, wherever you find them, <are> always <after money; always> say one thing, mean another. Villagers, gentry, clergy, all the same." (PH 401)

Woolf's phrase "[t]he rise of the professional class" shows her acutely aware of this social force in British society. Professionalisation – the specialisation of brainwork – is one particular and later manifestation of the general process of specialisation – the division of roles – throughout human history. Here, "[t]he rise of the professional class" is associated with mixed motives, which are caused by people being "always <after money>." This common true motive, however, splits people apart: It needs to be covered up with hypocrisy, so that people "say one thing, mean another." In the published version, Mrs Manresa responds to Bart's cynicism:

> "What's the object," said Bartholomew, suddenly rousing himself, "of this entertainment?"
> "The profits," Isa read out from her blurred carbon copy, "are to go to a fund for installing electric light in the Church."
> "All our village festivals," Mr. Oliver snorted turning to Mrs. Manresa, "end with a demand for money."
> "Of course, of course," she murmured, deprecating his severity, and the coins in her bead bag jingled.
> "Nothing's done for nothing in England," the old man continued. Mrs. Manresa protested. It might be true, perhaps, of the Victorians; but surely not of ourselves? Did she really believe that we were disinterested? Mr. Oliver demanded.
> "Oh you don't know my husband!" the wild child exclaimed, striking an attitude. (105)

Although in this village community, people can still assert "a right to enter" and be "sure of places, even if they came late" without having to pay "a shilling or a half crown," (*PH* 91), the pageant necessarily "end[s] with a demand for money."(*BA* 105). Not even this rural community, then, seemingly at some remove from fragmenting modernity, can claim the kind of disinterest Woolf hoped for – for the professions, and more generally for the whole of human society. The irony in Mrs Manresa's claim is that, as Maren Tova Linett has shown, Ralph Manresa, the absent Jewish businessman, is problematically associated with such negative aspects of modernity as money interests which threaten to transform the community. Linett points out that at the end of the pageant in the earlier typescript, Woolf writes: "'Liars and thieves.' (Ralph Manresa. Manresa was here exposed to view.)." Ralph is thus used to convey that English culture is unavoidably implicated, comprising "liars and thieves."[35]

Historically, specialisation was greatly helped by money, which enabled people to buy necessary products and services outside their own area of work. In *The Story of Money* (1930), Norman Angell, with whom

Woolf was acquainted,[36] and who was involved with Leonard Woolf on much political work on war and peace, writes that "division of labour immediately sets up the need for a medium of exchange.... If a man can in Robinson Crusoe fashion be entirely self-sufficient, producing all he needs, there is no reason for exchange."[37] Like specialisation, money, as a symbolic form of common value which people can use to meet their diverse needs, can both be used to build a diverse yet integrated whole (or what Woolf calls "civilization" in the novel), and can fragment excessively. The drive for money can destroy, as Woolf had detailed in *Three Guineas* by describing financially successful professionals as "cripple[s] in a cave" (197), and as the international conflict caused by the pursuit of financial interests by different countries in the 1930s had shown. A reason for German aggression in the late 1920s and throughout the 1930s was precisely "the economic question," as John Maynard Keynes had predicted in *The Economic Consequences of the Peace* (1919). Keynes had argued that the unrealistically harsh terms in the Treaty of Versailles, which demanded reparations which post–World War I Germany could not pay, would create international conflict.[38] It became increasingly clear that his predictions were accurate. For example, from 1928 to 1930, a policy of deflation in Germany – enacted to ensure that the German mark would retain a high value to enable Germany to pay off its war reparations and debts more efficiently – created massive unemployment and a plunge in wages.[39] Such economic instability contributed significantly to the rise of Nazism.[40]

Throughout history, the availability of money accelerated specialisation until the goal of work often became money itself, alienating people from the greater purpose of their work. This is a problem which Woolf was aware of, and which indeed also describes the problem of the professions. Leonard calls this "[t]he curse of the capitalist system," which "produces states of mind in individuals and classes which contaminate society by inducing a profound, instinctive conviction that the object and justification of everyone's work, trade, profession, in fact of nine-tenths of a person's conscious existence ... are and should be money."[41] The only type of society in which specialisation could exist with a more secondary use for money was the cooperative society which he had advocated in *Co-operation and the Future of Industry* (1918), where he describes an economy which would not be "geared to and judged by its ability to provide work, wages, and salaries," but instead "to produce what the community wants or needs to consume."[42] His vision is of a "Co-operative Commonwealth" in which everyone contributes their part to the greater whole of the community, even if this means there should be a system of "conscription ... for industrial labour," where "[e]very consumer, male and female, should be required to perform an equal share of this labour."[43] But this was not likely to be put into practice. It was such a radical departure from the way society had been run that it would "seem ridiculous and impossible," and that "many readers on a first hearing will either smile or shudder."[44] Later, in his autobiography, Leonard would write that "the psychology of capitalism" was "so firmly established in modern society that to most people the idea that the object of industry should be consumption, not production or profit, seems Utopian and even immoral. I never imagined, therefore, that my argument in favour of socialism controlled by consumers would cut any ice in the Labour movement."[45] There seemed to be few actualisable ways of separating specialisation and money.

Giles is the only major character in Woolf's novels who is a stockbroker, his profession the epitome of such a profit-driven, overspecialised society in which money-making has become disconnected from physical objects in the real world. Stockbroking makes use of money not in its earlier sense, as a common medium of exchange which allows the trading of goods, usually in the form of tokens which store value,[46] but in its subsequent sense, when money went beyond being a mere tool of exchange, and became a precious commodity in itself, inflating its exchange value with additional symbolic worth and power. But while making use of the derivative value of money, and earning money out of managing money, Giles is also a conscious captive of money: "Given his choice, he would have chosen to farm. But he was not given his choice. So one thing led to another; and the conglomeration of things pressed you flat; held you fast, like a fish in water" (*BA* 30–31). Because "he had no special gift, no capital, and had been furiously in love with his wife" (30), becoming a stockbroker had been his only option. This is the source of the antipathy which Giles feels towards his aunt. Where he has had to take up a city job, Lucy has been able to lead a free and quiet life in the countryside: "It was Aunt Lucy ... who made him change. He hung his grievances on her.... Aunt Lucy, foolish, free; always, since he had chosen, after leaving college, to take a job in the city, expressing her amazement, her amusement, at men who spent their lives, buying and selling – ploughs? glass beads was it? or stocks and shares?" (30).

The stigma attached to a profession which had its history in disrepute,[47] and which existed to allow people to make money out of money which was traded often in exchange for quick and large profits, had not disappeared. This was despite the fact that by the 1930s it had become a well-organised profession, with its own code of rules, an elected committee, and strict membership requirements.[48] Nicholas Davenport, in an article in the *New Statesman* in 1940, describes it thus: "I used to make some money on the Stock Exchange whenever it was possible to make it, which meant, of course, exploiting the follies of other investors more greedy than myself.... I do not know of any profession more soul-destroying than that of handling money for ungrateful and unimaginative capitalists."[49] He quotes from *The World of William Clissold* (1926) by H. G. Wells, which Woolf read in August 1926 (*L* 3: 286). Here, William, the protagonist, attacks the vacuousness of the City:

> Men follow science and art, pursue agriculture, organise manufactures ... because these things are profoundly and sustainingly interesting. But no one is in business in the City for the sake of business in the City. Men go there to come out of it again, successful.... The men who rush about [the City's] narrow ways do not know what they are up to.... [T]he sense of being a possible part of one complete organisation has not come to them.... Their great enterprises, their debts, their loans, their technicalities and methods, are solemn vast puerilities; it does not make them any the less puerilities that all mankind suffers because of them.[50]

Woolf's portrayal of Giles's occupation is informed by the wider fear in the 1930s that people and nations would develop into unthinking entities which pursued money for the sake of money without a consideration of a part to play in a greater whole, becoming, as noted earlier, "cripple[s] in a cave" (*TG* 197).

In the novel, money, disconnected from its material foundation, gives characters a common goal, yet also creates splits between and within them:

> "When we wake" (some were thinking) "the day *breaks us* with its hard mallet blows." "The office" (some were thinking) "*compels disparity. Scattered, shattered,* hither thither summoned by the bell. 'Ping-ping-ping' that's the phone. 'Forward!' 'Serving!' – that's the shop." So we answer to the infernal, agelong and eternal order issued from on high. And obey. "Working, serving, pushing, striving, earning wages – to be spent – here? Oh dear no. Now? No, by and by. When ears are deaf and the heart is dry." (*BA* 73; emphasis added)

"[E]arning wages," the final and foregrounded item in the series of activities described, is part of the "eternal order issued from on high." Money, from being an instrument of exchange and interconnectedness, has become something which people must "obey." Not even spending, the reward of earning, can bring any subsequent pleasure: It is deferred until it can no longer bring enjoyment, when people's physical and mental states have been wrung dry by the common pursuit of money. As excessive specialisation has left people with little sense of a greater belonging in modern society, so money, as a tool which developed alongside specialisation, has become the master, and people its servants. With Britain poised on the brink of another world war, the fear underlying the novel is that specialisation has disrupted beyond repair. The constant replaying of short phrases throughout the book, such as "dispersed are we," are like the constant "tick, tick, tick" and "chuff, chuff, chuff" of the haphazard gramophone, jaded and decrepit, and similar to the gramophone player in *Three Guineas* "whose needle has stuck," and whose "old tune" is "grinding out with such disastrous unanimity": "Here we go round the mulberry tree, the mulberry tree, the mulberry tree. Give it all to me, give it all to me, all to me. Three hundred millions spent upon war" (181).

On an international level, one perceived means to prevent this and create a meaningful global community was to encourage cooperation and interdependence through the specialisation of resources, industries and businesses, which would also link countries' financial systems together. This would prevent what Leonard, in the introduction to *The Intelligent Man's Way to Prevent War* (1933), which he edited, calls "economic imperialism," which could lead to the destructive ideals of "the self-sufficient state and economic nationalism."[51] In the final chapter in the book, Angell, quoting an academic at Leiden University, writes: "There was a time when man could live in a self-sufficient life, when the family, tribe or nation could live selfishly, with utter indifference as to the fate of other tribes or nations.... With the progress of science and of modern technique, with the advent of the machine or power age, all this changed."[52] For better or worse, in modern times, individuals and nations comprised a reciprocal system. The way to peace was to create the League of Nations, an international cooperative community which worked under "common rules of conduct and institutions," "apply[ing] to international relations the commonest, the most universal, the most conclusive human experience."[53] The idea behind this, as Angell puts it in the first chapter, is "to deprive the local states of their sovereignty for the benefit of society as a whole, without at the same time depriving them of their existence"[54] so that discreteness and unity can coexist in a peaceful state.

Leonard did not relinquish the idea of the League of Nations and its having a crucial role in building an international community, not even after its failure to handle the Italian-Abyssinian crisis, which according to him effectively destroyed the League's credibility at the time.[55] In 1940, he writes that the League had failed because of "the psychology of conflicting

interests and the organization of power politics," which needed to be
replaced by "the psychology of common interests and the organization
of international co-operation."[56] His view, in *The War for Peace*, is that
since the nineteenth century, "the lives we lead have demanded more and
more international co-operation and closer economic and political articulation of national communities." But because of "the lethal influence of
nationalist psychology," countries have worked against, instead of with,
this international system, so that there is "ever-increasing political and
economic conflict."[57]

Therefore, in the same book, Leonard acknowledges the need to change
the old League system, which assumed that nations were "completely
undifferentiated," and so "impos[ed] upon all the same obligations in all
cases and in all regions of the world."[58] The new League should at least
for now be run on a "confederate" system instead of under one single
federation: Smaller groups of nations that are economically and psychologically close could cluster together into smaller federations, which
could comprise a larger international confederation.[59] However, a uniform
"federate" system still seems Leonard's ultimate vision, one which would
"imply a colossal leap forward both from the organization and the psychology of the national state as they exist today,"[60] but "which is no doubt
ultimately the most logical and desirable form of international government."[61] Therefore, although he acknowledges that current psychological conditions do not yet allow this, if people and nations could remove
themselves from "the lethal influence of nationalist psychology,"[62] maximum international specialisation would ensure maximum cooperation
under a uniform federate system.

The problem throughout the 1930s, however, was not only that there
was no real sense of cooperation, but also that there was too much international specialisation, which of itself seemed to hinder cooperation, making nations highly yet uncomfortably interdependent. As a result, like the
villagers in *Between the Acts*, they were "too close, yet not close enough"
(41) – too close even to retreat temporarily into themselves and escape
each other's influence, beneficial or detrimental, yet not close enough
to create a comfortable whole. This, I suggest, is the basic question that
Between the Acts tries to consider before Leonard's solutions, although the
novel shares many of his ideas on the fundamental need for cooperation.
International specialisation in the novel seems immediately threatening.
Giles describes "the whole of Europe" as unbearably close, with its artil-
lery and planes which could at any moment "rake that land into furrows"
(34). It also meant that financial systems of different countries were closely

linked together, and the two references at the beginning and at the end of the novel to the newspaper article on the pegging down of the franc which Bart reads (11, 128) highlight these links. Such interconnectedness portended that when things went wrong, not even being, as Bart is, in the countryside or on the other side of the Channel could protect one from the disastrous effects of policies made elsewhere. With Europe compared to a "hedgehog" by Giles, "bristling with guns, poised with planes" (34), international cooperation and interdependence through specialisation, which had often been regarded as the best guarantors of peace, seemed so no longer.

An argument against excessive specialisation had in fact been put forward by Keynes, who advocated some level of national protectionism in a decade when free trade seemed to have pushed the international specialisation of industries and resources too far. In 1930, Keynes wrote to Ramsay MacDonald, the Prime Minister: "I am no longer a free trader ... in the old sense of the term to the extent of believing in a very high degree of national specialisation and in abandoning any industry which is unable for the time being to hold its own."[63] Excessive national specialisation put the industries in a country, and the wages of its workers, too much at the mercy of outside industry and market forces, when the world had not yet achieved an optimal international economic system in equilibrium. Keynes saw the need for national protectionism not as an end in itself, but rather as necessary in the 1930s, writing that "for the time at least and so long as the present transitional, experimental phase endures," it is best "to be our own masters, and to be as free as we can make ourselves from the interferences of the outside world," in order to transition more safely towards "an environment in which other ideals can be safely and conveniently pursued."[64] Keynes's views varied from Leonard's, who believed that because free trade, and the specialisation it entailed, created highly interdependent nations, it could be used to thwart the dangers of national sovereignty, making "the economically autarkic sovereign independent state an anachronism and an impossibility"; such free trade would have to be cooperative, not competitive as it had been in the nineteenth century.[65] The resultant specialisation could then serve as a cohesive force for world peace.

In "National Self-Sufficiency" (1933), Keynes continued to argue that "a greater measure of national self-sufficiency and economic isolation among countries than existed in 1914 may tend to serve the cause of peace, rather than otherwise." He sees the trends towards "the maximum of international specialization" and "the maximum geographical diffusion of capital wherever its seat of ownership" as resulting in "[t]he protection of a country's existing foreign interests, the capture of new markets, [and] the progress of economic imperialism." International specialisation disconnects what should be intricately linked: It aggravates the "remoteness between ownership and operation," "an evil in the relations among men, likely or certain in the long run to set up strains and enmities," which offsets any financial benefits.[66] Although Keynes admits that a "considerable degree of international specialization is necessary," he points out that it also leads to "the economic loss of national self-sufficiency," which disallows protection from turmoil in other countries. A balance is then needed between such specialisation and national sovereignty, so that nations have the freedom to conduct "different types of experiment" suited to their "different national temperaments and historical environments."[67] "[A]bove all," Keynes says, "let finance be primarily national."[68]

Like excessive specialisation in professional society and in *Between the Acts*, excessive international specialisation could then lead not to meaningful integration, but to destructive fragmentation. A high degree of interdependency before a cooperative mentality had been attained could backfire, provoking the worst in people and nations. Both Woolfs understood this problem. Leonard recognised that if interdependency did not lead to cooperation, it would result in war.[69] Virginia Woolf herself writes in *A Room* how "fear and bitterness" are removed from the narrator when she becomes financially independent from others (34). But where Leonard – also identifying the lack of "common international interest in law, co-operation, and peace"[70] as the cause of war – hoped ultimately that the "reason" and "common sense" which human beings were capable of would prevail,[71] *Between the Acts* suggests the need for some regression from overspecialisation, for the possibility of drawing back into oneself to allow some degree of insularity as a measure of protection and privacy. In what Julia Briggs has described as her "most English novel," Woolf both ridicules and parodies visions of Englishness and national insularity, yet retreats into them at the same time.[72]

Of course, as Woolf knew well, ideas of protectionism and insularity, if taken to their extreme, would be ruinous. In the specific case of Germany, the violent move towards *autarkie*, or complete self-sufficiency, began in 1933, the same year Keynes published "National Self-Sufficiency." The *New Statesman* at the time was filled with articles which discussed the economic rationale behind Germany's increasingly aggressive manoeuvres. One entitled "The High Road to Peace and Prosperity" in 1935 explains the close relationship between unbalanced specialisation and war. It argues that in advanced industrial countries, the rate of increase in the powers of production had been much greater than that of internal domestic consumption within a country, and that this had necessitated the search for external markets, which had hindered "a genuine political and economic co-operation that will establish the two pacific conditions of a fair and equal access of members of all nations to the resources of the common world."[73] Germany, which was "unfortunate, by comparison with the great imperial Powers, in that her industry has been developed out of all proportion to her territorial possessions, and cannot in the present condition of the world find an assured market," had instead resorted to "the economics of war" to establish the condition of *autarkie*. This included the policy of rationing certain types of imports, butter among them, in order to ensure that it had enough money to keep making armaments. Such a policy was clearly unsustainable: "the belly of a nation will not for ever be satisfied with cannon instead of butter."[74] Although unaware at the time of writing his essay that Germany would fully embark on such a programme, Keynes did caution about the possibility, saying that "[i]n those countries where the advocates of national self sufficiency have attained power, it appears to my judgment that, without exception, many foolish things are being done," and warning against implementing national self-sufficiency too hastily and irrationally.[75]

Autarkie would do away with the idea of a "whole" which accommodates the balanced existence of discrete nations, the vision of which I argue underlies *Between the Acts*, in pursuit of the almost impossible goal of becoming an entirely self-sustaining, isolated "whole" in oneself. Such a state of isolated wholeness is in different ways comparable both to the notion of the entirely solitary amateur discussed in Chapter 3, and the excessively successful, competitive and avaricious professional Woolf described in *Three Guineas*. The concept of complete self-sufficiency also links the idea of *autarkie* to the "[p]rehistoric man, … half-human, half-ape" (*BA* 129) who, according to Huxley, survived through "[g]eneralization". Advocating *autarkie* would be as destructive as advocating a return to the primeval. For Germany, this pursuit created an impossible financial predicament. The more Germany devoted its policies to its *autarkie* and armament programmes, the more its financial reserves suffered, and the more compelling it became for it to use armed force. It was a vicious cycle. The economic root of Germany's aggression led to proposals in Britain to combat it with economic sanctions. Louis Fischer analyses the dire situation in Germany in an article in the *New Statesman* in March 1936, in which he writes of the "economic impasse in Germany; capital is being frozen in armaments, in road building, in heavy Government subsidies, and in numerous other pursuits which bring no immediate financial return." Thus "if the League Powers desired, Hitler could be checked by a few well-aimed economic measures which would cost Europe much less than the billions it is spending on armaments and be at least as effective."[76] Ironically, it seemed that the most effective way to build up a whole would be first to break up the whole: War could be thwarted, this article suggests, with harsh economic measures such as threats of punitive trade sanctions, which capitalise on the specialisation in resources of the countries, and the impossibility of the German ideal of *autarkie*.

Between the Acts rethinks these debates on specialisation and money in society, putting them into the context of an English country village. Money defines many characters' relations, connecting them together but also separating them. Isa, for instance, is unhappily stuck in her marriage with Giles, whose "little trick" is to assume "the pose of one who bears the burden of the world's woe, making money for her to spend," which is why "[i]t made no difference; his infidelity – but hers did" (68). The links between Giles's occupation as a stockbroker, the setting for this occupation, and money, are even clearer in the earlier typescript: "Giles then did the usual trick; shut his lips; frowned; took up the pose of one who bears the burden. He had been in the City all week making money; on the Stock Exchange" (*PH* 119). Isa's hopes for alternatives to her financial dependence on Giles mainly rest on Haines, who is "a gentleman farmer" (*BA* 11).

Through Haines, Woolf depicts Isa's yearning for a pre-industrial society, before the excessive specialisation which characterises modernity. Unlike Leonard's description of modern society in which the sole purpose of work is money, Haines's occupation perhaps retains some of the last vestiges of what Angell described as "household" societies, in which money played a minimal role. In these societies in the Middle Ages, "the essence of the social arrangement did not depend upon an exchange, but upon everyone doing an assigned task and the product being divided by well-established custom or according to traditional hierarchical rights," and "for centuries during the Middle Ages," "all orderly life was organized on this household basis," when "monastery and manor and feudal estate remained practically moneyless because self-sufficient."[77] Angell argues against that the common belief that mankind "advance[ed] from the semi-animal and so barterless horde to tribes in which barter became common, and thence to a money economy, and thence to a credit economy." Instead, he explains, "[m]oney dates back to pre-history; the elements of credit – almost every form of it – to the very earliest history. Yet having discovered and adopted money ... man sometimes dropped it; lived a better life without it, returned to it, and bettered the betterment."[78] That communities rooted in farming were less influenced by fluctuations in the value of money was attested to by recent events. As Angell points out, "a few years ago in Central Europe, when the device of money had utterly broken down in the midst of the most orderly civilization in the world, and men hurried to get rid of money for goods, since it had lost all stable value," people in the cities, "helpless without money," "starved and froze," whereas "the peasants on the farms and in the forests recked little of the lack of money."[79] The secondary role of money in farming may account for Isa's attraction to Haines as an alternative to her stockbroker husband, as a regression from the fragmenting specialisation of modernity. He represents an older, simpler world order, which holds more romance in Isa's eyes: "the ravaged, the silent, the romantic gentleman farmer" (11). However, although Woolf contrasts the village community in the novel with that of a "London mob," it would not qualify as Angell's "'household' type of social organization" either; Isa, for example, thinks that everyone here is guilty of the ulterior motive of money: "none speaks with a single voice. None with a voice free from the old vibrations. Always I hear corrupt murmurs; the chink of gold and metal" (94). She herself hides her private thoughts in an object linked to financial interest, writing her poems in a book "bound like an account book in case Giles suspected" (12).

Zwerdling has written that Woolf was deeply aware of the problems in a vision of an old English community immune to the afflictions of the present.[80] Indeed, the appeal of "gentleman" farming as a return to simpler forms of society was not without its ambiguities. By aligning herself with Haines, Isa would merely be substituting one way of dependence for another. The hierarchy of "gentleman" farming is also problematic. But Isa deliberately refrains from deeper examination, instead always keeping a safe distance from which she can admire and idealise Haines. Throughout the pageant, she keeps turning around to look for him, because he is always separated from her: "She half turned in her seat. . . . Who was she looking for? William, turning, following her eyes, saw only a man in grey" (51). Apart from his occupation, readers only know that Haines has a "ravaged face" (6) and is married. In his fragmented representation he retains his "mystery" (6), which is necessary to maintain Isa's fascination, enabling him to serve as her icon. But it also ensures that he is a distant dream rather than a realistic alternative. Haines is as enigmatic to Isa as the prehistoric imagery is to the characters in the novel, and although both provide some imaginative relief from the predicament which excessive specialisation has led to, the narrative prevents the final vindication of either.

Between the Acts, therefore, shares to a certain extent Leonard's view that a wholly isolated, self-contained English culture and nationhood, suggestive of "the economically autarkic sovereign independent state," has in the present day been made an "anachronism and an impossibility" by the "large-scale industrialization of production" since the nineteenth century, which has made nations inextricably interdependent.[81] It also acknowledges that specialisation and money are necessary for building "civilization," or the "wall" (111) which the voice at the end of the pageant refers to, because, inevitably, "we are members one of another. Each is part of the whole" (114). The right balance of both is as fundamental to Woolf's aesthetic vision for the attainment of a meaningful human community, whether on the scale of the village, the nation or the world, as it is for enabling a meaningful life in the professions. But there are, as this chapter has suggested throughout, slight but significant differences between Virginia's and Leonard's views. In *Between the Acts*, there is, to a carefully limited degree, some relief to be found in visions of prehistory and pre-industrial England. The overspecialised state of modernity, which has created ever higher levels of interdependency, and an ever larger role for money, would, it seems, benefit from some regression. Such a partial retreat from excessive interdependency could in fact aid, rather than hinder, the goal of more cooperation.

A balanced use of specialisation and money can thus help reconcile the tension between discreteness and unity, so that people neither regress entirely to the undifferentiated mess of the primeval swamp, or become so specialised, without prior coordination and cooperation, that they are mere "orts, scraps and fragments" (*BA* 111), unable to fit together into a bigger whole. *Between the Acts*, although resonating with both Keynes's ideas of national protectionism and his criticism of overspecialisation, and Leonard's "renunciation of sovereignty"[82] and his approbation of maximum international specialisation, finally refuses conclusion with either. The novel contains a regressive yearning for the prehistoric, and a protectionist nostalgia for past national culture and Englishness; but it also does not accept these as final states, and where they threaten to consolidate they are broken up by fragmentation. It accepts that civilisation cannot be built without the modern discreteness of identity and individuals; but it also broods over the shattered state of modernity, in which discreteness has been taken too far without prior considerations of a greater whole. Woolf's own slightly modified vision, as suggested in the aesthetics of the novel, was of a balanced amount of specialisation and money: enough to build the meaningful whole that was civilisation, but not so much that the building materials could not fit together, or so little that there were not enough, propelling humanity towards primeval mess. In this lay her final effort at rethinking the implications of, and alternatives to, existing professional society. It is the hopeful message, always intermeshed with the darker sense of despair, in *Between the Acts*: "*Dispersed are we; who have come together. But*, the gramophone asserted, *let us retain whatever made that harmony*." (116). The aesthetics of simultaneous cohesion and fragmentation in the novel mirrors this precarious balance between the states of an absence of specialisation and overspecialisation, becoming a vehicle for averting the chaos of either extreme.

Novel Worlds

In her final novel, therefore, the question of how to create a new world containing a balanced amount of specialisation is raised and imagined, if not solved, in a new aesthetic approach. *Between the Acts* is the culmination of Woolf's engagement with the professions in her novels, in which she uses their creative space and her literary methods and experimentation to explore alternatives to the existing professional system. Combining the political with the aesthetic, Woolf wrote and rewrote throughout her career a philosophy of how "not to segregate and specialize, but to combine" (*TG* 155), of how people could live meaningful lives in modern society.

Because of its necessary interactions with the actual world, the complexities of which Woolf was only too conscious, parts of this philosophy were neither fixed nor stable. Although she could steadfastly express the human qualities and values to aspire towards, Woolf could not entirely satisfactorily articulate in her essays what practicable actions were to be taken so that people could be integral members of, and live a spiritually and intellectually rich life in, a real and realisable world, with the right amount of specialisation substantiated in a novel professional system. Nor could she ensure that her fiction expressed to the reader her whole vision, despite the relatively greater freedom of form that her creative writing accorded her. As Michael Whitworth writes, "Woolf's aestheticisation of the political" can be risky; without explicit commentary, readers can overlook or misunderstand the politics in her novels.[83] But this did not stop her from representing the issues in her writing, in which she continued to think through and search for improvements to the status quo of the existing professional system. As perhaps the best example of this dilemma, she imagined, but failed to articulate, a stable, ideal model for the profession of writing, at times used by her as a paradigm for other professions.

The attainment of the "perfect integrity" of vision in writing, its "most essential quality as a work of art" (*CE* 2: 145), could be striven for, but may not be consistently practicable because of material realities outside of the writer's complete control.

Many of Woolf's hopes rested on ideas of women's difference, and throughout this book, we have observed how her work has shown a careful, and perhaps perilous, balancing between both asserting and effacing the distinction between the sexes on which she built much of her rhetoric. But this difference could not be relied on for much longer as the catalyst for continuous improvement. Woolf writes in "Professions for Women": "Ah, but what is 'herself'? I mean, what is a woman? I assure you, I do not know. I do not believe that you know. I do not believe that anybody can know until she has expressed herself in all the arts and professions open to human skill" (*CE* 2: 286). In a circle of hermeneutics, her belief that "herself" has remained undiscovered due to external conditions means that there is little way to discover this essence unless external conditions are ideal. But since no one yet knows what a woman is, no one can know what the ideal environment is like in which she can find full expression. Upon women's entry into the professions, then, what would happen could only be speculated upon: women's traditions, education and values could adjust to approximate those of men; the existing professions could alter and orient themselves to women; or both possibilities could develop simultaneously. It is beyond the scope of this book, but because of the many changes which professional society has undergone since the 1940s, the time may have come when we are in a position to re-evaluate and update Woolf's arguments, when we can finally assess with the benefit of hindsight the results of a social experiment which she could only imagine.

The Introduction began with two quotations from the drafts which Woolf wrote for her talk for the London/National Society for Women's Service in January 1931, and so it is perhaps appropriate to end with the same text. Woolf, as mentioned, writes: "I have two proposals to put before you: the first is that all professional [*sic*] are to be avoided; & the second that several new professions must <at once> be invented."[84] The two suggestions are numbered, so she had the second in mind when she wrote the first. The contradiction of avoiding all professions yet still inventing new ones embodies both her aspirations for and her despondency about the possibility for a new world: Hoping that somehow, the professions might yet be changed and lead to a better future, she also despaired of a future in which they continued on in the same way; wanting to do away with their excessively restrictive specialisation, she was also unable to conceive of the world as she knew it without them. War, which she saw as the consequence of some professional values, realised her worst fears. Yet one of the key ideas in *Between the Acts* is that destruction and construction are two sides of the same coin, and her last novel contains the hope, however remote in the imminence of war, that the world would eventually be rebuilt differently. *Between the Acts*, like the other novels we have discussed, allowed her to explore these issues and respond to the status quo without always needing to present final executable answers or theories, to create novel worlds without always knowing exactly how they would look like in reality.

Notes

Introduction

1 "Articles, Essays, Fiction and Reviews" 145.

2 This comes from a different section of the same notebook, above which she wrote "Draft of Professions." The section is dated April 1935; the sentence is on p. 141.

3 "Articles, Essays, Fiction and Reviews" 145.

4 Ibid 141.

5 The *OED* lists the first meanings of the word as "senses relating to the declaration of faith [and] principles," and "any solemn declaration, promise, vow." All the instances it lists under these are religious. One particularly interesting example comes from a sermon in 1711, which captures the senses of both the public and the private in the word: "Not only in a private but a publick Profession of Obedience to all those Rules of Decency which they conceive to be most for his Honour." See "Profession, *n.*," *OED*.

6 The *OED* cites Walter Besant's *Fifty Years Ago* (1888): "New professions have come into existence, and the old professions are more esteemed. It was formerly a poor and beggarly thing to belong to any other than the three learned professions." See "Professional, *adj.* and *n.*," *OED*.

7 Corfield 244.

8 Ibid.

9 "Profession, *n.*," *OED*.

10 "Profess, *v.*," *OED*.

11 Ibid.

12 Woolf herself differed in this respect from Rachel and Katharine, although she preferred to portray herself as having been entirely self-educated. See Jones and Snaith, "'Tilting at Universities,'" where the authors show Woolf's attendance record between 1897 and 1901 at the university. Virginia Stephen was, they write, "not only registered for courses in a range of subjects, but reached degree-level standard in some of her studies, and also took examinations" (4).

13 Woolf would later return to this metaphor in *A Room of One's Own*: "Nick Greene, I thought, ... said that a woman acting put him in mind of a dog dancing. Johnson repeated the phrase two hundred years later of women preaching. And here, I said, opening a book about music, we have the very

words used again in this year of grace, 1928, of women who try to write music. 'Of Mlle. Germaine Tailleferre one can only repeat Dr. Johnson's dictum concerning a woman preacher, transposed into terms of music. "Sir, a woman's composing is like a dog's walking on his hind legs. It is not done well, but you are surprised to find it done at all."' So accurately does history repeat itself" (50).

14 McGee 236.

15 L. Woolf, *After the Deluge* 136.

16 *A Room of One's Own*, Alex Zwerdling writes, could have been renamed *Five Hundred Pounds a Year* because of the centrality of the central problem of women's incomes. See *Virginia Woolf and the Real World* 229.

17 V. Woolf, "Articles, Essays, Fiction and Reviews" 129.

18 Lee 598–601.

19 Ibid.

20 The first number refers to the volume number, and the second number to the page number.

21 Cucullu, "Exceptional Women" 172.

22 Snaith, *Virginia Woolf: Public and Private Negotiations*; Cuddy-Keane, *Virginia Woolf, the Intellectual, and the Public Sphere.*

23 Menand and Rainey, "Introduction" 6.

24 Pitcairn vii–x.

25 Ibid.

26 Hayward 103.

27 Ibid. 3–7.

28 Woolf and Carr-Saunders both signed, together with others, a letter to the editor of *The Times* to highlight the plight of the Spanish government and people in the Spanish Civil War, which appeared in *The Times* on 19 Aug. 1936. Carr-Saunders also co-authored the book *Consumers' Co-Operation in Great Britain* (1938), the title page of which states that it is written in consultation with, among others, Leonard Woolf, and which Leonard possessed copies of at both Monk's House and 24 Victoria Square London. See Holleyman 2 (Monks House, Section VI); 11 (Victoria Square, Section III).

29 Carr-Saunders and Wilson 3.

30 Ibid. 1.

31 Ibid.

32 Ibid. 299–302.

33 In *The Professions*, the section on law is divided into the history of barristers and solicitors. The authors write that "[u]p to comparatively recent times there was no organization representative of the Bar as a whole. But in December 1883 it was determined at a general meeting of the Bar to set up a body to be called the Bar Committee" (16). Likewise, the organisation of solicitors into what developed into the Law Society did not attain autonomy in examination and registration until 1877 (47–48). The history of medicine is divided into that of physicians, surgeons and apothecaries. Not until 1858, when the Medical Act was passed, which had remained "substantially

unamended" up till Woolf's time, was the "hierarchy with the physicians at the top, and below, in descending order of prestige, 'the three inferior grades of surgeons, apothecaries and even druggists'" consolidated into what became the massive body of the medical profession with "a single uniform medical qualification" (75–83). The Institution of Civil Engineers was founded in 1818, concerning itself initially with research, but in 1897 setting up its own examinations for qualification to different grades of membership. The establishment of a legal register of "Civil Engineers," however, had yet to come about by 1933 because of disagreement among different associations, and because of the debate about whether "existing trained engineers" who were not members of any association should be allowed on such a register (157–65). The Institute of British Architects, set up in 1834, received a charter in 1837 and became the Royal Institute of British Architects in 1866 (178). Stockbrokers, "chosen as an example of their group because their organization is elaborate," were governed by a committee set up in the eighteenth century with regulatory powers (273–74).

34 Smith 191–92.
35 Sutherland xxxiii.
36 Marx laid out the theoretical framework of this relationship in his most famous work, *Das Kapital* (1867).
37 Quoted in Perkin 83–84. The source is Arnold's "Report on the System of Education."
38 Chapter 3 will discuss the word "amateur" in more detail.
39 "Professionalism, *n.*," *OED*.
40 See *Abstract of the Answers and Returns: Occupation Abstract* 56.
41 *Census of Great Britain, 1851* cxxviii–cxxix.
42 *Census of England and Wales for the Year 1861* xl.
43 "Profession, *n.*," *OED*.
44 Ibid.
45 Ruth 4.
46 MacDonald 9–10.
47 Ibid. 13.
48 Ibid. 126–27.
49 Ibid.
50 Ibid.
51 Ibid.
52 Carr-Saunders and Wilson 302.
53 Perkin 3–4.
54 Ibid. 439.
55 Ibid. 390.
56 Ibid. 6.
57 Ibid. 4.
58 Hayward 27.
59 Ibid. 34.
60 Lee 328.

61 "The Fabian Society" 375.

62 Perkin 130–31. This is pointed out by Trotter 128–29. I am indebted to Trotter's work for directing me towards the Webbs and to Perkin's study.

63 "The Fabian Summer School" 448.

64 Lee 329.

65 Webb and Webb, "Special Supplement" 4–21.

66 Ibid. 1–31.

67 Webb and Webb, "What Is Socialism?" 301–02.

68 Webb and Webb, "Special Supplement (Part 2)" 48.

69 Ibid. 36–37.

70 Ibid. 48.

71 See Trotter, *Paranoid Modernism*.

72 Menand 123–30.

73 T. S. Eliot 61.

74 Menand 114; 132. For a discussion on professionalism as a reaction against capitalism, see also Perkin 120–23.

   Leonard Woolf defines capitalist society as one "founded upon economic competition," in which "the dominating influence in that competition is capital and the holders of capital." He also writes: "We live in an era which has been correctly called the age of capitalism.... The making of profits, buying cheap and selling dear, these are the principles of a capitalistic society." See *Economic Imperialism* 101. The professions operate under a different type of capital, what Perkin calls "human capital" (xv), and benefit from the artificial monopoly achieved by successful professional organisation.

75 Menand 114.

76 Strychacz 25–27.

77 Wexler 3.

78 Whitworth, "Virginia Woolf and Modernism" 147.

79 See, for instance, Kaufmann, "A Modernism of One's Own"; Collier 363–92.

80 Cucullu, *Expert Modernists*.

81 Ruth 15.

82 Schröder 6.

83 Ibid. 7.

84 As Holly Henry has pointed out in showing Bertrand Russell's influence on Woolf's thought, "The Mark" can be read as Woolf destabilising and calling into question single and fixed "genres and perspectives" which claim an absolute understanding of the physical world (79–84). Instead, reality, according to Russell, can be understood "as the interchange between material phenomena and the multiple perspectives of subjective experience" (80). See *Virginia Woolf and the Discourse of Science*.

85 Walker 158.

86 Alt 170.

87 Larson, *The Rise of Professionalism*; Witz, *Professions and Patriarchy*; Macdonald, *The Sociology of the Professions*. Also see Johnson, *Professions and Power* and Pavalko, *Sociology of Occupations and Professions*.

1 The Ethics and Aesthetics of Medicine

1 Hayward 93
2 Carr-Saunders and Wilson 26.
3 Loudon 155.
4 Pickstone 316.
5 Loudon 224. As a speaker in 1932 remarks, "[t]hough manners now seem to be less formal and pontifical, and the authority of mere seniority to be less dominant, human nature remains much the same," accounting for "the lure of the phrase 'the Harley Street specialist'" (Rolleston 129).

 This rivalry and hostility is depicted by Woolf in representing Holmes and Bradshaw's views: The former thinks that the difference between general practitioners like him and the Harley Street specialists is merely in the fees they charge (*MD* 103), whereas the latter considers general practitioners as blundering fools whose mistakes "took half his time to undo" (*MD* 105).
6 Berridge 179.
7 Porter 48.
8 Three earlier studies which look at Woolf's description of the medical profession biographically are Showalter, *A Literature of Their Own*, 276–78; L. Gordon, *Virginia Woolf: A Writer's Life*, 63–66; and Trombley, *All That Summer She Was Mad*. Such studies show how Woolf's depiction of doctors was based on her own experiences as a patient. I build on them by arguing that Woolf was doing even more than taking fictional revenge or releasing her bitterness: she was also trying to improve the medical profession.

 Poole's *The Unknown Virginia Woolf* is one of the earlier works to conscientiously avoid diagnosis of Woolf as mad, focusing instead on tracing her mental distress through documentation and her writing. In the chapter entitled "Was Septimus Smith 'Insane'?," Poole reads Septimus as Woolf, and writes, in a point similar to the one I make on medical diagnostic discourse, that "Sir William Bradshaw is closed to the subjective dimension of Smith's problem" (189). Hermione Lee's well-known biography on Woolf contains a chapter on "Madness," which is careful to distinguish between Woolf as a patient and as a victim, and not to portray Woolf as the latter (175–200). Lee also writes how Woolf was "extremely anxious that she should not be thought just to 'write essays about myself'" (192).
9 The phrase comes from the title of Trombley's book.
10 Childress 128–30.
11 Carr-Saunders and Wilson 102. As a high-profile example of such disputes, in 1918, four doctors took legal action against the BMA "for conspiracy to injure them in their profession and to libel and slander them." The accusation arose out of the boycotting by the BMA of the doctors who worked for a dispensary where "members paid a small subscription and in return they received from the dispensary medical attendance during illness" ("High Court of Justice" C4). The BMA objected to these "medical aid institutes" because doctors were salaried, and often paid at what they considered "entirely inadequate rates of payment for the medical officer." They also criticized the administration of

these institutes, which was "in the hands of a purely lay committee." The establishment of the dispensaries was seen as "a protest against efforts made by the local doctors to improve contract practice conditions, either by raising the rate of payment per head which in many cases was grossly inadequate, or by instituting a wage limit, or both" by non-medical societies ("Matters Referred to Divisions" 201–02).

12 "The Professional Mind" 907.

13 Historically, "conversion" referred specifically to religious conversion to Christianity. Jean Thomas, the proprietor of the nursing home at which Woolf stayed when she was ill, was a devout Christian who, as Poole points out, tried to do precisely this. In December 1910, Woolf wrote to Vanessa Bell: "She ... exhort[ed] me to Christianity, which will save me from insanity. How we are persecuted! The self conceit of Christians is really unendurable' (*L* 1: 25). See Poole 114.

14 Brian W. Shaffer has shown interesting parallels between Clive Bell's criticism of medicine in relation to his thoughts on civilisation and Woolf's. In *On British Freedom* (1923), for instance, Bell writes: "the attitude of these gentlemen who write to the papers and make speeches exhorting the Government to enforce their dogmas is about as unscientific as an attitude can be" (63–64), and that "I do think it preposterous that a gang of arrogant and ignorant human beings should presume not only to lay down the law in a science where there is hardly a conclusion which goes unchallenged, but, as though they had discovered incontrovertible principles of universal application, to bully the Government into applying their nostrums" (65–66, quoted in Shaffer 79). Although Bell's main target is not professionalism, but the more general term of "the enemies of freedom" (53), his censure comes close to criticism of the normative rules which medical professionalism creates. "[T]he common practitioner," he thinks, "puts his smattering of science and the prestige of a great calling at the service of the bullying instinct." For such a doctor, "[t]o differ from the commonplace, for instance to have genius or talent, to be sensitive to beauty, or to care greatly for truth, in fact to be exceptional in any way, is to be abnormal. And since the normal is the good, the normal life the good life, and normality (or normalcy) the true end of human aspiration, it follows that to be abnormal is to be wicked, and that abnormality (and abnormalcy too) should, so far as possible, be suppressed and eliminated by Act of Parliament" (63).

Shaffer's careful analysis points out that Woolf, for instance, disagreed with Bell on his emphasis on the necessity of a rigid class system, and that her more ambiguous representations of society and civilisation problematise Bell's (81–86). I would add that Bell's views on doctors do not correspond straightforwardly to those expressed by Woolf in the novel, who satirises the doctors yet at the same time shows them to be victims of their own fixed and limited ways of thinking. This is, I think, both a result of the difference in form (a novel versus an essay), and of the authors' different politics. Whereas Bell's argument reads in parts like an elitist diatribe (for instance when he says that he is not against the sterilisation of "people … least likely to produce children who will grow into intelligent, sensitive, happy and well-favoured men and women" [68–69]), Woolf balances her moments of harsh satire with a with-holding of authorial judgment throughout the novel.

15 Hayward 19.
16 "Publicity for Doctors" 437.
17 Dawson 26.
18 Ibid.
19 Drummond 103.
20 Ibid.
21 Ibid.
22 Dawson 26. Many of these arguments were also set in the larger context of the National Insurance Acts, which will be discussed later in the chapter.
23 "The Profession of Medicine" (1923): 354.
24 This law will be elaborated on later in the chapter.
25 Drummond 108.
26 Ibid. 110.
27 Thomas 54.
28 Zwerdling 30.
    Also see Knox-Shaw, "The Otherness of Septimus Warren Smith." Knox-Shaw provides useful historical information on the "Bill" Bradshaw refers to here, noting the heated debates in Parliament in 1922 because of plans to scrap the entitlement of shell-shocked ex-servicemen to their pensions for treatment, instead to be supported by the Poor Law (99). A bill to ensure that war pensions would continue to be paid to shell-shocked war veterans was "already in its preliminary stages by the mid-June day on which *Mrs Dalloway* is set" (100). Bradshaw's comment that "the deferred effects of shell shock" must be considered in such a bill could then be read as a mitigation of the severity of his views on mental illness. Alternatively, as Knox-Shaw thinks, it could be seen as "a nice irony," because it seems contrary to Bradshaw's "real views [which] clearly align him with that part of the Tory Party opposed to the reform." Bradshaw's suggestion then is possibly due merely to "the presence of his host," Richard Dalloway, "a sincere philanthropist" (101).
29 Thomson 61–84.
    Jane Marcus has used a later example, *Psychoanalysis and Medicine* (1935) by Karin Stephen, Woolf's sister-in-law, to argue similarly that psychoanalysis provided a more sympathetic account of mental illness than Woolf's doctor George Savage did, whom she primarily based her portrait of the fictional Bradshaw on. See J. Marcus 101; Trombley 100–01.
30 Eder 11.
31 Whitworth, *Virginia Woolf: Authors in Context* 170.
32 Eder 145.
33 Woolf had a few major mental breakdowns in her life: her first and second ones were in 1895 and 1904, following her mother's and father's death respectively; she also suffered from 1913–1915, when, according to Lee, they

consulted doctor after doctor to find help (177–83). For the first breakdown, she was attended to by Dr Seton, the family's doctor, who "put a stop to all lessons, ordered a simple life and prescribed outdoor exercise" (Bell 45). For the second, she was taken care of by three nurses, Vanessa, and her friend Violet Dickinson, at whose house in Burnham Wood she stayed until she was well enough to leave (89–90). When in 1910, she again showed symptoms of "acute nervous tension," she first entered a private home in Twickenham following the advice of Dr Savage (161). One letter she wrote to Vanessa during her stay there in the summer of 1910 reveals some of the characteristics of the rest cure which she had to undergo: "Savage wanted me to stay in bed more or less this week.... Then there is all the eating and drinking and being shut up in the dark." At the time she was writing the letter, she "had stayed in bed alone here for 4 weeks." It is perhaps not surprising that she felt that "I will soon have to jump out of a window" (*L* 1: 430–31).

34 Eder 140–41.
35 Ibid.
36 Jouve 252–56.
37 Ibid. 256.
38 Thompson 88.
    This is not to claim simplistically that Woolf was somehow anti-science or anti-empiricist. Rather, what Woolf seemed consistently against was the imposition of singular viewpoints which were taken as authoritative facts on "what, after all, we know nothing about – the nervous system, the human brain" (108), a position which characterised much of medical diagnosis of mental disorders, and to some extent also the self-proclaimed scientific position of psychoanalysis.
39 Winter 126.
40 Pointed out in Jouve 255.
41 Zwerdling 257. It may even be possible to see Woolf's fiction as drawing on the psychoanalytic method as well. Michael North, for instance, has pointed out that it is possible to read *Mrs Dalloway* as informed by psychoanalytic knowledge: The process of unconscious understanding of Septimus which Clarissa arrives at, and through which she also learns about herself in a moment of epiphany, mirrors the psychoanalytic process. See North 85–86.
42 "The Profession of Medicine" (1922): 412.
43 The word "vocation" will be discussed in more detail in Chapter 2.
44 "The Profession of Medicine" (1921): C11. We can compare this to what Hayward says: "Professionalism ... resents lay criticism or superintendence, claiming 'independence' ... in the alleged interests of the public, and denying, by implication, that the majority in its ranks are mediocre people who need guidance and oversight" (58).
45 Morris 798.
46 "Fabian Medicine" S81. Pointed out in Carr-Saunders and Wilson 101. See the discussion below on the BMA's role during the passage and implementation of the National Insurance Act of 1911.

47 Interestingly, in one of the drafts for *Mrs Dalloway*, Woolf wrote, and then crossed out: ~~'They had & they didn't mind paying three guineas [...] wh was what the great men of Harley Street payed for the same advice – They might go to see Dr. Bradshaw~~" (*H* 117).

48 Pickstone 309.

49 Ibid. 315.

50 Ibid. 319–20.

51 The establishment of a full state medical service would not be realised until the foundation of the National Health Service in 1948.

52 Hermann Levy 16–17.

53 A. Lyon 373.

54 Moore and Parker 86.

55 "The Profession of Medicine" (1923): 353.

56 "Fabian Medicine" S81.

57 Atkins 1096.

58 Gaffin and Thoms 69–70.

59 Ibid.

60 Blaszak 115; Lee 327. For a detailed summary of Woolf's participation in the WCG, see Black 39–41.

61 "Poverty and Maternity" 329.

62 Gaffin and Thoms 72.

63 *Maternity: Letters from Working-Women* 209–10.

64 Ibid. 210–11.

65 Ibid. 212.

66 Kennedy 107.

67 Sympathy, for the purposes of this chapter, refers to meaningful "affinity," "agreement," "harmony," and "community of feeling" (see "Sympathy, *n.*," *OED*), to the levelling of hierarchy which is antonymous to "tyranny," with its associations of forceful imposition based on the assumption of the existence of a hierarchical structure. In Woolf's representation in the novel, the doctors' lack of sympathy forms part of their professional tyranny.

68 Short 314–16.

69 Two recent examples of critics who have commented on this break in the otherwise nonjudgmental third-person narration in the novel are Herbert, "Mrs. Dalloway, the Dictator, and the Relativity Paradox" and Hite, "Tonal Cues and Uncertain Values". Herbert points out that "[i]n constructing her novel according to 'the negation of the absolute,' Woolf does of course proclaim one absolute: the rejection of absolutism itself," and that here, "the abolished omniscient narrator suddenly ... reappear[s] in her text for the specific purpose of analyzing and denouncing Sir William's perverted cult of Proportion and Conversion, according to which no relativistic indeterminacy is allowed" (118). Hite says that the narrator here "appears to be not only authoritative but authorial, a rare instance in Woolf's fiction of a third-person speaker unaffected by any character's point of view, stating what is the case in the narrative universe" (255).

70 However, even the aesthetics of sympathy in the novel may have its limits. Janet Lyon has argued that Woolf's "modernist subjectivism" has boundaries "beyond which [her] narrative sentience does not go." She sees Woolf's decision to kill Septimus as both a rescuing of Septimus "from the horrors of Dr. Bradshaw," to "prevent[] his institutional descent into the condition of un-man," and as a self-rescue, so that she does not have to confront "the condition of un-man," "beyond which her aesthetics cannot and will not go." This paves the way for Clarissa to share sympathetically Septimus's subjectivity when she hears of his death, bringing him under aesthetic and sympathetic control. See "On the Asylum Road" 569. An even more sceptical reading is provided by Karen DeMeester, who thinks that "[a]lthough Woolf's form is particularly well-suited for depicting trauma … it is ill-suited to depicting recovery." In order to recover, the patient must revert back to "a coherent, communicable narrative" and "social discourse," which is difficult within Woolf's form because of its intense subjective focus on the patient's consciousness. See "Trauma and Recovery" 652.

Read in view of the argument in this chapter, however, in both cases the limits of Woolf's aesthetics and narrative also serve a useful, and biased, purpose: to address the shortcomings of medical professionalism in its contemporary state. First, Woolf increases sympathy for Septimus by containing his condition to some extent, never allowing him to progress beyond a state where her readers would start to question his humanity and therefore agree with the doctors more than they feel connected to Septimus. Second, Woolf's point was to establish Septimus as an outsider to the dominant social discourse which is threatening to assimilate him. To have him recover entirely would again mitigate the horror of the doctors' oppression.

71 Skrbic 144.

72 For the chronology of these stories, see Susan Dick's notes in *CSF* 305.

73 Reynier 78.

74 Karen DeMeester has interpreted the doctors' appropriation of Septimus's stories as acts of "codifying them to affirm rather than condemn the status quo" ("Trauma, Post-Traumatic Stress Disorder, and Obstacles for Postwar Recovery" 87). Septimus is silenced, denied the communication in which the potential to heal lies (84–85). My points here about the importance of sympathy are similar, but I emphasise the potential disingenuousness of the use of professional conversation and communication.

75 Hayward 22.

76 Or, considering that Septimus calls him "human nature" (*MD* 107), the worst side of humanity.

77 Hayward x.

78 Perkin describes this as the "fiduciary" (16) nature of the services which the professions provide.

79 Beith 799–800.

80 Poole 144.

81 Bartlett and Sandland 17.

82 Theobald 143–44.

83 Ibid.
84 Ibid. 145.
85 "The Professional Mind" 908.
86 Ibid.
87 Ibid.
88 Ibid.
89 Furst 255.
90 Heather Levy 192.
91 Furst 255.

2 Virginia Woolf, Amateurism and the Professionalisation of Literature

1 Benedict 4.
2 Ibid. Benedict cites one of the definitions for the word in the *OED*: "[l]iterary productions as a whole; the body of writings produced in a particular country or period, or in the world in general." The first example of this definition documented in the *OED* is from Sir Humphry Davy's *Elements of Chemical Philosophy* in 1812, in which the word is used to refer to the literary endeavours in ancient Greece.
3 Ibid.
4 "Vocation, *n.*," *OED*.
5 "Calling, *vbl. n.*," *OED*.
6 See *Abstract of the Answers and Returns: Occupation Abstract* 56. Here the only three main categories under the heading "professional" are clerical, legal and medical occupations, under which are listed their subcategories. In the case of the medical profession, for instance, the list ranges from the physician to the midwife. In contrast, the census in 1831 had lumped professionals together in the category of "capitalists, bankers, professional and other educated men." See *Abstract of the Answers and Returns Made Pursuant to an Act* 3.
7 *Abstract of the Answers and Returns: Occupation Abstract* 31.
8 *Census of Great Britain, 1851* cxxix. There are also the smaller groups of "Reporter and Shorthand Writer" (207), "Literary, Private, – secretary" (137), "Fellow of College, Graduate or University" (755), and "Translator, Interpreter" (112).
9 Reader 147.
10 *Census of England and Wales for the Year 1861* xl.
11 Menand 117.
12 Carr-Saunders and Wilson 271.
13 Collier 372.
14 Guy and Small 378–79.
15 Court 85.
16 Eagleton 25.
17 See Court's work, which provides an excellent overview of the history of the institutionalisation of English literary studies in Britain. He writes that "[t]he first serious efforts to introduce English literary study into the university

curriculum in Britain were made in eighteenth-century Scotland," most notably by Adam Smith's "first formal series of lectures on the subject of English, its rhetoric and literature, at Edinburgh, from 1748 to 1751" (18). In England, English literary study was first introduced when London's University College opened in 1828 (41–52).

See also Palmer. The statute to set up an Oxford English School was submitted and approved in 1894 (111–12). At Cambridge, in 1878, English studies was part of studies for a degree in "Medieval and Modern Languages"; in 1917 the syllabus was changed so that one could study the English section of the degree "without any linguistic study and without any knowledge of literature before 1350"; and in 1926, "a degree in English alone became possible," and "the English Faculty Board was created" (151–52).

18 This essay first appeared in *Lysistrata* in May 1934.

19 At the University of London in 1919, "a cycle of courses in journalism" was created, "which entitle the members to a diploma at the end of two years." The National Union of Journalists was also encouraging "the supplementary education of journalists who are already practising their profession" in the form of "courses in history, economics, and sociology," and in 1927 "passed a resolution instructing its committee to undertake negotiations with newspaper proprietors with a view to arranging for the creation in journalism in various centres." See *Condition of Work and Life of Journalists* 16.

20 See Daugherty, who writes that Woolf's teaching style at Morley College is reflected in her essays, "creat[ing] a teaching/learning space where class can be muted, where access is encouraged, where being welcomed into the community of readers is more important than gatekeeping" (133).

21 V. Woolf, "Report on Teaching at Morley College" 203.

22 Cuddy-Keane, *Virginia Woolf* 86.

23 First published in *The Death of the Moth and Other Essays* (1942), the essay is based on her speech to the London/National Society for Women's Service in 1931.

24 Collier 377.

25 Clutton-Brock 49–50.

26 T. S. Eliot 61.

27 Ibid. Emphasis in the original.

28 "Amateur, *n.*," *OED*.

29 Bentley 461. Pointed out in "Amateur, *n.*," *OED*. Emphases in the original.

30 "Professional, *adj.* and *n.*," *OED*.

31 Ibid.

32 Dickens 15. Pointed out in "Professional, *adj.* and *n.*," *OED*.

33 T. S. Eliot 61.

34 Ibid.

35 Collier also points out that for Woolf, professionalism was a concept that included both "excessive commercialism" and "the more common associations of credentialing, rigor, and distinction that it held for Pound and Eliot" (377–78).

36 Wexler 123.

37 L. Woolf, *Beginning Again* 90; Lee 67.

38 Routh 60.

39 Ibid. 124.

40 L. Woolf, *Beginning Again*, 90; Lee 325–26.

41 L. Woolf, *Beginning Again*, 90.

42 Lee 557–58.

43 See the discussion later in this chapter on *D* 3: 221.

44 Collier makes a similar point when he writes that "Freed from the need to sell her work to pay for basic necessities, Woolf could use her literary earnings … to furnish herself with luxuries such as cars, properties, attractive clothing, and holidays," and that "[h]er voluntary, rather than compulsory, engagement with the literary marketplace saves her from the pressures that threaten her intellectual detachment" (368).

45 Melba Cuddy-Keane edited the transcript of the debate for publication in 2006. See Woolf and Woolf 236–37.

46 Ibid. 241.

47 In *Virginia Woolf: The Echoes Enslaved*, Allen McLaurin starts by similarly emphasising Butler's "anti-professionalism" (5), which he relates to Woolf's experimentalism and her aesthetics of "repetition and change" (11).

48 This first appeared as a review in *The Times Literary Supplement* in 1916 of Harris's *Samuel Butler, Author of Erewhon: The Man and His Work*.

49 Harris 257.

50 Ibid. 258.

51 From "A Man with a View."

52 Ruskin 41–42.

53 Butler 244.

54 Ibid. 250.

55 Ibid. 413.

56 Ibid. 427.

57 Ibid. 428.

58 This diary entry is pointed out in Collier 384.

59 "Amateur, *n.*," *OED*.

60 Pointed out in Collier 372–73.

61 Harris 258.

62 McLaurin 60–70.

63 This diary entry is pointed out in Collier 384.

64 Lee 559.

65 Perkin 7.

66 The trend of Woolf's journalism in the 1920s and 1930s, as well as her ability to demand more money for her articles "in the late 1920s, at the point of her greatest fame and success," are recorded by Lee 558–59. The diary entry in July 1927 and the letter to Helen McAfee are identified by Lee. For exact numbers and titles of articles published, see Kirkpatrick and Clarke. From 1927 to 1929, for example, sixty four of Woolf's articles appeared in periodicals, compared to the eighteen from 1932 to 1934. In 1935 and 1936, a mere two articles were published (282–93).

67 From that diary entry onwards, she was to publish three more articles in *Harper's Bazaar*, two in *The Atlantic Monthly*, one in *The Yale Review*, one in *The New Republic*, and one in *Hearst's International Combined with Cosmopolitan*. See Kirkpatrick and Clarke 293–96.
68 L. Marcus, "Virginia Woolf and the Hogarth Press" 145.
69 E. Gordon 108.
70 Ibid. 113–14.
71 Ibid. 113–15.
72 Quoted in Willis 63.
73 E. Gordon 122.
74 Ibid. 120.
75 Kenealy 242–43.
76 First published in March 1929 in *The Forum*.
77 Mullin 143–44.
78 See Huyssen.
79 Collier 377.
80 G. Eliot 310. Emphasis in the original.
81 Ibid. 317. Emphasis in the original.
82 The background to "An Unwritten Novel" is described in Hussey 322–23.
83 Moore 156.
84 Boumelha 177–78.
85 "Profession, *n.*," *OED*. The first instance the *OED* records of this use is in 1888.
86 See Bullough and Bullough 195; Fisher 85–86.
87 Bullough and Bullough 195.
88 Walkowitz 93.
89 These are words Woolf uses to describe the amateurism of Samuel Butler in her essay "A Man with a View."
90 L. Woolf, *Beginning Again*, 90; Lee 67.
91 Lee 557.
92 Paul Delany points out that despite Leonard's own criticism of imperialism in such works as *Economic Imperialism* (1920), he had "invested more than forty percent of his and Virginia's capital in imperial ventures like Shell Oil, Federated Selangor, Ceylon Para, or Bajoe Kidoel." See Delany 6–7.

3 Reconfiguring Professionalism: Lily Briscoe and Miss La Trobe

1 Booth 275.
2 Bridget and Wallace 71.
3 Lily is described as "amateur painter, unmarried, aged thirty-three" by Fleishman 97; as a "small, skimpy, amateur woman artist" by Blair 172; and as having "amateur interest in painting" by Ayers 89. La Trobe is called "an amateur scribbler" by Graham 392. Both are called "amateurs and outsiders" by Rodriguez 121.
4 Sypher "304.
5 Minow-Pinkney 111.
6 Greene 82.

7 This is the position which Bridget and Wallace tend towards. See Bridget and Wallace 71–75.

8 Booth 282.

9 These are key terms selected from the *OED* entry of "profession."

10 Ruth 18.

11 Caughie 392.

12 Ibid. 383–84.

13 Corfield 203.

14 Crackanthorpe 268–69.

15 Stott 116.

16 Phillimore 366.

17 Gollancz 7.

18 Royden 143.

19 Lovett and Hughes 451.

20 Koch 729.

21 Booth 276.

22 Ruth 5.

23 Jack Stewart has similarly suggested out that the colourlessness and austerity of the kitchen table represent Mr Ramsay's "abstract philosophy," and is "[t]he antithesis of her sensuous vision." Lily's task is "not to reject [the] empiricism" of his "masculine/intellectual tradition," "but to marry it to Mrs. Ramsay's mysticism," so that Lily's "dual way of seeing, at once true to the object and expressive of the subject" can come about, and she can think: "One wanted ... to feel simply that's a chair, that's a table, and yet at the same time, It's a miracle, it's an ecstasy" (*TTL* 218, 442–43). See Stewart, "Color in To the Lighthouse."

24 Critics who have focused on the relationship between Woolf and philosophical epistemology have tended to provide a more favourable reading of the kitchen table, and the most extensive argument to date is that by Ann Banfield. Banfield shows significant congruences between the thought and philosophy of Bertrand Russell and Woolf. The unseen table in Lily's mind symbolises an "impersonal truth" that is at once certain and uncertain, and reflects Russell's reaction against previous philosophical positions that saw reality as either purely mental (the idealism by such philosophers as Hegel and Bradley) or purely physical, in what is termed Russell's position of neutral monism. See Banfield 49–51. Here, I consciously revert back to a reading which is more feminist and in the spirit of the later *Three Guineas*. There is an ironical dimension to the invocation of the kitchen table that also supports my more political use of it here as a symbol for male academic specialism.

25 Alt has meaningfully related such acts in Woolf's writing to the "institutional tradition" in the life sciences of violence to nature, of taxonomic classification and control which destroy rather than respectfully observing and recording (79–80). The depiction of Brinsley's lack of sympathetic and imaginative engagement characterises Woolf's antagonism to the existing professions.

26 McLaurin 205.

27 Ibid. 191–206.
28 Ibid. 205.
29 Ibid.
30 Fry 347.
31 Ibid.
32 Ibid. 347–48.
33 Ibid. 348
34 Koppen 79.
35 Ibid. 375–78.
36 Quoted in Stewart, "A 'Need of Distance and Blue'" 79.
37 Koppen 378.
38 Banfield argues that Woolf was familiar with Russell's ideas, in particular his theory of sensibilia, or "phantom 'solid objects'" (49). Sensibilia are objects which exist prior to, or without, their occupation by subjects, "which have the same metaphysical and physical status as sense-data, without necessarily being data to any mind" because "there happen to be no observers to whom they are data" (Russell in *Mysticism and Logic*, quoted in Banfield 71). Banfield thinks Woolf should be seen as a philosophical realist who aspired to Russell's "subjectless subjectivity" based on this concept of sensibilia (70).

   Timothy Mackin describes this as a theory of "knowledge without reference to the self, even at the moment of perception," so that a conception of "generalized sense-datum" can be arrived at (119). He has argued against Banfield's view, instead going back more firmly to the view of Woolf as negotiating herself between the inner and the outer, the public and the private, so that she retains the benefits of both without the loss of either (Mackin 121). My argument on Lily's "professionalism" is more closely aligned with this position, with Lily becoming the essential site for such negotiations.
39 This, to me, indicates that Woolf found something lacking in Carmichael's method; although as I make clear, I do not mean to detract entirely from his methods and achievement. John Ferguson, for instance, has drawn correspondences between Carmichael and Woolf, writing that she "yearn[s] for the peaceful impersonality of Mr. Carmichael even as she remains busy, self-conscious, and tormented, like Lily at her easel" (60).
40 Steve Ellis 88.
41 Ibid. An earlier article by Mary Lou Emery argues similarly that at the end of the novel, Lily establishes "an independence that is at once tied to the past." Lily's "position as she paints in the garden, between the feminized house and masculinized lighthouse, suggests an androgynous space or perhaps a feminized public sphere. This potential for an alternative public space and the boundaries that ultimately restrict it are the contexts in which Lily's creativity acquires value" (229). Emery's focus – based on her reading of Lily's thought that "she will remain anonymous, [and] that her painting will be hung 'in the servants' bedrooms'" – is on how such "undo[ing] [of] an opposition of masculine/feminine" comes at the cost of establishing the dichotomy of "'Modern Woman'/'household drudge,'" through the servant Mrs McNab.

Lily's status as "meaning-giver depends on a servant unable to bestow meaning either through her voice or her gaze" (229–31). See Emery.

This is an interesting alternative feminist reading which highlights the impossibility of creating a perfect female artistic space, which I am certainly not trying to claim Woolf achieved in my argument that Lily reconfigured the notion of professionalism for her artistic needs. I will delve into the question of servants in more detail in Chapter 4.

42 Sarah Ellis 54, 61.

43 Ibid. 160. Emphasis in the original.

44 Jaffe 17.

45 Poovey. Pointed out by Kucich 230.

46 Elliott 10.

47 Ibid. 9–11.

48 Ibid. 77.

49 Ibid. 111.

50 Ibid. 77. Besides the sense of "profession" which Elliott points out, there may also be the sense of it as a calling which deserves serious recognition in its own right.

51 Ibid. 118.

52 Ibid. 128–30.

53 Mill 21–23.

54 Anderson 41.

55 Bradshaw xviii.

56 Silver 356.

57 Plain 133.

58 Froula 305.

59 Ibid. 297.

60 Ibid. 298.

61 Cuddy-Keane, "The Politics of Comic Modes" 278.

62 Cramer 176–78.

63 Jameson, *Civil Journey* 92.

64 This essay was originally called "Why Art Today Follows Politics," published in *The Daily Worker* in December 1936. See Hussey 9.

65 See Glynn and Booth. The authors write that "[w]ith the exception of unemployment, no single issue of interwar economic policy has received more attention than the gold standard" (130).

66 "The Daladier Franc" A16.

4 Translating the Fact of the Professions into the Fiction of Vision: *The Years* and *Three Guineas*

1 B. Shaw 15–16.

2 Ibid.

3 Ibid.

4 Webb 146. Pointed out in Perkin 182.

5 Webb and Webb, "Special Supplement (Part 2)" 48.
6 Berman 126–27.
7 Webb and Webb, "Special Supplement (Part 2)" 48.
8 Carr-Saunders and Wilson 319.
9 Ibid. 303.
10 Snaith offers an overview of existing criticism of *The Years* which "imply that *The Years* is flawed because of Woolf's original idea of using fact and fiction" (93–94).
11 Radin 118–21.
12 Plain 109.
13 Lee 677.
14 Naomi Black, for instance, points out that "*Three Guineas* is fiction as well as fact," and uses the correspondence Woolf drew on to show us how *Three Guineas* is based on both (77). The use of fictional elements is a characteristic of many of Woolf's essays. As Laura Marcus writes, "[h]er novels take up the images and imaginings of her pamphlets and essays; her 'non-fiction' uses strategies more often associated with fictional narrative" ("Woolf's Feminism" 217). Snaith has also discussed the merging of both genres in *The Years*, which is referred to later in this chapter.
15 M. Shaw 61. Shaw quotes from an unpublished letter in the Winifred Holtby Collection in the Hull Public Library, drawer I.18.
16 For a detailed description of the entire revision process of *The Years*, see Radin.
17 Snaith 110–11.
18 "Press Cuttings" 24–25.
19 Phillips 44. Phillips sees the reference to North's sheep farming in Africa as part of the larger criticism of colonialism which the novel contains, and concludes that "North's income in Africa is steeped in blood – not only of sheep but of Africans" (44).
20 L. Woolf, *Empire and Commerce in Africa* 343–48. He writes: "In their [English settlers'] opinion the native has no right to land and no right to live his life for himself; he should be compelled to work on the white man's land for a wage fixed at twopence per day by law by the white man" (348).
21 This is discussed in Radin 103.
22 Lee 349.
23 Ibid.
24 Ibid.
25 Strachey 124.
26 Childers 66.
27 Ibid. xviii.
28 Ibid.
29 Ibid. xvii.
30 Ibid. xvi.
31 Ibid.
32 Snaith 117.

33 Childers 71.
34 In *Flush*, Woolf provides a brief biography of Lily Wilson, Elizabeth Barrett Browning's maidservant, in a footnote, stressing at the same time that "[t]he life of Lily Wilson is extremely obscure and thus cries aloud for the services of a biographer" (109–13).
35 See Light for an account of Woolf's ambivalent relationship with her servants.
36 Childers points out that Woolf's rigid separation of the two classes ignores the dependence of the middle and upper middle classes on the lower classes, something that cannot be taken for granted, "[j]ust as no feminist discussion of women having professional careers *and* families today should leave out information about the careers and families of houseworkers" (73). Her point about the modern-day dependence of the professional woman on domestic workers is one that she does not trace to Woolf's time, but this dependence was – although less prevalent because there were fewer professional women – also applicable to the 1930s, as I will show further on.
37 Beddoe 61–63; Lewis 191.
38 Beddoe 51–53.
39 "Domestic Work a Profession?" A7.
40 Ibid.
41 "Women's Highest Profession" B9.
42 Ibid.
43 "A Domestic Servant Problem" D11.
44 Light 251.
45 *The Woman's Leader*, 1 Apr. 1920; quoted in Beddoe 61.
46 V. Woolf, "Memories" 124.
47 See Firth. Firth writes that "[t]here is no reason why one woman in a household should sit in idleness while another attends to the needs of both. Specialisation of labour is legitimate, but avoidance of labour is contrary to the national interest. As long as we have an idle and unproductive class we will have social unrest" (66). She does not discuss the possibility of a class of professional women supported by domestic servants.
48 "Women's Highest Profession" B9.
49 "Women in the Civil Service" F11.
50 Brittain, *Testament of Youth* 610; emphasis added.
51 Ibid.
52 Ibid. 653.
53 Brittain, *Honourable Estate* 616. This is a book referred to by Lewis 105–06. Lewis here writes that "[t]he small number of married women who pursued an active public life between the wars continued to assume that home and family were part of their natural responsibilities and solved the problem ... through the employment of domestic servants."
54 Brittain, *Honourable Estate* 591.
55 Ibid. 619.
56 Ibid. 544–45.
57 Jameson, "Combining a Career with a Home" 7.

58 Light 186.

59 Ibid.

60 Ibid. 194–95.

61 Light (169) describes, for example, Woolf fantasising about a house "entirely controlled by one woman, a vacuum cleaner, & electric stoves" (*D* 2: 281) and her sense of liberation at doing temporarily without a live-in servant (Light 195). However, almost immediately after dismissing Nellie Boxall, who had been her live-in servant in London for eighteen years, Woolf took on another live-in servant, Mabel Haskins (229).

5 A Balancing Act: *Between the Acts* and the Aesthetics of Specialisation

1 Beer, "Introduction" xix.

2 Laurence 245.

3 Pridmore-Brown 411–12.

4 De Gay 210.

5 Esty 107.

6 Ibid. 93.

7 Pridmore-Brown 418–19.

8 Froula 312–21.

9 Huxley 260. Emphasis added.

10 Beer, "Virginia Woolf and Prehistory" 121–22.

11 Ibid. 171.

12 Ibid. 180.

13 A review of *A Dictionary of Occupational Terms* (1927) in the *New Statesman* entitled "Tinker, Tailor" uses it to refer to "[t]his immense diversity of modern industrialism," the results of the specialisation process in the foregoing century ("Tinker, Tailor" 668).

14 Mitchell Leaska, who edited the typescripts of the novel, has named the three existing versions the earlier, later and final typescripts, the former two of which Woolf was working on from April 1938 to October (?) 1940, and to November 1940 respectively (*PH* 25–29).

15 Zwerdling 308–11.

16 For a recent discussion of the relationship between modernity and fragmentation in the novel, see Linett 84–97.

17 Special, *adj., adv.,* and *n., OED Online.*

18 J. Marcus 57.

19 "Species, *n.," OED Online.*

20 See Beer, "Virginia Woolf and Prehistory."

21 Beer writes that "[r]hyme is one of the last things; it stays – a final skill – when other ordering principles have fled the mind," and that it "offers connection still, even when semantic clues may have been voided." See Beer, "Rhyming as Resurrection" 203.

22 Beer, "The Island and the Aeroplane" 285.

23 Beer also writes of nursery rhymes that they hint at the "primitive" in their association with our childhood past. See Beer, "Rhyming as Resurrection" 191.
24 Ibid.
25 Huxley 260.
26 Tate 125.
27 Beer, "The Island and the Aeroplane."
28 See 643.
29 L. Woolf, *Quack, Quack!* 109.
30 Ibid. 40.
31 L. Woolf, *The War for Peace* 222.
32 Ibid. 105.
33 Angell, *The Story of Money* 147.
34 Leaska estimates that Woolf started writing the later typescript in October 1940, finishing it the next month (*PH* 29).
35 Linett 92.
36 Woolf mentions seeing him in a letter to Julian Bell, in which she says that "Norman Angell was rather fun" (*L* 5:33). They also both signed, together with others, a letter to the editor of *The Times* to highlight the plight of the Spanish government and people in the Spanish Civil War, which appeared in the newspaper on 19 Aug. 1936. In addition, Leonard Woolf cooperated with Angell on such books as *The Intelligent Man's Way to Prevent War* (1933) and *Does Capitalism Cause War?* (1935).
37 Angell 22.
38 Keynes, *The Economic Consequences of the Peace* 103–210.
39 Skidelsky 336.
40 "The percentage of votes cast for the Nazis rose from 2.6 in 1928 to 18.3 in 1930" (Skidelsky 336).
41 L. Woolf, *Downhill* 85–86.
42 Ibid. 86.
43 L. Woolf, *Co-operation and the Future of Industry* 126–27.
44 Ibid.
45 L. Woolf, *Downhill* 88.
46 "Money, *n.*," *OED*.
47 Carr-Saunders and Wilson write: "Stockbroking was first heard of towards the end of the seventeenth century, and several attempts were made to suppress the practice. In 1697 an Act was passed 'to restrain the Number and ill practice of Brokers and Stock Jobbers'" (273–74).
48 Carr-Saunders and Wilson 273–74.
49 Davenport 376. See also Killik, *The Work of the Stock Exchange*. Killik writes that "[m]embers of the Stock Exchange are divided into two classes, brokers and jobbers. The broker is familiar to the public as the agent who is employed by them to purchase or sell stocks and shares. The jobber is the person to whom the broker goes to deal" (32). The jobber's aim was to profit from the difference in buying and selling prices of stocks to brokers, whereas brokers earned money from the commission fee they charged the public.

50 Wells 220–22.
51 L. Woolf, "Introduction" 16–17.
52 Angell, "Educational and Psychological Factors" 488.
53 Ibid. 491.
54 Angell, "The International Anarchy" 29.
55 L. Woolf, *Downhill*, 241–43.
56 L. Woolf, "Utopia and Reality" 181.
57 L. Woolf, *The War for Peace* 238–39.
58 Ibid.
59 Ibid. 202–09; 23.
60 Ibid. 211.
61 Ibid. 225.
62 Ibid. 238.
63 Keynes, *Collected Writings*, vol. 20, 379–80.
64 Keynes, *Collected Writings*, vol. 21, 240.
65 L. Woolf, "De Profundis" 469.
66 Keynes, *Collected Writings*, vol. 21, 236–37.
67 Ibid. 238–39.
68 Ibid. 236.
69 L. Woolf, "De Profundis" 469.
70 L. Woolf, *The War for Peace* 202.
71 Ibid. 241–44.
72 Briggs 201–03.
73 Hobson 67.
74 "Hunger Breeds War" 4.
75 Keynes, *Collected Writings*, vol. 21, 243.
76 Fischer 446–47.
77 Angell, *The Story of Money* 22–27.
78 Ibid. 20.
79 Ibid. 21.
80 Zwerdling 308–11.
81 L. Woolf, "De Profundis" 468–69.
82 L. Woolf, "Introduction" 17.
83 Whitworth, "Virginia Woolf and Modernism" 161.
84 V. Woolf, "Articles, Essays, Fiction and Reviews" 145.

Bibliography

Abstract of the Answers and Returns Made Pursuant to an Act, Passed in the Eleventh Year of the Reign of His Majesty King George IV. Enumeration Abstract. Vol. 1. House of Commons, 1833.

Abstract of the Answers and Returns: Occupation Abstract, M.DCCC.XLI. Part I. England and Wales, and Islands in the British Seas. London: Her Majesty's Stationery Office, 1844.

Alt, Christina. *Virginia Woolf and the Study of Nature.* Cambridge: Cambridge University Press, 2010.

"Amateur." *OED Online.* 25 Mar. 2008. <http://dictionary.oed.com/cgi/entry/50006818>.

Anderson, Amanda. *Tainted Souls and Painted Faces: The Rhetoric of Fallenness in Victorian Culture.* Ithaca, NY: Cornell University Press, 1993.

Angell, Norman. "Educational and Psychological Factors." In *The Intelligent Man's Way to Prevent War.* Ed. Leonard Woolf. London: Victor Gollancz, 1933. 482–91.

"The International Anarchy." In *The Intelligent Man's Way to Prevent War.*

The Story of Money. London: Cassell & Company, 1930.

Arnold, Matthew. "Report on the System of Education for the Middle and Upper Classes in France, Italy, Germany, and Switzerland." *Report of the Commissioners.* Vol. 6. London: Her Majesty's Stationery Office, 1868.

Atkins, H. J. B. "State-Organized Medicine: A Point of View." *British Medical Journal* 1.3881 (1935). 1095–96.

Ayers, David. *English Literature of the 1920s.* Edinburgh: Edinburgh University Press, 2004.

Banfield, Ann. *The Phantom Table: Woolf, Fry, Russell and the Epistemology of Modernism.* Cambridge: Cambridge University Press, 2000.

Bartlett, Peter, and Ralph Sandland. *Mental Health Law: Policy and Practice.* London: Blackstone Press, 2000.

Beddoe, Deirdre. *Back to Home and Duty: Women between the Wars, 1918–1939.* London: Pandora Press, 1989.

Beer, Gillian. "Introduction." In *Between the Acts.* London: Penguin, 2000. ix–xxxv.

"The Island and the Aeroplane: The Case of Virginia Woolf." In *Nation and Narration*. Ed. Homi K. Bhabha. London: Routledge, 1990. 265–90.

"Rhyming as Resurrection." In *Memory and Memorials, 1789–1914: Literary and Cultural Perspectives*. Eds. Matthew Campbell, Jacqueline M. Labbe, and Sally Shuttleworth. London: Routledge, 2000. 189–207.

"Virginia Woolf and Prehistory." In *Arguing with the Past: Essays in Narrative from Woolf to Sidney*. London: Routledge, 1989. 117–37.

Beith, John Hay. "The Privileged Profession." *The Lancet* 226.5849 (1935): 799–800.

Bell, Clive. *On British Freedom*. London: Chatto and Windus, 1923.

Bell, Quentin. *Virginia Woolf: A Biography*. Vol. 1. London: Pimlico, 1996.

Benedict, Barbara M. "Readers, Writers, Reviewers, and the Professionalization of Literature." In *The Cambridge Companion to English Literature, 1740–1830*. Eds. Tom Keymer and Jon Mee. Cambridge: Cambridge University Press, 2004. 3–23.

Berman, Jessica. *Modernist Fiction, Cosmopolitanism, and the Politics of Community*. Cambridge: Cambridge University Press, 2001.

Berridge, Virginia. "Health and Medicine." In *The Cambridge Social History of Britain, 1750–1950: Social Agencies and Institutions*. Ed. F. M. L. Thompson. Cambridge: Cambridge University Press, 1993. 171–242.

Black, Naomi. *Virginia Woolf as Feminist*. Ithaca, NY: Cornell University Press, 2004.

Blair, Emily. *Virginia Woolf and the Nineteenth-Century Domestic Novel*. Albany: State University of New York Press, 2002.

Blaszak, Barbara J. *The Matriarchs of England's Cooperative Movement: A Study in Gender Politics and Female Leadership, 1883–1921*. Westport, CT: Greenwood Press, 2000.

Booth, Alison. *Greatness Engendered: George Eliot and Virginia Woolf*. Ithaca, NY: Cornell University Press, 1992.

Boumelha, Penny. "The Woman of Genius and the Woman of Grub Street: Figures of the Female Writer in British *Fin-de-Siècle* Fiction." *English Literature in Transition: 1880–1920* 40.2 (1997): 164–80.

Bradshaw, David. "Introduction." In *To the Lighthouse*. Oxford: Oxford University Press, 2006. ix–xliii.

Bridget, Elliott, and Jo-Ann Wallace. *Women Artists and Writers: Modernist (Im)positionings*. London: Routledge, 1994.

Briggs, Julia. *Reading Virginia Woolf*. Edinburgh: Edinburgh University Press, 2006.

Brittain, Vera. *Honourable Estate: A Novel of Transition*. London: Victor Gollancz, 1936.

Testament of Youth: An Autobiographical Study of the Years 1900–1925. 1933. London: Virago, 1978.

Bullough, Vern, and Bonnie Bullough. *Women and Prostitution: A Social History*. Buffalo, NY: Prometheus Books, 1987.

Butler, Samuel. *The Way of All Flesh*. 1903. Ed. Michael Mason. Oxford: Oxford University Press, 1993.

"Calling, *vbl. n.*" *OED Online*. 21 Jun. 2010. <http://dictionary.oed.com/cgi/entry/50031666>.

Carr-Saunders, A. M., and P. A. Wilson. *The Professions*. Oxford: Clarendon Press, 1933.

Caughie, Pamela L. "The Woman Artist in Virginia Woolf's Writings." In *Writing the Woman Artist*. Ed. Suzanne W. Jones. Philadelphia: University of Pennsylvania Press, 1991. 371–97.

Census of England and Wales for the Year 1861: Population Tables. Vol. 1. London: Her Majesty's Stationery Office, 1863.

Census of Great Britain, 1851. Population Tables. II. Ages, Civil Condition, Occupations, and Birthplace of the People. Vol. 1. London: Her Majesty's Stationery Office, 1854.

Childers, Mary M. "Virginia Woolf on the Outside Looking Down: Reflections on the Class of Women." *Modern Fiction Studies* 38.1 (1992): 61–79.

Childress, Marcia Day. "Practically Speaking: *Mrs. Dalloway* and Life in the Professions." In *Approaches to Teaching Woolf's Mrs. Dalloway*. Eds. Eileen Barrett and Ruth O. Saxton. New York: The Modern Language Association of America, 2009. 128–32.

Clutton-Brock, Arthur. "Professionalism in Art." *The Times Literary Supplement*. 31 Jan. 1918: 49–50.

Collier, Patrick. "Virginia Woolf in the Pay of Booksellers: Commerce, Privacy, Professionalism, *Orlando*." *Twentieth Century Literature* 48.4 (2002): 363–92.

Conditions of Work and Life of Journalists. Vol. 2. Geneva: International Labour Office, 1928.

Corfield, Penelope J. *Power and the Professions in Britain 1700–1850*. London: Routledge, 1995.

Court, Franklin E. *Institutionalizing English Literature: The Culture and Politics of Literary Study, 1750–1900*. Stanford, CA: Stanford University Press, 1992.

Crackanthorpe, Hubert. "Reticence in Literature." *The Yellow Book* 2 (1894): 259–69.

Cramer, Patricia. "Virginia Woolf's Matriarchal Family of Origins in *Between the Acts*." *Twentieth Century Literature* 39.2 (1993): 166–84.

Cucullu, Lois. "Exceptional Women, Expert Culture, and the Academy." In *Rhetorical Women: Roles and Representations*. Eds. Hildy Miller and Lillian Bridwell-Bowles. Tuscaloosa: University of Alabama Press, 2005. 158–86.

 Expert Modernists, Matricide, and Modern Culture: Woolf, Forster, Joyce. Basingstoke: Palgrave Macmillan, 2004.

Cuddy-Keane, Melba. "The Politics of Comic Modes in Virginia Woolf's *Between the Acts*." *Modern Language Association* 105.2 (1990): 273–85.

 Virginia Woolf, the Intellectual, and the Public Sphere. Cambridge: Cambridge University Press, 2003.

"The Daladier Franc. Stabilization at New Level. 175 to the Pound. Britain and U.S. Agree. Dollar Unchanged." *The Times*. 5 May 1938: A16.

Daugherty, Beth Rigel. "Morley College, Virginia Woolf and Us: How Should One Read Class?" In *Virginia Woolf and Her Influences: Selected Papers from the Seventh Annual Conference on Virginia Woolf.* Eds. Laura Davis and Jeanette McVicker. New York: Pace University Press, 1998. 125–39.

Davenport, Nicholas. "State Capitalism." *New Statesman and Nation.* 19 Oct. 1940: 375–76.

Davies, Margaret Llewelyn, ed. *Maternity: Letters from Working-Women.* London: G. Bell and Sons, 1915.

Dawson, Bertrand. "An Address on the Future of the Medical Profession." *British Medical Journal* 2.3002 (1918): 56–60.

De Gay, Jane. *Virginia Woolf's Novels and the Literary Past.* Edinburgh: Edinburgh University Press, 2006.

Delany, Paul. "A Little Capital: The Financial Affairs of Leonard and Virginia Woolf." *Charleston Magazine* (1993): 5–8.

DeMeester, Karen. "Trauma, Post-Traumatic Stress Disorder, and Obstacles for Postwar Recovery." In *Virginia Woolf and Trauma.* Eds. Suzette A. Henke and David Eberly. New York: Pace University Press, 2007. 77–93.

"Trauma and Recovery in Virginia Woolf's *Mrs Dalloway.*" *Modern Fiction Studies* 44.3 (1998): 649–73.

Dickens, Charles. *Dombey and Son.* 1848. Ed. Andrew Sanders. London: Penguin, 2002.

"A Domestic Servant Problem. Search for a Better Name." *The Times.* 1 Feb. 1937: D11.

"Domestic Work a Profession? Status and Training. Mistresses and Maids in Conference." *The Times.* 9 Dec. 1921: A7.

Drummond, David. "The Medical Profession: A Horizon of Hope." *British Medical Journal* 2.3160 (1921): 103.

Eagleton, Terry. *Literary Theory: An Introduction.* 2nd ed. Cambridge, MA: Blackwell, 1996.

Eder, Montague David. *War-Shock: The Psycho-Neuroses in War Psychology and Treatment.* London: William Heinemann, 1917.

Eliot, George. *Essays of George Eliot.* Ed. Thomas Pinney. London: Routledge and Kegan Paul, 1963.

Eliot, T. S. "Professional, Or ..." *Egoist* 5.4 (1918): 61.

Elliott, Dorice Williams. *The Angel out of the House: Philanthropy and Gender in Nineteenth-Century England.* Charlottesville: University Press of Virginia, 2002.

Ellis, Sarah Stickney. *The Women of England, Their Social Duties and Domestic Habits.* London: Fisher, Son, & Co., 1839.

Ellis, Steve. *Virginia Woolf and the Victorians.* Cambridge: Cambridge University Press, 2007.

Emery, Mary Lou. "'Robbed of Meaning': The Work at the Center of *To the Lighthouse.*" *Modern Fiction Studies* 38.1 (1992): 217–34.

Esty, Joshua. *A Shrinking Island: Modernism and National Culture in England.* Princeton, NJ: Princeton University Press, 2004.

"Fabian Medicine." *British Medical Journal* 1.3452 (1927): S80–81.

"The Fabian Society" [Advertisement]. *New Statesman*. 16 Jan. 1915: 375.

"The Fabian Summer School (Seventh Session)" [Advertisement]. *New Statesman*. 12 Jul. 1913: 448.

Ferguson, John. "A Sea Change: Thomas De Quincey and Mr. Carmichael in *To the Lighthouse*." *Journal of Modern Literature* 14.1 (1987): 45–63.

Firth, Violet M. *The Psychology of the Servant Problem: A Study in Social Relationships*. London: C. W. Daniel, 1925.

Fischer, Louis. "The Economic Crisis in Germany." *New Statesman and Nation*. 21 Mar. 1936: 446–47.

Fisher, Trevor. *Prostitution and the Victorians*. New York: St. Martin's Press, 1997.

Fleishman, Avrom. *Virginia Woolf: A Critical Reading*. Baltimore, MD: Johns Hopkins University Press, 1975.

Froula, Christine. *Virginia Woolf and the Bloomsbury Avant-Garde: War, Civilization, Modernity*. New York: Columbia University Press, 2005.

Fry, Roger. *A Roger Fry Reader*. Ed. Christopher Reed. Chicago, IL: University of Chicago Press, 1996.

Furst, Lilian R. *Women Healers and Physicians*. Lexington: University Press of Kentucky, 1997.

Gaffin, Jean, and David Thoms. *Caring & Sharing: The Centenary History of the Co-operative Women's Guild*. Manchester: Holyoake Books, 1993.

Glynn, Sean, and Alan Booth. *Modern Britain: An Economic and Social History*. London: Routledge, 1996.

Gollancz, Victor. "Preface." In *The Making of Women: Oxford Essays in Feminism*. Ed. Victor Gollancz. London: George Allen and Unwin, 1917. 7–8.

Gordon, Elizabeth Willson. "How Should One Sell a Book? Production Methods, Material Objects and Marketing at the Hogarth Press." In *Virginia Woolf's Bloomsbury, Volume 2: International Influence and Politics*. Eds. Lisa Shahriari and Gina Potts. Basingstoke: Palgrave Macmillan, 2010. 107–23.

Gordon, Lyndall. *Virginia Woolf: A Writer's Life*. Oxford: Oxford University Press, 1984.

Graham, J. W. "The Drafts of Virginia Woolf's 'The Searchlight.'" *Twentieth Century Literature* 22.4 (1976): 379–93.

Greene, Sally. *Virginia Woolf: Reading the Renaissance*. Athens: Ohio University Press, 1999.

Guy, Josephine M., and Ian Small. "The British 'Man of Letters' and the Rise of the Professional." In *Modernism and the New Criticism*. Eds. A. Walton Litz, Louis Menand, and Lawrence Rainey. Cambridge: Cambridge University Press, 2000. 377–88.

Harris, John F. *Samuel Butler, Author of Erewhon: The Man and His Work*. London: Grant Richards, 1916.

Hayward, F. H. *Professionalism and Originality*. London: George Allen and Unwin, 1917.

Henry, Holly. *Virginia Woolf and the Discourse of Science: The Aesthetics of Astronomy*. Cambridge: Cambridge University Press, 2003.

Herbert, Christopher. "Mrs. Dalloway, the Dictator, and the Relativity Paradox." *Novel: A Forum on Fiction* 35.1 (2001): 104–24.

"High Court of Justice. King's Bench Division. Doctors' Action against The British Medical Association. Pratt and Others v. British Medical Association and Others." *The Times*. 16 Jul. 1918: C4.

Hite, Molly. "Tonal Cues and Uncertain Values: Affect and Ethics in *Mrs Dalloway*." *Narrative* 18.3 (2010): 249–75.

Hobson, J. A. "The High Road to Peace and Prosperity." *New Statesman and Nation*. 19 Jan. 1935: 67–68.

Holleyman, G. A. *Catalogue of Books from the Library of Leonard and Virginia Woolf*. Brighton: Holleyman and Treacher, 1975.

"Hunger Breeds War." *New Statesman and Nation*. 2 Jan. 1937: 4.

Hussey, Mark. *Virginia Woolf A to Z*. New York: Facts on File, 1995.

Huxley, Aldous. *Beyond the Mexique Bay*. London: Chatto and Windus, 1934.

Huyssen, Andreas. "Mass Culture as Woman: Modernism's Other." In *After the Great Divide: Modernism, Mass Culture, Postmodernism*. Basingstoke: Macmillan, 1986.

Jaffe, Audrey. *Scenes of Sympathy: Identity and Representation in Victorian Fiction*. Ithaca, NY: Cornell University Press, 2000.

Jameson, Storm. *Civil Journey*. London: Cassell and Company, 1939.

"Combining a Career with a Home." *Evening Standard*. 2 Dec. 1926: 7.

Johnson, Terence J. *Professions and Power*. London: Macmillan, 1972.

Jones, Christine Kenyon, and Anna Snaith. "'Tilting at Universities': Woolf at King's College London." *Woolf Studies Annual* 16 (2010): 1–4.

Jouve, Nicole Ward. "Virginia Woolf and Psychoanalysis." In *The Cambridge Companion to Virginia Woolf*. Eds. Sue Roe and Susan Sellers. Cambridge: Cambridge University Press, 2000.

Kaufmann, Michael. "A Modernism of One's Own: Virginia Woolf's *TLS* Reviews and Eliotic Modernism." In *Virginia Woolf and the Essay*. Eds. Beth Carole Rosenberg and Jeanne Dubino. Basingstoke: Macmillan, 1997. 137–55.

Kenealy, Arabella. *Feminism and Sex-Extinction*. London: T. Fisher Unwin, 1920.

Kennedy, Finola. *Family, Economy, and Government in Ireland*. Dublin: Economic and Social Research Institute, 1989.

Keynes, John Maynard. *The Collected Writings of John Maynard Keynes*. Ed. Donald Moggridge. Vol. 20–21. London: Macmillan Press, 1981–82.

The Economic Consequences of the Peace. 1919. London: Macmillan, 1924.

Killik, Stephen. *The Work of the Stock Exchange*. 2nd ed. London: Committee for General Purposes, Stock Exchange, 1934.

Kirkpatrick, B. J., and Stuart N. Clarke. *A Bibliography of Virginia Woolf*. 4th ed. Oxford: Clarendon Press, 1997.

Knox-Shaw, Peter. "The Otherness of Septimus Warren Smith." *Durham University Journal* 87.1 (1995): 99–110.

Koch, Vivienne. "The 'One-Making' of Virginia Woolf." *Sewanee Review* 54.4 (1946): 727–31.

Koppen, Randi. "Embodied Form: Art and Life in Virginia Woolf's *To the Lighthouse*." *New Literary History* 32.2 (2001): 375–89.

Kucich, John. "Intellectual Debate in the Victorian Novel: Religion, Science, and the Professional." In *The Cambridge Companion to the Victorian Novel*. Ed. Deirdre David. Cambridge: Cambridge University Press, 2001.

Larson, Magali Sarfatti. *The Rise of Professionalism*. Berkeley: University of California Press, 1977.

Laurence, Patricia. "The Facts and Fugue of War: From *Three Guineas* to *Between the Acts*." In *Virginia Woolf and War: Fiction, Reality, and Myth*. Ed. Mark Hussey. Syracuse, NY: Syracuse University Press, 1991. 225–45.

Leaska, Mitchell A. "Dating the Manuscript." In *Pointz Hall: The Earlier and Later Typescripts of Between the Acts*. New York: University Publications, 1983. 25–30.

Lee, Hermione. *Virginia Woolf*. London: Chatto and Windus, 1996.

Levy, Heather. *The Servants of Desire in Virginia Woolf's Shorter Fiction*. New York: Peter Lang, 2010.

Levy, Hermann. *National Health Insurance: A Critical Study*. Cambridge: Cambridge University Press, 1944.

Lewis, Jane. *Women in England 1870–1950: Sexual Divisions and Social Change*. Brighton: Wheatsheaf, 1984.

Light, Alison. *Mrs Woolf and the Servants*. London: Penguin, 2007.

Linett, Maren Tova. *Modernism, Feminism and Jewishness*. Cambridge: Cambridge University Press, 2007.

Loudon, Irvine. *Medical Care and the General Practitioner*. Oxford: Clarendon Press, 1986.

Lovett, Robert Morss, and Helen Sard Hughes. *The History of the Novel in England*. London: Harrap, 1933.

Lyon, Ann. *Constitutional History of the UK*. London: Cavendish, 2003.

Lyon, Janet. "On the Asylum Road with Woolf and Mew." *Modernism/Modernity* 18.3 (2011): 551–74.

Macdonald, Keith M. *The Sociology of the Professions*. London: Sage, 1995.

MacDonald, William. *The Intellectual Worker and His Work*. London: Jonathan Cape, 1923.

Mackin, Timothy. "Private Worlds, Public Minds: Woolf, Russell, and Photographic Vision." *Journal of Modern Literature* 33.3 (2010): 112–30.

Marcus, Jane. *Virginia Woolf and the Languages of Patriarchy*. Bloomington: Indiana University Press, 1987.

Marcus, Laura. "Virginia Woolf and the Hogarth Press." In *Modernist Writers and the Marketplace*. Eds. Ian Willison, Warwick Gould, and Warren Chernaik. Basingstoke: Macmillan, 1996. 124–45.

"Woolf's Feminism and Feminism's Woolf." In *The Cambridge Companion to Virginia Woolf*. Eds. Sue Roe and Susan Sellers. Cambridge: Cambridge University Press, 2000.

"Matters Referred to Divisions. Memorandum by the Joint Medico-Political and Hospital Committees Concerning the Question of Medical Aid Institutes." *British Medical Journal* 1.2779 (1914): 201–04.

McGee, Patrick. "Woolf's Other: The University in Her Eye." *Novel: A Forum on Fiction* 23.3 (1990): 229–46

McLaurin, Allen. *Virginia Woolf: The Echoes Enslaved*. Cambridge: Cambridge University Press, 1973.

Menand, Louis. *Discovering Modernism: T. S. Eliot and His Context*. Oxford: Oxford University Press, 1987.

Menand, Louis, and Lawrence Rainey. "Introduction." In *Modernism and the New Criticism*. Eds. A. Walton Litz, Louis Menand, and Lawrence Rainey. Cambridge: Cambridge University Press, 2000.

Mill, Harriet Taylor. *Enfranchisement of Women*. 1851. London: Virago, 1983.

Minow-Pinkney, Makiko. *Virginia Woolf and the Problem of the Subject*. Brighton: Harvester, 1987.

"Money, *n*." Def. 1. *OED Online*. 27 Oct. 2009. <http://dictionary.oed.com/cgi/entry/00313968>.

Moore, Benjamin, and Charles A. Parker. "The Case for a State Medical Service Re-stated: By the President and Honorary Secretary to the State Medical Service Association." *The Lancet* 192.4951 (1918): 85–87.

Moore, Jane. "Plagiarism with a Difference." In *Beyond Romanticism: New Approaches to Texts and Contexts, 1780–1832*. Eds. John C. Whale and Stephen Copley. London: Routledge, 1992. 140–59.

Morris, Sir Malcolm. "The Medical Profession and the Nation's Health." *The Lancet* 194.5018 (1919). 795–98.

Mullin, Katherine. "Modernisms and Feminisms." In *The Cambridge Companion to Feminist Literary Theory*. Ed. Ellen Rooney. Cambridge: Cambridge University Press, 2006. 136–52.

North, Michael. *Reading 1922: A Return to the Scene of the Modern*. Oxford: Oxford University Press, 2001.

"On the Hindoo Systems of Astronomy, and their Connexion with History in Antient and Modern Times." *Edinburgh Review* 10.20 (1807): 459–71.

Palmer, D. J. *The Rise of English Studies*. Oxford: Oxford University Press, 1965.

Pavalko, Ronald M. *Sociology of Occupations and Professions*. Itasca, IL: F. E. Peacock, 1971.

Perkin, Harold. *The Rise of Professional Society*. London: Routledge, 1989.

Phillimore, R. C. "Women in Social Life." In *Good Citizenship: A Book of Twenty-three Essays by Various Authors on Social, Personal, and Economic Problems and Obligations*. Ed. J. E. Hand. London: George Allen, 1899.

Phillips, Kathy J. *Virginia Woolf against Empire*. Knoxville: University of Tennessee Press, 1994.

Pickstone, John. "Medicine, Society and the State." In *The Cambridge Illustrated History of Medicine*. Ed. Roy Porter. Cambridge: Cambridge University Press, 1996. 304–41.

Pitcairn, E. H., ed. *Unwritten Laws and Ideals of Active Careers*. London: Smith, Elder, and Co., 1899.

Plain, Gill. *Women's Fiction of the Second World War: Gender, Power and Resistance*. Edinburgh: Edinburgh University Press, 1996.

Poole, Roger. *The Unknown Virginia Woolf*. 1978. Cambridge: Cambridge University Press, 1995.

Poovey, Mary. *Uneven Developments: The Ideological Work of Gender in Mid-Victorian England*. Chicago, IL: University of Chicago Press, 1988.

Porter, Roy. *Disease, Medicine and Society in England, 1550–1860*. 2nd ed. Cambridge: Cambridge University Press, 1993.

"Poverty and Maternity." *The Times Literary Supplement*. 30 Sept. 1915: 329.

"Press Cuttings, Manuscripts and Typed Extracts Collected or Copied by Virginia Woolf Relative to *Three Guineas.*" *The Virginia Woolf Manuscripts from the Monks House Papers at the University of Sussex.* B.16f. 3 vols. Brighton: Harvester Microform, 1985.

Pridmore-Brown, Michele. "Of Virginia Woolf, Gramophones, and Fascism." *PMLA* 113.3 (1998).

"Profess, *v.*" *OED Online.* 3 Jun. 2010. <http://dictionary.oed.com/cgi/entry/50189437>.

"Profession, *n.*" *OED Online.* 3 Jun. 2010. <http://dictionary.oed.com/cgi/entry/50189444>.

"The Profession of Medicine." *British Medical Journal* 2.3218 (1922): 411–13.

"The Profession of Medicine." *British Medical Journal* 2.3270 (1923): 351–54.

"The Profession of Medicine." *The Times.* 26 Aug. 1921: C11.

"Professional, *adj.* and *n.*" *OED Online.* 21 Jun. 2010. <http://dictionary.oed.com/cgi/entry/50189445>.

"The Professional Mind." *British Medical Journal* 1. 3828 (1934): 907–08.

"Professionalism, *n.*" *OED Online.* 3 Jun. 2010. <http://dictionary.oed.com/cgi/entry/50189446>.

"Publicity for Doctors." *New Statesman and Nation.* 25 Sep. 1937: 436–37.

Radin, Grace. *Virginia Woolf's* The Years*: The Evolution of a Novel.* Knoxville: University of Tennessee Press, 1981.

Reader, W. J. *Professional Men: The Rise of the Professional Classes in Nineteenth-Century England.* London: Weidenfeld and Nicolson, 1966.

Reynier, Christine. *Virginia Woolf's Ethics of the Short Story.* Basingstoke: Palgrave Macmillan, 2009.

Rodriguez, Laura. "Contradiction and Ambivalence: Virginia Woolf and the Aesthetic Experience in 'The Duchess and the Jeweller.'" *Journal of English Studies* 3 (2001–02): 115–29.

Rolleston, Sir Humphrey. "The Changes in the Medical Profession and Advances in Medicine during the Last Fifty Years." *British Medical Journal* 2.3733 (1932): 129–34.

Routh, Guy. *Occupation and Pay in Great Britain 1906–79.* 1965. London: Macmillan, 1980.

Royden, A. Maude. "The Woman's Movement of the Future." In *The Making of Women: Oxford Essays in Feminism.* Ed. Victor Gollancz. London: George Allen and Unwin, 1917.

Ruskin, John. *Selected Writings.* Ed. Dinah Birch. Oxford: Oxford University Press, 2004.

Ruth, Jennifer. *Novel Professions: Interested Disinterest and the Making of the Professional in the Victorian Novel.* Columbus: Ohio State University Press, 2006.

Schröder, Leena Kore "Who's afraid of Rosamond Merridew?: Reading Medieval History in 'The Journal of Mistress Joan Martyn.'" *Journal of the Short Story in English* 50 (2008). 29 Oct. 2012 < http://jsse.revues.org/pdf/719>.

See, Sam. "The Comedy of Nature: Darwinian Feminism in Virginia Woolf's *Between the Acts.*" *Modernism/Modernity* 17.3 (2010): 639–67.

Shaffer, Brian W. "Civilization in Bloomsbury: Woolf's Mrs. Dalloway and Bell's 'Theory of Civilization.'" *Journal of Modern Literature* 19.1 (1994): 73–87.

Shaw, Bernard. "Socialism and Superior Brains." *Fabian Tract.* Nov. 1909: 1–23.

Shaw, Marion. "From *A Room of One's Own* to *A Literature of Their Own.*" *South Carolina Review* 29.1 (1996): 58–66.

Short, Mick. *Exploring the Language of Poems, Plays and Prose.* Harlow: Longman, 1996.

Showalter, Elaine. *A Literature of Their Own: British Women Novelist from Brontë to Lessing.* Princeton, NJ: Princeton University Press, 1977.

Silver, Brenda R. "'Anon' and 'The Reader': Virginia Woolf's Last Essays." *Twentieth-Century Literature* 25.3 (1979): 356–441.

Skidelsky, Robert. *Politicians and the Slump: The Labour Government of 1929–1931.* 1967. London: Macmillan, 1994.

Skrbic, Nena. *Wild Outbursts of Freedom: Reading Virginia Woolf's Short Fiction.* Westport, CT: Praeger, 2004.

Smith, Adam. *An Inquiry into the Nature and Causes of the Wealth of Nations.* 1776. Ed. Kathryn Sutherland. Oxford: Oxford University Press, 1998.

Snaith, Anna. *Virginia Woolf: Public and Private Negotiations.* New York: Palgrave, 2000.

"Special, *adj., adv.,* and *n.*" *OED Online.* 16 Jan. 2010. <http://dictionary.oed.com/cgi/entry/50232614>.

"Species, *n.*" *OED Online.* 16 Jan. 2010. <http://dictionary.oed.com/cgi/entry/50232637>.

Stewart, Jack. "Color in *To the Lighthouse.*" *Twentieth Century Literature* 31.4 (1985): 438–58.

"A 'Need of Distance and Blue': Space, Color, and Creativity in *To the Lighthouse.*" *Twentieth Century Literature* 46.1 (2000): 78–99.

Stott, Anne. "Women and Religion." In *Women's History: Britain, 1700–1850.* Eds. Hannah Barker and Elaine Chalus. London: Routledge, 2005. 100–23.

Strachey, Ray, ed. *Our Freedom and Its Results, by Five Women.* London: Hogarth Press, 1936.

Strychacz, Thomas. *Modernism, Mass Culture, and Professionalism.* Cambridge: Cambridge University Press, 1993.

Sutherland, Kathryn. "Introduction." In *An Inquiry into the Nature and Causes of the Wealth of Nations.* By Adam Smith. 1776. Oxford: Oxford University Press, 1998. ix–xiv.

"Sympathy, *n.*" *OED Online.* 27 Mar. 2009. <http://dictionary.oed.com/cgi/entry/50245127>.

Sypher, Eileen. "Shifting Boundaries: 'New' and Traditional Women in Virginia Woolf." *Women's Writing* 3.3 (1996): 297–310.

Tate, Trudi. *Modernism, History and the First World War.* Manchester: Manchester University Press, 1998.

Theobald, Sir Henry Studdy. *The Law Relating to Lunacy.* London: Stevens, 1924.

Thomas, Sue. "Virginia Woolf's Septimus Smith and Contemporary Perceptions of Shell Shock." *English Language Notes* 25.2 (1987). 49–57.

Thompson, Michael Guy. *The Truth about Freud's Technique: The Encounter with the Real.* New York: New York University Press, 1994.

Thomson, Mathew. "'The Solution to His Own Enigma': Connecting the Life of Montague David Eder (1865–1936), Socialist, Psychoanalyst, Zionist and Modern Saint." *Medical History* 55.1 (2011): 61–84.

"Tinker, Tailor." *New Statesman.* 3 Mar. 1928: 668.

"To the Editor of the Times." *The Times.* 19 Aug. 1936: C6.

Trombley, Stephen. *All That Summer She Was Mad: Virginia Woolf, Female Victim of Male Medicine.* New York: Continuum, 1982.

Trotter, David. *Paranoid Modernism: Literary Experiment, Psychosis, and the Professionalization of English Society.* Oxford: Oxford University Press, 2001.

"Vocation, *n.*" *OED Online.* 20 Jun. 2010. <http://dictionary.oed.com/cgi/entry/50278694>.

Walker, Charlotte Zoë. "The Book 'Laid Upon the Landscape': Virginia Woolf and Nature." In *Beyond Nature Writing: Expanding the Boundaries of Ecocriticism.* Eds. Karla Armbruster and Kathleen R. Wallace. Charlottesville: The University Press of Virginia, 2001. 143–61.

Walkowitz, Judith R. *Prostitution and Victorian Society.* Cambridge: Cambridge University Press, 1980.

Webb, Beatrice. *Beatrice Webb's Diaries, 1912–1924.* Ed. Margaret Cole. New York: Longmans, 1952.

Webb, Sidney, and Beatrice Webb. "Special Supplement on Co-operative Production and Profit-sharing." *New Statesman.* 14 Feb. 1914: 1–31.

"Special Supplement on Professional Associations (Part 2)." *New Statesman.* 28 Apr. 1917: 25–48.

"Special Supplement on the Co-operative Movement." *New Statesman.* 30 May 1914: 1–34.

"What Is Socialism? X.– Co-Partnership Between Producer and Consumer." *New Statesman.* 14 Jun. 1913: 300–302.

Wells, H. G. *The World of William Clissold.* 1926. London: Heron Books, 1969.

Wexler, Joyce Piell. *Who Paid for Modernism: Art, Money, and the Fiction of Conrad, Joyce, and Lawrence.* Fayetteville: University of Arkansas Press, 1997.

Whitworth, Michael. "Virginia Woolf and Modernism." In *The Cambridge Companion to Virginia Woolf.* Eds. Sue Roe and Susan Sellers. Cambridge: Cambridge University Press, 2000. 146–63.

Virginia Woolf: Authors in Context. Oxford: Oxford University Press, 2005.

Willis, J. H. *Leonard and Virginia Woolf as Publishers.* Charlottesville: University Press of Virginia, 1992.

Winter, Sarah. *Freud and the Institution of Psychoanalytic Knowledge.* Stanford, CA: Stanford University Press, 1999.

Witz, Anne. *Professions and Patriarchy.* London: Routledge, 1992.

"Women in the Civil Service: Need of Marriage Bar." *The Times.* 16 Dec. 1930: F11.

"Women's Highest Profession. Domestic Service Ideal." *The Times*. 16 Jun. 1923: B9.

Woolf, Leonard. *After the Deluge: A Study of Communal Psychology*. Vol. 2. London: Hogarth Press, 1939.

  Beginning Again: An Autobiography of the Years 1911–1918. London: Hogarth Press, 1964.

  Co-operation and the Future of Industry. London: George Allen & Unwin, 1918.

  "De Profundis." *Political Quarterly* 10.4 (1939): 463–76.

  Downhill All the Way: An Autobiography of the Years 1919–1939. London: Hogarth Press, 1967.

  Economic Imperialism. London: Swarthmore Press, 1920.

  Empire and Commerce in Africa. London: Labour Research Department; Allen and Unwin, 1920.

  "Introduction." In *The Intelligent Man's Way to Prevent War*. London: Victor Gollancz, 1933. 7–18.

  Quack, Quack! London: Hogarth Press, 1937.

  The War for Peace. London: G. Routledge and Sons, 1940.

  "Utopia and Reality." *Political Quarterly* 11.2 (1940): 167–82.

Woolf, Leonard, and Virginia Woolf. "Are Too Many Books Written and Published?" Ed. Melba Cuddy-Keane. *PMLA* 121.1 (2006): 235–44.

Woolf, Virginia. "'Anon' and 'The Reader': Virginia Woolf's Last Essays." Ed. Brenda R. Silver. *Twentieth-Century Literature* 25.3 (1979): 356–441.

  "Articles, Essays, Fiction and Reviews." In *The Virginia Woolf Manuscripts: From the Henry W. and Albert A. Berg Collection at the New York Public Library*. M.1.6. Vol. 6. Woodbridge, CT: Research Publications International, 1993.

  Between the Acts. 1941. Ed. Gillian Beer. London: Penguin, 2000.

  Collected Essays. Ed. Leonard Woolf. 4 vols. London: Hogarth Press, 1966–67.

  The Complete Shorter Fiction of Virginia Woolf. 2nd ed. Ed. Susan Dick. San Diego, CA: Harcourt, 1989.

  The Diary of Virginia Woolf. 5 vols. Ed. Anne Olivier Bell. London: Hogarth Press, 1977–84.

  The Essays of Virginia Woolf. Ed. Andrew McNeillie and Stuart N. Clarke. London: Hogarth Press, 1986–2009.

  Flush. 1933. Ed. Kate Flint. Oxford: Oxford University Press, 2009.

  "Introductory Letter to Margaret Llewelyn Davies." In *Life as We Have Known It*. Ed. Margaret Llewelyn Davies. London: Hogarth Press, 1931. xvii–xxxxi.

  The Letters of Virginia Woolf. 6 vols. Ed. Nigel Nicolson and Joanne Trautmann. London: Hogarth Press, 1975–80.

  "Memories of a Working Women's Guild." *The Yale Review*. Sept. 1930: 121–38.

  Mrs Dalloway. 1925. Ed. Stella McNichol and Elaine Showalter. London: Penguin, 2000

  Night and Day. 1919. Ed. Julia Briggs. London: Penguin, 1992.

  On Being Ill. 1930. Ed. Hermione Lee. Ashfield, MA: Paris Press, 2002.

  Orlando. 1928. Ed. Sandra M. Gilbert and Brenda Lyons. London: Penguin, 2000.

The Pargiters: The Novel-Essay Portion of The Years. Ed. Mitchell A. Leaska. London: Hogarth Press, 1978.

Pointz Hall: The Earlier and Later Typescripts of Between the Acts. Ed. Mitchell A. Leaska. New York: University Publications, 1983.

"Report on Teaching at Morley College." In *Virginia Woolf: A Biography.* By Quentin Bell. 2 vols. London: Hogarth Press, 1972.

Roger Fry: A Biography. 1940. Ed. Diane F. Gillespie. Oxford: Shakespeare Head 1995.

A Room of One's Own/Three Guineas. 1929/1938. Ed. Michèle Barrett. London: Penguin, 2000.

"*Three Guineas*: Holograph Fragments." *The Virginia Woolf Manuscripts: From the Henry W. and Albert A. Berg Collection at the New York Public Library.* M28. Woodbridge, CT: Research Publications International, 1993.

To the Lighthouse. 1927. Ed. Hermione Lee and Stella McNichol. London: Penguin, 2000.

Virginia Woolf "The Hours": The British Museum Manuscript of Mrs Dalloway. Ed. Helen M. Wussow. New York: Pace University Press, 1996.

The Voyage Out. 1915. Ed. Jane Wheare. London: Penguin, 1992.

The Waves. 1931. Ed. Kate Flint. London: Penguin, 2000.

Women & Fiction: The Manuscript Versions of A Room of One's Own. Ed. S. P. Rosenbaum. Oxford: Blackwell, 1992.

The Years. 1937. Ed. Jeri Johnson. London: Penguin, 2002.

"*The Years*: Holograph." *The Virginia Woolf Manuscripts: From the Henry W. and Albert A. Berg Collection at the New York Public Library.* M42. 8 vols. Woodbridge, CT: Research Publications International, 1993.

Zwerdling, Alex. *Virginia Woolf and the Real World.* Berkeley: University of California Press, 1986.

Index

Lightning Source UK Ltd.
Milton Keynes UK
UKOW01f0000160917
309240UK00001B/119/P